D1265217

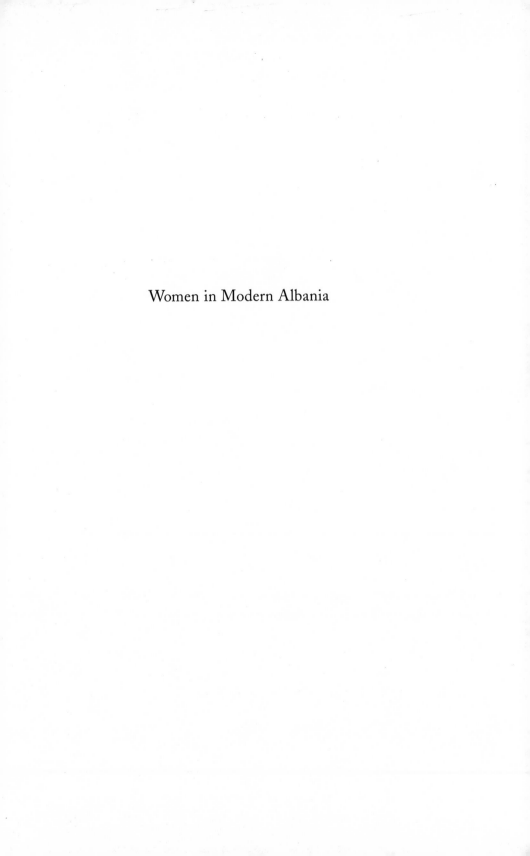

Women in Modern Albania

Women in Modern Albania

*Firsthand Accounts of Culture and
Conditions from Over 200 Interviews*

by

SUSAN E. PRITCHETT POST

McFarland & Company, Inc., Publishers
Jefferson, North Carolina and London

Except where otherwise indicated, all photographs are by the author. The map of Albania on page ix is courtesy Ismer Mjeku/IDM Design.

British Library Cataloguing-in-Publication data are available

Library of Congress Cataloguing-in-Publication Data

Post, Susan E. Pritchett, 1950–
   Women in modern Albania : firsthand accounts of culture and
conditions from over 200 interviews / by Susan E. Pritchett Post.
      p.   cm.
   Includes index.
   ISBN 0-7864-0468-X (library binding : 50# alkaline paper) ∞
      1. Women—Albania—Social conditions.   2. Women—Albania—
Interviews.   I. Title.
HQ1710.5.P67   1998
305.42′094965—dc21   97-50579
                                                                          CIP

Manufactured in the United States of America

McFarland & Company, Inc., Publishers
   Box 611, Jefferson, North Carolina 28640

With love to my daughter,
Rosalie Claudianna Post ("Anna"),
born October 5, 1992,
in Laç, Albania

Contents

Map   ix

Acknowledgments   1

Introduction   3

Part I: Bread, Salt, and Good Hearts

  1. Albania as I Found It   15

  2. The Albanians as I Found Them   31

Part II: The Challenge and the Sacrifice

  3. The Older Generation of Women in Albania   47

  4. The Lives of the Village Women   59

  5. The Lives of the City Women   75

  6. Dhora Leka: I Have Remained a Soldier All My Life   87

  7. Margarita Xhepa: A Life Nourished by a Great Gift   99

  8. Drita Kosturi: Broken but Not Bent   107

Part III: The Grinding Out of Communism

  9. The Middle Generation of Women in Albania   119

 10. The Lives of Typical Women   131

 11. Atypical Women of the Middle Generation:
     Lives of Persecution   165

 12. Floresha Dado: The Sacrifices of a Mother and a
     Passionate Scientist   173

 13. Diana Çuli: A Life of Art and Service   179

 14. Kozeta Mamaqi: The "Sins of the Father,"
     the Life of the Child   185

 15. Liri Kopaçi: Born and Bred to Succeed   197

Part IV: Chaos and Hope

16. The Younger Generation of Women in Albania   207
17. The Lives of Young City Women   219
18. The Lives of Young Village Women   233
19. Valbona Selimllari: Instant Stardom   253
20. Magnola Liço: The Transformation of a Life   259
21. Juliana Kurti: Poetic Promise   265

Part V: Some Conclusions

22. The Role of Faith in Albania   273
23. The Spirit of the Albanian Women   285

Epilogue   289
Index   299

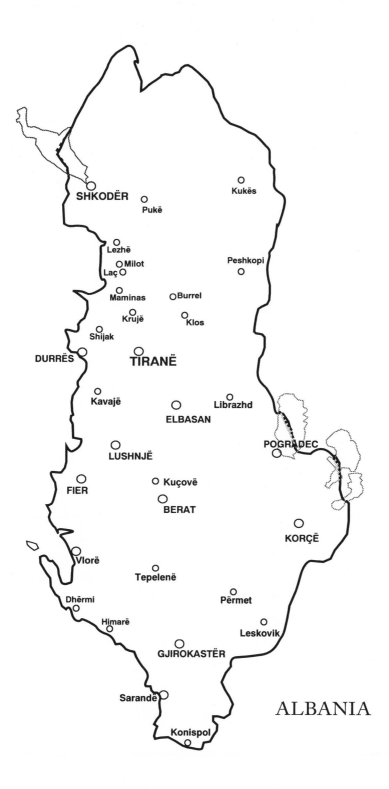

SHKODËR

Kukës

Pukë

Lezhë

Milot
Laç

Peshkopi

Maminas

Burrel

Krujë

Klos

Shijak

DURRËS

TIRANË

Kavajë

Librazhd

ELBASAN

POGRADEC

LUSHNJË

FIER

Kuçovë

BERAT

KORÇË

Vlorë

Tepelenë

Dhërmi

Përmet

Himarë

Leskovik

GJIROKASTËR

Sarandë

ALBANIA

Konispol

Acknowledgments

I am grateful to all the people who made it possible for me to gather the information contained in this book and to write it. In chronological order, I would like to thank Matty Thimm and the women of her group who first heard the idea and encouraged me to go forward with the manuscript. I would next like to thank all of the women who hosted me in my travels and helped arrange the interviews: Fitore Sulejmani in Berat, Flutra Cevani and her family in Perondi, Anita Jella and her family in Homesh, Sanije Batku in Peshkopi, Marie and Pjerin Sheldia in Shkodër, Nikoleta Konomi and Nikoleta Polena in Korçë, and Bukurie Rapo in Himarë. I would also like to thank the women in Tiranë who headed up women's groups and who provided moral support and many ideas, especially Diana Çuli, Delina Fico, Liri Mitrovica, and Flutra Hasko. Many thanks also to Andromaqi Gjergji for sharing information about Albanian traditions and customs. Most of all I would like to thank Ksanthipi (Ksanthi) Dodi, whose example first inspired me to write this book. I particularly wish to thank her for her innumerable contributions throughout the writing process: for making arrangements for our travel, for accompanying me in dilapidated buses and slogging through muddy streams, for interpreting faithfully the words and the context of the women's responses, for being my therapist during the times when I was trying to make sense out of what I was hearing and wondering how to present it, and for reading countless drafts. Finally, I would like to thank my friend Tanner Gay for encouraging me and for editing a draft of the manuscript.

I am also grateful to the people in my personal life who made it possible for me to follow my heart. Especially, I thank my husband Everett for taking me to Albania and encouraging and supporting me throughout the two years it took to complete the book and my children Jacko and Anna, who were so charming with "Mama's Tetas"* and were very patient

---

*"Teta," aunt, is an Albanian term of respect used by children when addressing an adult woman who is not a relative.

1

during my work time. I also wish to thank Edie (Dije) Mersini, who inspired me to learn enough Albanian so that we could be friends, who loved my children as a second mother throughout our time in Albania, and who gave me ideas and insights into the problems of everyday Albanian life.

I give this book to the women of Albania with thanks for their kindness to me and their participation in the interviews, with the hope that it will increase the world's understanding and admiration of them and lead to healing within their society.

Introduction

Drita, aged 78, is the daughter of an intellectual family who served her country as a partisan in the War of Liberation.* She was arrested just after the war, accused of being a spy, and was tortured cruelly with electric shock and deprivation. Drita was imprisoned for 13 years and exiled for almost 30 years. She now has nowhere to live. She stays in her niece's apartment while her niece and her family are living elsewhere, but knows that her niece will need to move back with her family soon. Although she says that she never smiles or laughs anymore, she remembers the good things that people did for her in her years of trial. She even recounts humorous stories of events that took place during her years of torture and interrogation, and—despite her age and physical disabilities—she burns with desire to be of service to her country today.

Safide, aged 53, lives in a village that has water once a month. It comes out of a pipe that is about 3 inches off the ground. On other days, Safide's daughter or husband used to walk each day to the spigot at the edge of a nearby town (about 20 minutes away from their home) and haul home the family's water for bathing, washing, drinking, and cooking. She and her husband and daughter also used to carry home on their backs and heads all of the produce and the animal feed from the plot of land they were given during this new democratic period, as many of their neighbors still do. They are thankful that they now have a donkey to help them carry the water and the produce. Safide works the land, keeps the house clean and orderly, and prepares excellent meals for her family. She has a life filled with hard work and uncertainty. Despite this, she remains kind and optimistic, with a ready smile and eagerness to help others.

Vjollca is 50 years of age and sells bananas in the street near the fruit

---

*Albanians refer to the Second World War as the War of Liberation because they themselves were not engaged in warfare outside their country and Allied troops were not active in the war in Albania (other than a small contingent of British soldiers). Therefore they view the conflict as a personal one in which their country single-handedly overcame the occupiers and oppressors.

3

market in Tiranë. When we met, after not seeing each other for a long time, she greeted me with a smile and asked about myself and my children. I would never have known, unless I asked, that her husband had been ill and had an operation. Their only source of income is a monthly pension of $20. She has no children to help her, and she makes only 1 or 1.5 lekë (about 1 cent) on each banana she sells. When she stays home to care for her husband, she can't even supplement the family income with that small amount.

Teuta, 18, lives in a village in Peshkopijë. She is the third of 5 children. Despite her desire to continue studying, Teuta's father took her out of school after eighth grade to work on the family land, help her mother with the housework, and await an arranged marriage. Teuta hopes that she will be able to meet her future husband before she marries him, and she dreams of being able to move to a city.

Throughout modern history, as these brief stories show, Albanian women have led extraordinarily difficult lives, characterized by deprivation and repression (both political and social). Despite the challenges in their lives, the women raise clean and educated children and they are hospitable, good-hearted, and optimistic. They have done more than merely survive. This book is an inside view of a culture that was isolated from the outside world (both East and West) for a period of 45 years. It reports, in their own words, the life stories of Albanian women of all ages and backgrounds.

This work is not a scientific study of Albanian women, but is their story told unabashedly from their hearts and mine. Their stories and mine are interwoven. I am both a facilitator and a participant, because it is inevitable that the reader will see these women through my eyes, filtered through my perceptions and experiences. Therefore, it is important that the reader know where I have come from, how I happened to find myself in Albania, and what Albania was and is like in this period.

How I Came to Albania

I grew up in New York City and, after spending the summer of 1968 in Luxembourg on the Experiment in International Living, wanted to live for a time overseas. I thought that Paris or London might be great for an adventure. More recently, I even thought of living somewhere more challenging (a developing country, perhaps), but I was daunted by the idea. When my husband started doing consulting work in Albania in 1993, we were both apprehensive because we knew so little about the country and what we had heard was frightening. The only image I had was that portrayed in news photos of hundreds of young Albanian men hanging onto boats arriving in Italy, fleeing their homeland in 1991. While my husband was in Albania for 10 days in February 1993, I did not hear from him until he was back in Italy and had access to a telephone. He came home talking of a country that was a throwback to an earlier age: rudimentary telecommunications, almost no cars, few shops and little merchandise, inadequate housing, erratic electricity and water, and no heat.

After his second trip to Albania in July of that year, during which we were able to talk on the phone, my husband spoke of all the changes: a working traffic light in the center of town; shops and kiosks; and the intense desire on the part of the people to improve their conditions. At the same time, he started discussing the possibility of finding full-time employment somewhere in Eastern Europe and moving our family there for a time.

At the end of the year, and after several more trips, it was clear that my husband felt called to Albania, to help in the area of critically needed housing. The actual call came in January, and we arrived in Albania in April 1994 when my husband was hired to manage the Housing and Urban Services' contracts for the U.S. Agency for International Development in Albania. I came with a contract to work on a part-time basis to provide technical assistance in sales and credit training to the National Housing Agency for the apartment units that were being constructed under a World Bank program.

I felt very brave and adventurous leaving suburban America, a career in banking, and friends and family to move to a country that many Americans had never heard of and couldn't find on a map. I sat in my car at the intersection of 18th and K streets, NW, in Washington, D.C., on my way home every evening for weeks wondering how my life would be different living in Albania: I could never have imagined what it would be like. It was also clear that we were to have an adventure and an opportunity to make a difference in a very real way in a country that was at a clear turning point in its history. So my husband moved to Albania in March 1994 and my son (then our only child, though we would later adopt an Albanian daughter) and I arrived in April.

The Road to Writing This Book

It is clear to visitors and newcomers to Albania that there are social differences between men and women. Although shortly after my arrival I remarked to a friend in the United States, "It appears that in Albania the men drink coffee and the women work," I found out quickly that this was hardly an original comment (see the quotation from the writings of Çajupi that opens Part I of this book). It was, however, the beginning of my quest to understand better the lives of the Albanian women.

It is true that in Tiranë—and indeed in all the towns and villages in Albania—a great number of coffee bars have sprung up and represent the largest proportion of shops in the retail sector. It continues to be a relatively rare occurrence to see a woman in a coffee bar, while the men spend a great deal of time there drinking coffee and talking. The women are either at home or in their offices, working. Although some of this can be explained by the high rate of unemployment, it is a feature of the culture and an inheritance from the time of Turkish rule. The pattern also exists in private homes, mostly in the rural areas and in the northern part of Albania. There, the woman may even wash the man's feet (and those of the men accompanying him) prior to serving coffee, and then return to her housework.

From the beginning of our stay in Albania we were invited into Albanian homes and spent time with our Albanian neighbors. I became aware of their everyday problems: inadequate and polluted water and washing facilities; erratic electricity; a dirty and decaying environment; poor medical care; unemployment; and inadequate clothing in winter. I was surprised by the orderliness and cleanliness of their homes, by the excellence of the food they prepared in their tiny cooking areas, by their eagerness to include me in their conversations and activities, by the education and general cleanliness of their children, and by their own efforts to dress and present themselves in an attractive manner. I began to wonder how they survived with such difficulties in their lives. Later, I realized that they were not just surviving: that they were also living meaningful lives filled with optimism and energy. I wondered how this was possible. There were people I had known in the United States whose lives were dominated by grinding, or even moderate, poverty and deprivation, and I reflected on their bitterness and pessimism. I thought about the alcoholism and negativity rampant among the people in the United States and I wondered what was the difference.

In Albania there is a strong sense of community and there is a special community of women. Women live with and help their husbands and children, their extended family members, and their neighbors. There is not the sense of isolation many experience in the United States. On the one hand, this is due in part to the overcrowded living conditions (based both on tradition that dictates that the oldest or youngest son remain in the parents' home even after marriage so that he and his wife can care for them, and on the unavailability of housing), a resulting lack of regard for privacy, and the historically static nature of the society both economically and geographically. On the other hand, there is pride among the women due to their accomplishments over time. Clearly, they have not only held their individual families together though all adversity, but they have also contributed their enormous strength to maintaining the society and the economy. In part, it is the pride that they feel in this sacrifice that has allowed the Albanian women to accomplish these things and remain kind, generous, and hospitable, as well as generally optimistic.

I am not suggesting that Albanian women have more difficult lives than many other women in the world. There are multitudes of women in all parts of the world, even in the United States, who struggle to survive. It is my intention to present only what I have seen of the Albanian women and to express the admiration that I have for them and the inspiration I have drawn from their lives. The impetus for writing this book, however, came from the question that remained in my mind: "What has given the Albanian women the strength, the force, not only to survive, but also to live meaningful and fulfilled lives with good-heartedness and optimism?"

I was struggling with this question in April 1995 when I happened to hear the CNN coverage of the Oklahoma City bombing. At one point a reporter interviewed the mayor of Oklahoma City and asked him, "What will get the people of this city through this terrible disaster? How will they live with this tragedy?" The mayor's response was, "Their faith will see them through." I realized that this is a very common answer in our society. When you read the story of an old woman on welfare who has managed to raise her children well, inspire them to learn (and is now caring for her grandchildren to allow the parents to work), maintain her optimism, and even manage to help others, we are frequently told that it was her faith that gave her the strength not only to survive but also to touch the lives of others in a significant way.

If it is so frequently faith that supports and gives people strength in our culture, what is the source of the strength of the Albanian women? How do they maintain their good-heartedness and optimism? Albania was an officially atheistic country from 1967 through 1991, with cruel persecution of those who practiced their faith. Prior to that, there were many families who had adopted atheism as the modern, communist ideal. Is it possible that faith has survived? Is there another explanation of where this strength has come from, such as tradition and the role of women in the family and in society or the will to survive, or the replacement of religious or spiritual faith with faith in the dictator or communism?

I wanted to know. In addition—out of my respect and growing admiration for the Albanian women—I wanted to present my findings to the outside world as an inspiration to others. I wanted to give something back to the Albanian women themselves as a thanksgiving for their kindness and inspiration. Finally, it was also important to me that the women of Albania wrote their own book. I wanted to incorporate as much as possible the words of the women themselves as they told their stories. Therefore, I interviewed women from all over the country, about 200 in all, and recorded their words faithfully so that I could present them here. I also interviewed a number of prominent or simply more articulate women. These are women who for one reason or another exemplify the Albanian woman or who have had experiences that highlight the difficulties that women of different ages, backgrounds, and political viewpoints have experienced in Albania.

The first challenge was to find an Albanian woman to be my partner in this project. I chose the one who had been my Albanian language teacher, Ksanthipi (Ksanthi) Dodi, because she exemplifies for me so much of what I admire. Also, she has had translating experience, she is empathetic, and I felt confident that our friendship could withstand the rigors of traveling and working on a book together. The next problem was to find out if there was a simple answer to the question I was asking or if the subject warranted additional research. Finally, I had a concern as to whether or not the Albanian women could or would answer my questions.

To resolve some of these issues, Ksanthi and I met with a women's group in Tiranë on an informal basis to explore possible theories and to refine the idea. I was not truly committed to the project until this point. There were ten Albanian women there with a variety of backgrounds. The group was articulate and eager to share their experiences with a lack of reserve and an eagerness to speak from the heart about personal issues. There also appeared to be a significant amount of catharsis involved in simply telling the stories and a positive effect on the participants that someone cared enough to ask about them and their lives. The outpouring of support and gratitude for my even thinking to undertake such a project was exciting and exhilarating. I also felt that I had been given a huge responsibility when one woman said, "This is a book that must be written and the Albanian women are counting on you to do it." This sentiment was strongly affirmed by the other participants. Afterward, I had the same enthusiastic response in meetings I had with women from all different walks of life, although some interviews were given to us for background only and not for attribution.

The interviews themselves took the form of guided conversations in which we asked the women to tell us something about their family backgrounds and significant people and events in their lives. After hearing their stories, we asked them what had given them strength to cope with the difficulties in their lives and, if faith was not raised as a primary source of their strength, we asked what role faith had played in their lives.

Although at first I had wanted to interview only "everyday" women, we quickly found that such women are not always articulate enough to provide the information we needed. This was either because of a lack of education or simply because we were asking questions that they had never been asked before or even thought about.

Ksanthipi Dodi, the author's faithful companion and interpreter.

Therefore, I decided to do in-depth interviews with articulate women, many of whom are prominent in Albania for their artistic or other professional contributions or for their personal sacrifice for their country.

We also found distinct differences in the responses of women of different generations. As a result, this book is structured by generation with the ordinary women serving as the context for their generation and the prominent and more articulate ones providing detailed examples of women in that same generation.

In order to interview the women in the villages and cities outside of Tiranë, Ksanthi and I traveled by public and private transportation to those locations and interviewed the women in the conditions in which they lived: either in their own homes or in the homes of friends, and sometimes in the fields or shops where they worked. I have included descriptions of our adventures on the road with the interviews because they provide some perspectives on the general way of life of the women.

Clearly, we applied no real science to the interview process or selection of the women. We did, however, strive for balance in terms of socioeconomic level, political orientation, geographical location (within Albania and between village and city), and religious background. It must be noted that since the majority of the population of Albania is nominally Muslim, most of the women we interviewed were from Muslim families, whether or not they currently practice their faith.

The Issues Raised

Finding the women and setting up the interviews turned out to be one of the easiest problems to solve as ever more issues—logistical and philosophical—were raised.

Being an American, how could I really understand the life of the Albanian woman? As challenging as my experience in Albania has been in terms of becoming accustomed to not having water and light occasionally or coping with the other infrastructure problems, my life is not the life of the ordinary Albanian woman. I have so many ways of cushioning the impact of these difficulties, not the least of which is the opportunity to travel outside of Albania when the problems of life overwhelm me. I have not shared fully in their experience, I have only tasted it. I have only experienced a realization and understanding of their lives in stages without ever seeing the full picture. I needed to know what specific challenges the Albanian women have faced and what events have shaped these women's lives.

The issues of justice and culpability, particularly, brought me to a great deal of personal soul-searching. After we had done a number of interviews, I found that there were people who were eager to talk to me to justify themselves in some way or other. Either they wished for me to portray them as politically persecuted—when in fact they were no more persecuted than the mass of people in Albania—or they wished somehow to be exonerated for their roles as Communist Party members or for somehow benefiting from the communist system. In a country where the persecution and repression by a ruling class were so extreme and cruel and where the wounds are still gaping and raw, where there is as yet no healing, how could I fully understand and navigate through the minefields?

While it has always been my intention to present the women of Albania simply as women, it was impossible to ignore the political issues.

I began somewhat naively aspiring to a balanced presentation in which I would include the stories of persons of all political persuasions. However, I quickly ran into the moral dilemma of how to express the later intense personal suffering of someone who, while serving as a high official in a repressive government at some earlier point in her life, had signed death warrants and the orders for imprisonment of innocent persons. Then I found myself wondering about the activities and guilt of the more ordinary women I interviewed. What activities represented doing what you had to do in order to keep your family safe and to give them the best life you could? What constituted guilty involvement in the system and the repression of others for personal gain?

I was and still am in conflict concerning the issue of culpability. However, I frequently think of the wording of a law that was passed shortly after the election of the Albanian Democratic Party in 1992. This law committed the government to providing benefits to formerly persecuted persons and identified five categories of people who would receive these benefits. The categories reflected the severity of the persecution, with the idea that persons who had received the most severe punishments would receive the greatest benefits under the new law. Although there are clearly persons whose crimes against their fellow Albanians are undeniable and documented, I could not help thinking that the last category—"All persons who had their civil rights denied or abridged by the former communist regime"— described the vast majority of Albanians whether or not they were members of the Communist Party and whatever their role. This feeling was further reinforced by two stories:

A young woman whose father had just died at 58 years of age told me,

My father was a very outspoken man who could see the abuses of the communist system from an early time. When he finished school, he was sent to a village to teach. Later, because he was an attractive and well-liked man, the Sigurimi* came to him and told him that if he would become one of their agents they would send him with his family to the United States to live for the rest of his life. Despite the attractiveness of this offer, my father was an honorable man and refused. They tried again to get him to become an agent by force and again he declined. Later, a friend told him, 'Be careful. They are trying to find something to get you for.' He lived with that fear all of his life, fear for himself and for his family, but he would not accept to do a thing that would hurt others. He bore this burden and died early because of the toll it took on him physically.

Another woman told me this story of when she was being taken to exile:

*The Albanian secret police in the communist era.

With me on the trip was a woman with her young son. Throughout the trip the child begged his mother for water and of course there was none to give him. He cried and cried, but there was nothing the mother could do to comfort him. Finally, as the road turned to follow the sea coast, the child pointed to the water and cried for something to drink. The agent of the secret police who was guarding us went to the sea and scooped up some water for the child and gave it to him. When the boy drank the water, he turned to his mother smiling and said to her 'how sweet this water is!' The Sigurimi turned away in shame and said "what a terrible job I have that I cannot even give a child a drink of decent water."

My conclusion is that it is impossible to judge and that it is not my role to judge. That being said, while I have not undertaken to judge the vast majority of women whose stories are included here, I felt that I could not include interviews with persons whose culpability was known or whose commitment to the prior regime was unquestioning. This is not because the stories of some are not moving and their courage in the face of their own subsequent persecution is not extraordinary. I cannot include them rather because they do not exemplify the majority of Albanian women. I have also kept politics out of the book as much as possible and have focused on the life experiences of these women and their responses to those experiences. My hope is that my presentation of the Albanian women is balanced and that this book will bring healing to this wounded society and pride to the strong and courageous women who have held it together.

Part I

BREAD, SALT, AND GOOD HEARTS*

Men under the shade of the tree
Play cards and talk together,
Cursed they should be because
They live on what their women do.
The women go to the field, to the vineyard,
They harvest and do all kinds of
Work day and night

They leave the house before dawn
and come back home after the setting of the sun.

Çajupi: "My Village"

*Bukë dhe kripë dhe zemër të mirë, *literally translated "bread and salt and good hearts,"* is an Albanian saying that is frequently applied to the people in general, but most frequently to the women. This saying expresses the idea that although they have had only "bread and salt" to live on, the people have remained generous, open-hearted, and optimistic.*

Chapter 1

Albania as I Found It

It has been said that there are two reactions that people have when they arrive in Albania for the first time: either they demand to know when is the next flight out, or they fall in love with the country and the people instantly. I fell in love. Bleary-eyed and exhausted by the transatlantic flight with a screaming almost two-year-old, I was still awed by the beauty of the land, especially the mountains that dominate the valley where the airport is situated and almost surround the city of Tiranë. The landing on the cobblestone runway was bumpy and frightening and the airport itself was a nightmare of pushing and chaos. However, I became enthralled with the scene in that hypersensitive but remote way that comes with exhaustion.

My husband plucked us and our baggage from the crowd and tried to talk with me as we traveled to the city and to the house he had rented for us. I could not, however, take my eyes off the sights outside the windows of the car. It was a grey, cold, and drizzly day, but the land was lush and spring green. Everywhere there were people and animals—together—in the road, by the side of the road, down the lanes, by the rivers, and in the fields. There were small herds of goats, a few sheep, or single dirty cows accompanied by old women dressed in black with their heads wrapped in white or dark cloth, old men with white wool caps, or very young children. As we approached Tiranë, the number of horse-drawn vehicles increased and the taxi progressed haltingly. Everywhere in the city—in the parks and on the streets—there were people with their animals grazing wherever there was a stray blade of grass.

I recognized from my husband's photographs some of the sights that he pointed out as we passed through the center of town. However, I was mostly numb from the cold by the time we arrived at our house. I was eager to get inside and get warm. That's when I had my first personal shock. Our landlady and her sister had been working all morning to clean the house and make it nice for me when I arrived. The stone floors were damp from the mopping and the windows were wide open. In addition, the house was under construction because we were having some alterations made to make it more comfortable for our family. As a result, the house was piercingly cold and damp! After closing the windows and putting the one electric heater on high, I became aware that in Albania cold and damp is the way things are indoors when that is what the weather is like outdoors; even when the floors aren't freshly washed.

The First Months

Our goals for the first months in Albania were to survive, to set up our household, and to start work. At first we were so focused on these critical issues that we only gradually became aware of the life of the people around us. As this awareness dawned, we began the search for understanding of them and their lives.

My first task was to buy some groceries, so I asked our landlady if she would take me shopping. I knew that there would not be much to buy, but I had no idea what there would be. First she took me to the open-air fruit and vegetable market nearby. There were stands set up in a muddy area next to a traffic circle, which I later came to know as the Pazar i Ri (the new market). There was a choking smoke coming up from behind the stalls as the vendors burned trash to keep warm in the continuing cold and drizzle. It was difficult to see and breathe, but I detected that there were potatoes and onions along with some olives that my landlady wanted me to taste. We walked around the neighborhood some more, through streets that were more like mud bogs and proved to be a particular challenge to navigate with a stroller. In the course of this shopping expedition I bought a few things—including sugar and flour—but we still didn't have enough to make what I thought of as a meal, especially as there appeared to be no meat other than sausages, which I didn't trust.

Although the prices were very low and the quality of the available fruits and vegetables was excellent, obtaining other foodstuffs consumed a great deal of our time in the first few months. Long-life milk from Holland, Slovenia, or Italy would be available everywhere in the stores and from sidewalk vendors for a few weeks, and then would disappear for a while. Local milk was available from the village people who sold it in recycled soda or mineral water bottles that they scavenged from the trash piles around town. I was not ready to accept the cleanliness of the bottles and was informed by an expatriate who was working on a dairy project that 100 percent of the cows in Albania had either brucellosis or tuberculosis. For these reasons, I avoided local milk and other dairy products entirely.

I was horrified by the idea of going into the meat market, where the smell was repulsive and there were carcasses strung up. Bloodstained men simply hacked a chunk of meat off using a tree trunk as a chopping board. I learned just how much of a hypocrite I am: I love meat, but want it to come wrapped neatly in plastic so I don't have to think about the beast it comes from. Fortunately, however, pastas and tomato sauce were in abundant supply and we found that the bread was the best anywhere. Bread is the mainstay of the Albanian diet, and I learned quickly how to handle the pushing in lines at the bakeries. One of the first words I learned was *Avash!* (meaning slowly, and delivered with a disdainful look). We also found olive oil from Italy and butter from the United States and Ireland that were sent as food aid. After we had been here for about four months, we were able to move away from a primarily vegetarian diet when reasonably safe, frozen U.S. chicken legs became available. This did not occur, however, before we became desperate for some meat and asked our babysitter to help us. Her father bicycled to a place that had chickens for the diplomatic community and her mother killed and plucked the bird for us. When it was presented to me, I was horrified that this scrawny bird had given its life for our dinner when there was hardly enough meat on it for our family. It also turned out to be the world's toughest chicken which, of course, spawned many rubber chicken jokes. I later understood that I was supposed to boil it before I roasted it.

Another challenge during these first few weeks was the construction project that was going on in our home. Progress was slow, as it is in any construction project, but it was also done in a poor manner using inferior quality materials. The young man who served as the general contractor was very responsive and had many creative ideas for solving problems that arose. He had worked for a Canadian firm and had been exposed to Western building and construction techniques. Frequently he would listen and consider carefully what we were suggesting then he would say, "Yes. It can be done. I have seen it." He would then shrug, smile, and say, "But this is Albania." It was clear that nothing could be done and that would be the end of the conversation. The expression "This is Albania" quickly became our motto whenever things were difficult or frustrating.

Despite the daily challenge of finding food and coping with the construction, I became more enthralled each day with the physical setting of the city and more horrified by the living conditions of the people. I have heard Tiranë described as a heap of "rubble at the base of Mount Dajti."* While this description does the city an injustice, it is true that the physical

*Lloyd Jones, Biographi: A Traveler's Tale *(New York: Harcourt Brace, 1993), p. 26.*

A woman at her loom in the village of Vithkuq demonstrates an occupation typical for women throughout the country.

attributes of the city are decrepit and decayed. In addition, trash was every-where when we arrived. The accepted method for trash collection was that the people threw their trash on a large pile located in a strategic place on the street. About once a week a horse-drawn cart would come by and men would shovel the trash up onto the cart. The trash pile at the end of our street was so high that we used it as a landmark for telling people how to find our house (as in "turn right at the trash pile"). We were pleased that within nine months of our arrival, and partly as a result of the U.S. Agency for International Development's technical assistance, the city of Tiranë had signed contracts for formal trash collection. As a result, dark green plastic trash dumpsters and big orange garbage trucks arrived in February 1995, leading to somewhat cleaner streets. However, many Albanians think noth-ing of throwing trash on the ground: leading to hazardous walking in the cities where banana peels and papers are strewn all over. The ultimate dis-posal of trash has not changed since we arrived: it is taken to a spot along the river and dumped in. The tides carry it out to the Adriatic Sea at Durrës.*

*One of our consultants who visited the spot as part of the solid waste project observed that there were sheep grazing on the trash at the point where it was dumped into the river and dubbed it the "lambfill."

The sensation of dirtiness is heightened by the fact that more than 150,000 cars flooded into the country in one year between 1993 and 1994* and by the presence of the open sewer that runs through the middle of town. We also learned quickly that Albania has two seasons: dust season and mud season. After the first few weeks of mud, we went into a relentless, and hot, dust season. Our faces and bodies as well as the furniture in the house were gritty and dusty for months.

It was during the first few weeks that we began to be introduced to our neighbors and to learn something about Albanian hospitality. The little alley (*rrugica*) we lived on was full of children and we were greeted warmly whenever we went out. On the morning of Orthodox Easter, which fell on May 1 that year, our neighbor directly across the alley invited us to come by for a "red egg" later in the day. We eventually got there around 6 P.M., thinking that we would just drop in and wish his family a Happy Easter. That's not the way things work in Albania! After they served us candy and raki, a powerful brandy made from grapes, they brought out a multilayered cake with Joy-Cola (the Greek-produced competitor to Coca-Cola) to go with it, and then set out fresh oranges. While we were in the process of consuming what was put before us, our neighbors showed off their television and satellite dish, demonstrating a preference for MTV. Meanwhile, the children bombarded us with questions in English, like "How much money do you make in the States?" "Who are the best actors and pop singers in the U.S.?" and "What kinds of machines do you own?" (translation: "What kind of cars do you drive?") We learned in this first experience that the Albanians are hospitable and generous and that they are also unabashedly curious.

The best summary of our first few weeks in Albania comes from my journal entries at the end of May 1994.

There are times when I feel that we live in what must have been at one time the Garden of Eden. The physical setting is so spectacular, the weather has been so perfect, and our house is such a marvelous oasis. In addition, the market is almost at our front door and it is filled with the most amazing and exotic sights, sounds, and smells not to mention the freshest and most delicious fruits and vegetables. One of the great luxuries in this world is also on our doorstep—fresh bread still hot from a wood oven almost anytime during the day. I have a sense of contentment and well-being, security and comfort, that I have rarely experienced at "home." Also, we find the Albanians to be good-hearted, warm and hospitable.

That being said, I also have the sense of being an outsider in the land of lotus

---

Private cars, trucks, mini-vans, and buses have continued to pour into Albania, resulting in air pollution and traffic jams as well as enormous stress on the road system. Prior to the democratic reform, during the period of communism, Albania is reported to have been cleaner because private cars were not allowed, there was little disposable packaging, and people were severely punished for littering.

eaters. The transition that the Albanians are making is very difficult and both their experience with the former regime and their natural Mediterranean style make them very much mañana people. It's important to state your opinion, usually loudly and with much movement of the hands, but at the end of the day or whenever the deadlines come it is also important to leave your work behind and say "I've done what I can." The attitude is "*s'ka problem*" (no problem) and their question to me is "Why do *you* worry?"

Also, there are many assaults to the senses and the soul—the exhaust fumes from all of the vehicles, the ever-present sewage smell and body odor, the crumbling buildings and roads, the piles of trash at intersections and the discarded banana peels and candy wrappers everywhere, the dirty children sleeping on the sidewalks or pressing their faces against the car window as they beg for food or money, the stories (and almost all of the Albanians have them) of political persecution, imprisonment, and poverty. There is such a disparity between the beauty of the land and the decay of the infrastructure and such a gulf between my experience and expectations and that of the Albanians. It's very hard to integrate or make sense of. In the first two or three days that I was here I was too overwhelmed by what I saw—at first I couldn't take it all in and then I just cried, and that was before I knew or had seen very much. Sometimes the way I deal with it is by viewing it all as a movie set, a backdrop, but then the reality resonates in my soul.

Some weeks later I hit my real culture shock week, during which I described life in Albania as follows:

I had a relatively sleepless night last night and that may have influenced my state of mind and induced a negative feeling in me. Also, on my way to work, I passed the trash pile at the corner and heard soft mewings in it and looked to see a small litter of newborn puppies left there. I had to turn around and go home and cry before I could continue to work.

This incident touched off recollections of other sad sights I've collected in the past two months and haven't really let into my consciousness. For example, the man who kicked his sheep all the way to the market like a tin can, the skeleton-like horses hauling large loads of goods, people, and furniture all over town, and the dogs, cats, and people routing in the trash for anything salvageable. It is hard to feel too sorry for the animals when you know that the people have as difficult a life. Many of them have been thrown on the trash pile of life, too.

After spending the day noting every crumbling building (including the one I work in, where part of the wall actually crumbled on me today), complaining about the holes in the sidewalk, the ubiquitous banana peels, and the smell of the "river," and yelling (in my head, of course) at the careless and/or arrogant drivers, I came home and hugged my son and cried for Albania and the people in it.

It was at this point that our landlady, whose husband was spending three months in Washington, D.C., on a training program, said to me, "My husband tells me that in Washington people will kill you for $20." That single comment put my experience into perspective and single-handedly turned my focus back to the reality of life in Albania, rather than either the rosy glow of the honeymoon period or the negativity of the culture shock period.

Other Early Observations
About Life in Albania

HOUSING

The majority of people in Tiranë and the other cities in Albania live in mid-rise apartment buildings (known as *pallati*, or palaces) that are crumbling around them. There are also many houses made of dried mud bricks and these are squeezed into alleys all over town. Every time I thought I had seen the worst of the living conditions, I found yet another part of the city where they were even worse. Some people live as they might in the country, sharing their homes, gardens, or even apartments with animals, including sheep, cows, chickens, roosters, and horses. At first I wondered why the country people brought their animals into the city to graze, but within the first few weeks it began to dawn on me that the animals lived in the city too. All I had to do was listen to the early morning sounds of the capital city to know that some of them were my neighbors.

Even though I had been working on the housing program for several months and had been inside some of the units the National Housing Agency was building, I didn't really understand how the average Albanian person lived until our family spent a weekend in the southern city of Korçë in July 1994. Our friend and his family arranged for us to stay in a friend's apartment, and staying there was probably our single most educational Albanian experience up to that time. It was what is called here a "one plus one": one bedroom and a kitchen (a large room with a small alcove on one side where there is a sink). Since the bedroom was locked, we stayed in the kitchen. We slept on two sofas made in Albania that are specially designed to be used as both sofas and beds and we put our son in a portable crib in the middle of the floor. There was no room to move after the crib was set up. Fortunately, we were not obliged to prepare any meals other than breakfast in the apartment, but even that was challenging as there was just a small, two-burner stove and some old pots and pans. The bathroom seemed primitive to me then, but we have seen much more primitive facilities since. In any event, it had one spigot with cold water and a leaking toilet with no seat. There was a shower rigged up in typical Albanian style where there is no separate stall. (Apparently, there was some sort of water heating arrangement that required lighting a match to some unidentified fuel, but we decided not to risk trying it). Since there was no tub except a large metal pan, we took frigid sponge baths for the few days we were there.

Outside Tiranë, and most especially in the port city of Durrës, it was more obvious that there was still a critical and urgent housing problem in Albania. It was not that uncommon to see people living in some of the larger bunkers that dot the landscape, and in Durrës it was heartbreaking to see whole families living in single rooms of former motel units along the beach road. The conditions in both types of habitation were crowded and unsanitary, but there was no option for the people who lived there: most of them were former political prisoners whose property or apartments were confiscated by the communist government and turned over to others,* and there were not many affordable apartments or homes for purchase or rent.†

It wasn't until some time late in our first year in Albania that I learned that some of the people we worked most closely with—who were currently or formerly university professors—were living in similar conditions. They had come to Tiranë from other areas of the country to work at the university or for the government and many of them lived with their entire families in single dormitory rooms with a communal bathroom and no cooking facilities. The only positive thing that could be said about the students' quarters was that the electricity and water to these buildings were more dependable than in any other part of the city (with the possible exception of the area around the president's house). This was reputedly because the government knew that the students and professors were the first to protest against the government if they were unhappy.

WATER AND ELECTRICITY

Water is a major problem in Albania. This country is reputed to have the cleanest water at the source of any country in Europe. However, the water lines are laid next to the sewer lines and both systems are old and the pipes have decayed. In addition, because there is not sufficient water production and there is much leakage in the system, the water is turned

*Under a restitution law applications for the return of much of this confiscated property have been received, but the actual restitution process has been slow due to the unavailability of records and conflicts over ownership. Often the actual property is not restituted and there is no house associated with the restitution.

†Conditions have improved since 1994 as many people, particularly those living in the worst of these conditions and those who have moved from the remote areas of the north to the larger cities, have taken land and constructed houses on it. These houses range from primitive sheds made of various materials to relatively elaborate concrete and brick homes with small gardens around them. This illegal housing, on state land or property owned by others with no municipal services, has mushroomed on the peripheries of the cities and even in the city centers. It now represents the dominant source of new housing.

on and off in various parts of the city at different times during the day. The pressure created when the water is turned off sucks wastewater into the broken freshwater pipes. Fortunately, imported mineral water for drinking is readily available, although expensive for the Albanian people.

Although we had an electric water pump giving us water with adequate pressure 24 hours a day, I learned early on of the troubles of my Albanian women friends. One told me that her building had water once a day at 4 A.M. Even then the water pressure was insufficient to reach her fifth-floor apartment. When I asked her why it was she who rose each morning to haul water and not her husband, she told me that it was her job and his job was to work in trade. However, she was also obliged to prepare her son to go to school, to work a full day in her government position, to return home and prepare a large meal for her family, and to do all of the housework and caring for her son.*

Erratic electricity is another daily problem. Electricity is called *dritë* (light) in Albanian for a good reason. Until 1992 the primary use of electricity was for lighting. Typically, each room is constructed with only one electrical socket and an overhead light. It was not the norm to have refrigerators, washing machines, or other electrical household appliances, including hot-water heaters. Predictably, these have been the most demanded retail products, along with electrical space heaters, since the advent of the free-market economy. Power is provided primarily by hydroelectric means and is carried across an antiquated system of wires that is not able to support the vast increase in the demands for electricity in the past four years. Therefore, it is not unusual to lose power during the summer for a few minutes or a few hours. However, in the winter when all of the heaters are plugged in, the situation becomes critical as the frequency and duration of the blackouts increases. We anticipated these problems and had a generator installed. This initially gave me a sense of security: a false sense as it turned out.

RETAILING

The industrial base of Albania prior to the fall of communism was characterized by obsolescent, inefficient, and clearly unhealthy factories that were "gifts" from the Russians or Chinese, almost all of which are closed, waiting to be privatized. Agriculture is now the only really productive business in Albania, and this is hampered by the inefficiency created in the redistribution of the land to the villagers. What is produced in the agricultural

---

*This story was true in July 1994 and is true today. Although Ana and her husband bought and installed a hydraulic pump in August 1995, it was stolen five months later. She now has twin daughters as well as a nine-year-old son to care for.

area cannot be processed or distributed effectively, so the income potential is limited.

The retail sector of the economy is by far the most active and successful industry in the country. Albania has made a full transition to a market economy in this sphere and, as a result, there is quite a lot to buy and many places in which to buy it. That being said, there is also an inconsistency of supply and it can be difficult to find what you want when you want it. For example, there are several different types of retailers. Some stores carry only specialty goods, such as electronics, household appliances, clothing, food, jewelry, and souvenirs; other stores have general jumble. However, these businesses are fairly reliable and provide some limited guarantees on what they sell. Then there are the kiosks. They have erupted all over Tiranë, wherever there are a few square meters to build on.* This includes the verge of the "river" (the open sewer that runs through the city), the parks, parking lots, and sidewalks. They range from very elaborate to not much better than makeshift booths (some of the earliest ones even look like converted trash dumpsters). Many of them are bars and restaurants and others sell a variety of products. In 1994 what was available in the kiosks, and to some extent in the stores, was whatever arrived by truck that week. It was available until it ran out and then it wasn't available until another truckload came in. Then the same kiosk might not sell it again.† The rule was to buy a case of things used on a regular basis because you never knew when you would be able to find that item again. Similar to kiosks are the people who have knocked a hole in the side of the wall in a first-floor apartment and are selling things from their kitchens, living rooms, and basements.

Then there are the people who just spread their wares out on the street (with or without a sheet or blanket under them). This is especially true of the banana vendors who pile up a couple of boxes of bananas and then sit by them until they are sold. (Initially, I found it remarkable to find a person sitting for hours waiting to sell just one or two bananas, but I learned later that the Albanians are used to waiting in long and endless lines and have spent much of their lives doing so.) Many times the products sold in this manner are foodstuffs or new items, but frequently they are just old clothes that a family is selling to raise money.§

*In mid–1996 there were reported to be 4,000 kiosks in Tiranë, approximately 1 for every 100 inhabitants.

†While this was true in early 1994 when we arrived, there are still times in mid–1996 when this is the case. However, the supplies of staple goods has become much more consistent.

§I learned later that when I saw better-quality clothes sold in this manner that these were aid packages from Western countries that had been diverted from the government ministry responsible for distribution to entrepreneurs. There are now also people, primarily gypsies, who get used clothes from other countries to sell in this manner.

A roadside vendor of sodas and candies.

MEDICAL FACILITIES AND CARE

Within the first two weeks that we were in Albania I had my introduction to the nature of medical care in the country. I was obliged to go to a hospital, at the request of a friend in Washington, to deliver some documents to the chief of ophthalmology. Somehow I had expected that the hospital would be a shining and clean place in an otherwise gritty city. I was shocked to see both how dirty and how totally unequipped it was. At the gate to the hospital there was a throng of people pushing and shoving to get by a uniformed guard. However, I was shown through first, apparently because they thought that my son was sick and they were showing deference to a foreigner with a sick child. I was taken into the eye clinic where people were jostling with each other to get a chance to see a doctor. The doctor was seated in a dingy room with only a few instruments at hand on a small table in front of him. There was no privacy for the patients.

Medical care is an ongoing problem in Albania. We were all relatively healthy during the first few months that we were there and, after the first months, had access to a health clinic set up by a missionary group and staffed by Scottish and U.S. doctors. Thus, we were fortunate that we only had limited opportunity to assess the quality of Albanian medical practice. However, one funny episode took place during the cholera epidemic in October 1994. Our baby-sitter at the time was a young woman who had recently graduated from medical school. One day when I was sick, she pronounced that I wasn't really sick, but was just experiencing stress. An hour later when I was sound asleep she came into my room, woke me up, and asked "You don't suppose you have cholera, do you?"

Less amusing is the experience of the Albanian people in obtaining health care. The following three stories we heard were appalling. One friend had a brother-in-law who died of a heart attack at age 45 after seeing the doctor three days in a row complaining of chest pains and pains down his left arm. The doctor's diagnosis was indigestion and arthritis. Another friend took his seriously dehydrated baby to the hospital for care and had to stay next to the child continuously over two days to protect her from the roaches. During this time the hospital had no supplies (such as diapers), heat, or food for the patients. A woman I know delivered a baby with birth defects, including fused fingers and a deformed head. The baby was taken away from her at birth to be placed in an incubator for three weeks and she was not allowed to see the child throughout this time. When the child was handed to her for the first time after the three weeks, she was horrified, but was told that the child was normal and that there was no need to follow up on her condition.

Although health care is supposedly free of charge, the doctors and nurses routinely charge additional sums under the table for treatment. For example, if injections are required, the nurse might refuse to give them unless the family pays her 200 lekë (about $2.00) per injection. A doctor will treat those who pay extra rather than those who do not or may provide only half-hearted care. My neighbors routinely collect money from friends and neighbors to help them in meeting such health-care costs. Drugs are another problem because they are so expensive, especially compared with salaries, which when we first arrived averaged $60 or $70 a month for a professional. In the villages there is frequently no health care at all.

TRAVEL AND ROADS

Traveling in Albania is challenging because the roads, which are rutted and sometimes unpaved in the capital city, are full of potholes outside of town and are very narrow and heavily traveled by villagers with all sorts of conveyances and beasts. On our first trip to Korçë we had a hair-raising ride with one of the drivers from the ministry of construction. The road is about two-thirds of the width of a secondary rural road in the United States, there are no shoulders, and there are hairpin turns over the mountains with sharp drop-offs on either side. It gave me no sense of security to see a fair number of guardrails with big gaps in them where people had gone through and the guardrails had not been replaced. Since the road in the second part of the trip from Elbasan to Pogradec was also the main transportation route for Macedonia at that time (during the Greek embargo of Macedonia), there were large trucks to contend with as well. When we got to Korçë we were surprised because this city, like the others in Albania, just starts.* There is no gradual increase in the number or density of buildings. The first apartment complexes just appear out of the fields.

On another occasion we spent the weekend on the Ionian Coast in the town of Dhermi, a beautiful beach spot with a distant view of Corfu. The road to the village is good until you get to the port city of Vlorë, about four hours from Tiranë. The next 59 kilometers take another hour and a half. Llogarë, a rustic resort development in a cool pine forest high up in the mountains, is at the highest point on the road. After that the trees stop abruptly and there is a precipitous drop. Forty kilometers of switchbacks, which provide a breathtaking drive, in all senses.

Travel outside of Tiranë is interesting, not only because of the challenges offered by the roads but also because of sights that make the capital city look like a sophisticated cosmopolitan center. There are small groups of animals and people, such as those I had seen on the way into Tiranë from the airport, as well as horse carts on and beside most roads. A frequent sight is people leading their donkeys home so loaded with hay that the bales look as if they have grown hooves and are walking by themselves. In addition, I have seen horse carts pulled by young boys, 10 or 12 years old, but looking old and worn out, straining to pull the cart and the heavy load while their fathers walk along beside them. The most common sights on roads

---

This is becoming less true as construction, both legal and illegal, is booming. Both in-filling of space in cities and sprawl on the periphery of the cities is increasing at a rapid pace.

in Albania are people carrying heavy loads on their shoulders and walking along the roadside or balancing a large load on the back of their bicycles; young couples with a small child in the woman's arms; and groups of people going to or returning from the market. Only the style of the people's clothes differs from one area to another. People in the central section of the country wear more modern or Western styles (although it is not uncommon to see a woman in a skirt with pants worn underneath and her head wrapped in a manner distinctive to the region); whilst the people of northern Albania frequently wear the traditional costumes of their regions, with brightly colored and embroidered skirts and vests for the women and the distinctive woolen caps for the men, indicating the region of the country they are from.

Kiosks and roadside vendors are also present in all parts of Albania, as are markets for produce, livestock, and household goods in and near most large towns. There are also persons who slaughter animals and hang the carcasses by the side of the road ready to hack off a piece as you require. There are also many auto service places now: carwashes (a pull-off on the side of the road where there is some water and a person who will use the water to clean your car), tire sales and repairs, and the occasional gas station. However, a driver has to be prepared to perform most repairs himself since real mechanics are few and far between and some stretches of road have no services at all.

One of the most talked about features of the Albanian landscape is the omnipresence of concrete bunkers: 700,000 in likely and unlikely locations throughout Albania. These defensive structures decorate the landscape everywhere you can imagine: in clusters on hillsides, along the roads, at the end of valleys, along the coast, in front of people's houses, in the parks, and in the fields. Visitors frequently stop to photograph the first bunkers they see and then find that subsequently they have difficulty taking photos that don't include bunkers. An enterprising artisan has even started crafting alabaster replicas of the bunkers, which have proven to be popular souvenir items.

Our Life in Albania as the Year Progressed

It is amazing how quickly everything exotic and new becomes normal. Within weeks we had developed a pattern for our lives and had learned to accept and resolve the challenges of everyday life. I shopped almost daily for milk, vegetables, and bread with a more substantial shopping outing on Saturday or Sunday mornings for less perishable items.

The heat of the summer was almost unbearable that first year from late May through mid–October and we learned to cope by taking cool showers and standing in our son's wading pool. The heat was accompanied by dust and there were only two or three rain storms from late May through August. Although these storms brought no lasting relief from the heat, we enjoyed them.

Thunder (or *bubullim* as it is called in Albanian) is like a concert in this city surrounded by mountains. Each boom is immediately echoed by the closest mountains and then it rolls down the mountain ranges in both directions. You feel as if you could look out and see it just bouncing along, all the way to the south and north of the country. Sometimes one boom is still rolling to the end when another occurs: then there is harmony and counterpoint rhythms.

Our first trip out of the country in August was both a shock and a welcome relief. We left Tiranë on a day in mid–August when the temperature was 105 degrees and had been that high all week. When we arrived in Luxembourg City the temperature was in the sixties and there was a light misty rain falling. We had relatively cool temperatures, rain, and overcast skies for the entire vacation and were very thankful for this weather. It made it easier to cope with the heat when we got back. We also felt like country bumpkins being back in what we had thought of as civilization. I went into the hyper-market outside Luxembourg City and just stood there gaping at all the things to buy. The relatively affluent Western world is such a sharp contrast to life in Albania, where you are thankful for every blessing, however small.

We maintained our appreciation for Albania until winter came. Nothing in this world prepared me for the cold of that first winter. We burned out the generator motor by the middle of January 1995 after temperatures in December as low as 28 degrees and severe municipal power outages. During this period, there were frequently no street lights and many neighborhoods were without power for weeks on end. A close friend told me that she had not had power for six weeks by the end of this cold period. The culmination was that in mid–December the entire power system of Tiranë failed and was not operational until January 1. During this time, the bread factory was unable to operate; people were forced to go to neighborhood bakeries that used wood or other fuels to bake with; and there were significant shortages of bread. Even after the worst of the electrical crisis was over, there were frequent power outages that we learned to live with in the absence of the generator. We used the wood stove that was provided with the house for heating, cooking, and boiling water. Using the wood stove we could warm the kitchen to 60 degrees, but the rest of the rooms that

A scene near the village of Homesh that is characteristic of the Albanian country-side.

we were trying to heat with electrical heaters never got above 55 degrees. We felt fortunate to have an opportunity when we were in the United States for Christmas that year to buy lots of gear, including mud boots and long johns, to help get us through the rest of the winter in Albania.

Chapter 2

The Albanians
as I Found Them

It is presumptuous to make pronouncements about the character of the Albanians in general, especially without having done exhaustive testing and research. However, there are certain observations about the Albanian people that are inescapable and serve as context for understanding the society in which the women live. Early in our life in Albania I began to make observations about the Albanians and had a desire to understand them better. My first impressions were only of their good qualities and my admiration of them for the transition in which they are involved. However, the longer I lived in the country the more insights I had into both their strengths and weaknesses, including both attractive and unappealing qualities. I became increasingly aware as well of how their history—especially the profound isolation of the recent past—has shaped the people and their outlook.

The Albanians appear to many foreigners as incredibly complex people. In the early days I never felt that I really knew the truth about any given situation or what my Albanian counterparts were thinking. Other expatriate advisers have literally run from Albania in hysteria, totally shattered by this impression. I have concluded that the best preparation I had for living and working in Albania was reading the works of Karl Marx and Franz Kafka in graduate school. So often I have felt as if I were trapped in some sort of maze that had no logical solution, and yet my intense desire to understand the people better was the impetus for beginning this book.

The Historical Situation

There are two virtually universal personality characteristics that can be ascribed to the Albanian people: the importance of the clan and hospitality.

Throughout their history and even today, the Albanian people have defined their place in society by the tribe or clan to which they belong. This explains why, when Albanians meet each other, they seem to establish each other's genealogy before they enter into more general conversation. Although some foreign observers have suggested that individuality is a characteristic of the Albanian people, this is a misapprehension. Self-interest exists, but it encompasses the family or clan, excluding others. For example, an Albanian will recommend or hire a person for a job based not on the appropriateness of the person's background and capabilities but exclusively because he is a friend or family member.

Albanian hospitality is legendary and has been raised to such a high level of importance in the society that it forms an underpinning of the national consciousness. From the earliest historical observations about the Albanian people, hospitality has been cited as one of their most common attributes. The nature and responsibilities of that hospitality have been recorded in stories from ancient times and codified in the Kanun, the Code of Lekë Dukagjini.*

Although the traits of clan identification and hospitality have been remarked upon from the earliest times, knowing the Albanian people today requires an understanding of the history that has formed them. As their history is one of conflict and occupation, it can be argued that the Albanians display the adaptive behaviors of occupied peoples, including an ability to subvert the intentions of the occupier and obtain the maximum benefit for themselves in the process. However, it is the communist period extending from 1945 through 1991 that appears to have been especially formative. Throughout our time in Albania it has been difficult for me to fathom the full impact of the oppression of the people of this country—to grasp what a lifetime of such experience means to the people today. However, in order to understand the behavior and character of the Albanians I undertook the critical task of trying to understand the communist regime and the persecution of the people. The key aspects that were most influential on the formation of the Albanian outlook and behavior are as follows:

1. Enver Hoxha, the dictator for 40 years, was ruthless and paranoid. While he purported to maintain a high standard of communism based on the Marxist-Leninist ideal, he was in fact inspired by Stalinism to purify the society to ensure adherence to his vision. From the earliest days of his ascendancy to power—in the early days of the rise of communism just prior to the War of Liberation coinciding with World War II—he engineered the slaughter of

*See chapter 3 for a fuller discussion of the Kanun.

some of his fellow partisans: the best educated, most charismatic, and therefore the most threatening to his leadership.

2. During his 40-year rule, Hoxha maintained his position of sole leadership by routinely purging the ranks of his closest advisers and other senior government officials by fabricating accusations. Therefore, even total dedication to "I Madhi" (the Big One) was rewarded with death and persecution. No one existed who could take his place. Former partisans who were decorated for their bravery in the fight for national independence and were later senior government officials fell from power, and were expunged overnight from the history books and even from photographs, based on Hoxha's own declaration that they were not actually patriots but traitors to the country.

3. In addition to Hoxha's personal involvement in identifying and denouncing traitors and other enemies of the people, there was a well-organized and highly motivated secret police called the Sigurimi. These people, many of whom worked in normal jobs as well, were responsible for filling quotas of persons to be punished for various crimes. These crimes included such things as being suspected of observing religious holidays or feasts, having a bad biography,* trying to escape from Albania, complaining of not having enough to eat, or in some other way criticizing the government. The level of activity of the Sigurimi varied, depending on the intensity of what Hoxha termed the class struggle. From time to time, when Hoxha sought to increase his hold on the people, he would declare that the country was engaged in an intense class struggle and then would use this as a pretext for rounding up more "criminals."

4. The Sigurimi was assisted by everyday people—some to curry favor and some under duress—who reported on the activities of their neighbors or coworkers.

5. Persons accused of crimes were punished in various ways, including surveillance, hard labor in work camps, exile to remote villages, imprisonment, cruel and horrifying torture, and death (sometimes by firing squad and sometimes by "suicide").

6. The country was closed to the outside world for much of the communist period. Hoxha terminated the early alliance with the Soviet Union after the death of Stalin. His rationale for this was the

A biography was kept on each person. A bad biography resulted from being related to a person who was already convicted or suspected of political crimes, being from a formerly wealthy or politically influential family, or undertaking activities that were considered to be unpatriotic (that is, against Hoxha and his government).

Soviet adaptation of revisionist policies, which denounced Stalin for his repression of the Russian people and for what was called "the cult of the personality"—Stalin's ruthless insistence on total loyalty to him and his philosophy. Hoxha then formed an alliance with the People's Republic of China, but in 1978 this alliance was also terminated because Hoxha felt that the Chinese government was also becoming revisionist and betraying the Marxist-Leninist ideals. Although Albania benefited somewhat in a material sense from these alliances, there was little or no discourse with other countries, except for some exporting of goods and electricity to other communist countries. At the time of the breaking of each of these alliances the isolation of Albania was increased, and foreign literature and other Western influences in dress, culture, and thought were particularly repressed and punished. Such influences were not allowed into Albania, and the Albanian people were not allowed to leave the country; they were not even allowed to resettle or move freely within their own country. Therefore, the people were isolated and limited in the acquisition of knowledge. Such isolation brought with it increasing poverty, as Albanians tried to live up to Hoxha's ideal that the country should be entirely self-supporting. The result was that ever more goods were exported for currency to support the country and not enough goods remained to meet the needs of the Albanians. With a demoralized workforce and the obsolete technical contributions of the Soviet Union and China, the self-support goal proved impossible.

7. Although religion was officially outlawed in 1967—leading to punishment of believers who practiced their faith—priests, hoxhas,* and other religious figures had been tortured and killed from the beginning of the regime. Mosques and churches were turned into museums or sports arenas, or were desecrated and locked up.

The result of the policies and practices of the communist regime was vast poverty, both spiritual and physical. The circumscribed world in which the people lived was a frightening place where no one else could be trusted, with the possible exception of the immediate family. People lived constricted lives with almost no control over their environment. Everything was decided for them. They were told whether or not they would be able to study, where they could study, what type of work they would do, and what city or village they would work in. In effect, they even had their clothes chosen for them because they could only buy clothing produced in

*Muslim priests.

Albania, and this was limited as to style, color, and fabric. Their choices were further constrained by their very low salaries and the scarcity of food and other products.

In the workplace a person's job depended on doing what he or she was told to do. Mistakes—such as breakage of equipment—were severely punished, including payment for the damage from the miserably low wages. Much of the office work was tediously bureaucratic and limited in scope; the manual work was backbreaking and almost totally unassisted by machinery; the intellectual work was frequently limited by the unavailability of texts and reference books from foreign countries and the requirement that the results comply with the official propaganda; and the factory work was boring and hazardous due to the obsolescence of the plants and the inadequacy of health protection.

In the home—behind the closed walls of their gardens or the locked doors of their apartments—the people had a little more freedom, but only in their immediate family, as even the extended family represented a risk. Extended family members could be spies, or they could represent another danger in that if one of them, however distant, were found guilty of a crime, it was not unusual for the entire family to be punished. This was true even for families who had no direct contact with each other for years. Sometimes an individual could escape punishment by divorcing a spouse who was part of such a family, and this naturally created other strains within the family. Family life revolved around housework and survival issues, such as obtaining the rations of food for the family. The joy of living for most people came primarily from their children and simple family activities. Even with the children, however, the parents had to be careful to teach them what they needed to know to keep themselves and the family safe from persecution.

Life was further complicated by "voluntary" activities in which all of the citizens were required to participate. The people were required to volunteer their time for military exercises and manual labor to build irrigation systems and apartment buildings, to terrace the hills to provide more arable land, and to construct the concrete bunkers for national security.

The Impact of History on the People and Their Behavior

It is important to understand how much the communist experience influenced the people and how recently the situation has changed: to comprehend how this system, under which the vast majority of people who are alive today grew up, formed their present-day personalities or at least their behavior in business and personal matters.

It is also important to note that there have been positive as well as negative responses to the circumstances of the past. Almost without exception the Albanians now have apparently unbounded eagerness to learn and to improve their lives. I learned early on that my coworkers and neighbors spent long hours after work learning other skills, especially languages. There is a thirst for knowledge on the part of young and old alike that comes from the years of deprivation and the desire to improve their conditions. Due to those years in which most of the joy and precious entertainment came from their children, the Albanians continue to treasure their own and other people's offspring. Even on the streets and in the shops this is clear: many people were eager to speak with our children, to pat their heads or pinch their cheeks, or to offer them candy. The Albanians' love of children makes the country a wonderful place in which to raise young children because they are welcome almost everywhere.

In working with the National Housing Agency I attacked the problems of the sales of the completed units and the loans that were expected to be extended with my usual enthusiasm and energy. I asked questions—the same ones—over and over again, only to be given the same answer for three months and then suddenly a new answer. I had the sense of working with a moving target. I was frequently promised information for tomorrow that never appeared. The people with whom I worked were either unable—for political or other reasons—or unwilling to work with me in the manner envisioned by the World Bank. After about four months on the job I reviewed the situation, thinking about the obstacles—mostly government policy—that hindered the progress of the project. Then, after eight months, I began to explore the mentality more carefully for clues as to what was going on. I developed—informally and in jest—a model of Albanian work activity that describes the progress of the work flow. If the agreed-upon objective is to go from point A to point B, it is possible to start at A, if you can truly understand what and where A is. You then wander off radically, revisiting the direct path only by accident and after many desultory conversations over coffee. There is then a great deal more wandering off and only after some time, maybe even years, you arrive at a destination that might vaguely approximate B, but would not actually be B!

After more months in which there was a singular lack of progress, I took a senior person from the housing agency out for a coffee and confronted him. I asked him why he and I, as well as others, had been working so hard and yet nothing seemed to be happening. He thought about it for a while and I was beginning to think that he would sidestep the question, but then he leaned across the table confidentially and stated quite simply, "Susan, you don't understand. If you don't do anything, you can't make a mistake." This crystallized for me the essence of the problem and spoke more about the working lives of the Albanians over the past 50 years than anything else I have heard. In the prior regime your job depended not on taking initiative, but on adherence to the direct orders of the person at the top. If no direction came from that source or if the direction was confused, it was better to do nothing, then you couldn't make a mistake for which you would be severely punished.

Based on my experiences, I also concluded that Albanians, especially the bureaucrats, love the convoluted. At one point the organization I was working with was described to me by someone who worked there as *lëmsh*, a tangled mess. The word described precisely my view of the organization, but I was surprised to hear one of the employees say it so directly. I was even more surprised by the pride with which he said it, although I shouldn't have been since I had been working there long enough to suspect that the people I was working with were intentionally making things more complex than necessary. Nothing is simple in Albania! For example, the laws are written in an intentionally vague manner to allow for various interpretations and serve more as guidelines or good intentions than as binding rules. Policies and procedures are meaningless in a country where there is a constant conflict between the person's need—based on historical precedent— to carry out only the express orders of people above him, and the person's own desire to satisfy his self-interest and the interests of his clan. Therefore, discussions about structure, planning, and rules become circular. The results are invariably not implementable in a rational manner. This serves the need of leaving the door open for resolving the conflict in any given situation as seems appropriate and possible at the time.

Due partly to the historic need to obscure matters for one's own protection and to the general confusion in which Albanians are living now, it is easy to conclude that Albanians do not always tell the truth in either their business or personal lives. This particular characteristic bothers foreigners more than any other single characteristic of the Albanians. It has also led many advisers and business people to abandon Albania, based on the paranoid assumption that the Albanians were systematically lying to them for their own purposes. I don't believe that this is the case, although at one time I had also come to the same conclusion. There is a code that you have to learn in order to understand what is really being said. It helps to learn the language and to live in the country and among the people for a while, to become part of the community and earn the respect and confidence of the Albanians. It also helps to understand where this tendency not to tell the truth comes from. There are those who argue that the Albanians have not made the developmental leap from symbolic to rational thought. Therefore, if they have the symbols, they treat the symbols as evidence of fact. For example, there is a danger in projecting events or financial results because once the projections are made they become real, whether or not they correspond with reality. Therefore, Albanian economists have difficulty in preparing projections only partly because it is a new skill for them. After a week of working intensively with me on the concept of projected cash flows, one person asked, "How can you prepare projections when you do not know how much you will earn or spend until it happens?" Estimating or guessing is not possible when to do so creates reality. In addition, it seems to be a common practice to accept the word of people that they will do something *as if* the thing has been done, without holding them accountable to do it. Therefore, if you ask if something has been done, you are likely to hear that it has, because the people know that you want them to do it, not because it actually has been done.

Whether or not this characteristic existed prior to the communist period, living a lie became the norm during the communist regime. Then it was necessary to inculcate children with an understanding of how to respond to questions in order to keep the entire family safe. The government propaganda told the Albanians one thing—such as how well they were fed and how prosperous they were—when even the simplest people could tell that this was not true. People did not dare to contradict for fear of being put in prison. The safest thing to do was to repeat the words in parrot fashion, to learn by rote what the party had to offer, and to lie to yourself, to your children, and everyone around you: to accept the symbols rather than search for meaning. Survival depended upon it. Original thoughts were not encouraged and adherence to doctrine and propaganda was necessary. Conformity, enforced conformity, was the goal rather than learning and intellectual exploration.

Related to this characteristic is the Albanian's mistrust of information: it can be valuable and dangerous. In all aspects of life, information has been a source of both power and punishment. People were not used to speaking to each other, working together, or sharing information with each other in a work setting. I noticed in my early months on the job that people sitting in the same office frequently did not know what the other people in the office did, much less work together on a common project. The most striking evidence of this was that the financial manager of the organization was working on a historical analysis and had not consulted with the bookkeeper to obtain the numbers. Instead she was using the numbers that were established as objectives (again making the estimates or objectives "real").

In addition, almost all efforts we and other technical advisers made to install information systems in government offices and enterprises met—at least initially—with strong resistance and suspicion. This is directly traceable in most instances to the communist period. If you had information, you might be asked to use it against your neighbor or friend. If your friend, neighbor, or coworker had information about you, that gave him power over you and your family. Therefore, the best thing was not to have or give information. In the democratic period this problem has been compounded sometimes by the desire for personal financial gain (for example, illegal activities masquerading as free enterprise) from information. This is illustrated by the reluctance of the staff of a large bank to set up an on-line program that would allow the tellers instantaneous access to currency exchange rate information. The reluctance turned out to be that some staff members in the bank were taking advantage of the delay to inform the black-market traders of the change and were receiving kickbacks in compensation. Frequently, where there is resistance to a proposal there is personal gain at stake. Slowing or halting the project may turn out to be the objective rather than the stated objective of implementing the program.

What I have also found here is a nation of people with excellent intellectual capabilities and great pride in themselves, their culture, and their ability to survive, yet who have lived a restricted existence in vast ignorance. Albanians have a reputation for being dirty and impolite by Western European and U.S. standards. It is unavoidable living in Albania not to be exposed to behaviors and habits that are shockingly unattractive. Walking through the streets of Tiranë one is likely to witness men spitting, blowing their noses, and urinating on the ground. Many of the men are also unshaven and dirty, there are dirty street urchins, and the smell of body odor is overwhelming at times. What some outsiders view as a lack of civic pride in Albania can be seen more as reaction to years of restraint and sheer ignorance. Many people, the young particularly, interpret democracy and freedom as license and, as a result, act in an antisocial manner: driving aggressively and without respect to traffic laws or the safety of pedestrians, throwing trash on the ground, and wearing suggestive or scanty clothes and excessive makeup.

While I have come to understand that this superficial view of the population does not define the people in general, I have learned that even among the most educated people there are behaviors that are shocking. Competition for the necessities of life—such as the earlier need to line up for small rations of food supplies that could run out before one reached the front of the line—has created a survival mentality among many of the people that now shows up in certain actions. For example, every Sunday morning there is a show at the puppet theater in Skanderbeg Square in the center of Tiranë. On the one occasion that the children and I went with a group of mothers and children from our neighborhood, a neighbor bought tickets for all of us and we joined the crowd of parents and children outside the door of the theater. As we waited for the doors to open, the pressure of pushing from behind and both sides became intense. When the doors opened, the crowd pushed so hard that I was afraid that the children who were not being carried in their parents' arms would be crushed. Inside, the people who had paid for standing-room tickets sat in the seats and there were people who had paid for seats who, despite entreaties from the announcer, had to stand through the performance.

The ignorance of some people extends to their dealings with others on a social level as well. Foreigners frequently find questions they are asked as guests to be overly direct and personal, lacking in tact and politeness. However, Albanians do not themselves respond well to direct questioning. They have a million responses to such questions that range from a sudden lack of understanding of whatever language you are speaking to answering with irrelevant information or ignoring you. My favorite story on this subject is one recounted by Elizabeth and Jean-Paul Champseix in their book *57, Boulevard Staline.** They noted in 1982, their first year teaching in Albania, that there were no birds, not even pigeons, in Tiranë. They asked the students directly "Do you eat the birds?" and received no response. The next year, they say, they got smart and asked, "How do you cook the birds?" and received a response "On the stove."

The direct questioning of outsiders also indicates the curiosity of the Albanians about other people in the world. For so long their isolation and the resulting ignorance of the world and its people kept them from knowing anything about others. This curiosity is even more extreme with African, Asian, and other racially different people. However, on the whole, Albanians now interact with pride with foreigners. One day some other advisers and I met with a highly placed government official who was clearly pleased to be meeting with us. At the end of the meeting he told us one of the reasons for his pleasure, "I can hardly believe this. Just a few years ago I could have gone to prison for speaking to or of Americans and here I am today meeting openly with Americans with no threat of punishment."

*Elizabeth and Jean-Paul Champseix, 57, Boulevard Staline: Chroniques Albanaises, *Paris: Editions La Découverte, 1990, p. 42.*

Despite their cultural and national pride, however, many Albanians also seem to feel inferior to other people. Although individual Albanians are, in general, self-confident and apparently have good self-esteem, this apparent sense of inferiority has been historically that of an occupied people and this has intensified in recent years. Throughout the Hoxha regime the people were given encouragement regarding their capabilities, but they realized as soon as they were able to see Western television shows that Albania was far behind the development of the other countries in Europe.

A significant legacy of the isolationism imposed by the Hoxha regime is that the Albanian people think in terms of inside (*brënda*) and outside (*jashtë*). This exacerbates the force of their comparisons between themselves and others. While the policy of isolationism no longer exists—in fact, the new government has placed great emphasis on working with and obtaining funds from other countries and international organizations—the Albanians still have a great deal of difficulty leaving their country for any reason, given the mistrust of Albanians in other countries. The governments of other countries fear that if they allow an Albanian to enter the country, even for studies or for vacation, that that person will never leave. In many cases they are correct, since the Albanians' desire to find work and improve their living conditions has led them to emigrate, legally and illegally, in large numbers. However, this restraint on travel has a significant impact on the ability of Albanians to do business and obtain education and medical care beyond what is provided in their own country. As might be expected, such travel restraints also affect the Albanian mentality. On several occasions we witnessed the extreme desire of the people to cross borders to other countries and the difficulties they had in doing so.

The first and most moving such experience was our first trip to Greece. Through a variety of mishaps and miscommunications we found ourselves having to walk from the Albanian side of the border to the Greek side through Albanian passport control and the customs area. The Albanian passport office is in a large concrete building that looks like a squat prison tower. The office itself is a grungy little room on the ground floor with peeling wallpaper, two dirty couches, and a miserable-looking passport control guard sitting behind an equally miserable-looking old desk. After the guard recorded our names and passport numbers in a huge registry book and waved us on, we dragged our luggage to the actual border gate, where we found ourselves standing with about 100 Albanian men all pushing and pressing to be let into Greece. When a Greek passport official noticed that there were Americans in the crowd, he came and opened the gate for us. At this moment scores of people grabbed our arms and pulled on us asking to go with us to carry our bags. We ended up being pushed through

The author with daughter Anna (photograph by Mary Johnson).

the gate and stumbling into Greece. Later, as we drove away from the border in a Greek taxi, we were stopped at a border guard checkpoint and were
required to present our passports again. The guards checked the car thoroughly, including the trunk and underneath, and sent us on our way. As
we approached the main road some miles later, we were stopped again by

some police who shined flashlights into our eyes, checked our passports, and questioned our driver. It is clear that they really don't want Albanians coming into Greece.

Later, after we had adopted our daughter, Anna, in Albania, we had many more unpleasant personal experiences trying to get a visa for her when we wanted to travel outside the country. These ranged from the frustrating (long waits and repeated visits to one embassy or another) to the frightening (being threatened with clubs by the police, along with the throng of Albanians seeking visas).

Another effect of the recent history of the country on the personality of the Albanians is that many of the people seem to see things in terms of black and white only. As a result, they have an endless need to assess blame and tend to be unforgiving. I have heard it said that when Albanians meet each other for the first time they not only exchange genealogical information but also determine who is to blame before they continue with any conversation. This is an overstatement, but it illustrates a central characteristic of the people.

Albanians are highly critical and unwilling to accept the good part of something if they find other parts to be faulty. This critical nature results in one of the most immediately noticeable characteristics of the Albanians: their argumentativeness. They love to talk and arguing is almost a national pastime. It is common to see people face to face arguing with great physical energy and heat in the workplace and on the street. Fortunately, most such arguments end in laughter and embracing.

My first attempts to understand the most negative of these behaviors led to my hypothesis that if you treat people like animals for long enough they will begin to act like animals. As time has passed, however, I have seen more directly the poverty of the people, experienced living in the conditions in which they live, and heard the stories of the women of the challenges they have faced in their lifetimes. So I have developed an understanding and acceptance of these behaviors and have learned to look past them to the people and their spirit.

Part II

THE CHALLENGE AND THE SACRIFICE

Chapter 3

The Older Generation of Women in Albania

Definition

The older generation are women who were over 60 at the time of the interviews. Since the oldest woman we interviewed was 98, all of the women represented were born between 1897 and 1936. Historically and socially they were born in a momentous and tempestuous period in their nation's existence and this had an influence on them to a greater or lesser extent throughout their lives. For some, the effect of growing up in this critical period was to instill nationalistic and humanitarian ideals for which 6,000 women fought in the War of Liberation. For others, the political or social positions of their families would lead to lifelong persecution under the communist regime. For still others, the changes in their lives from the lives of their mothers were almost imperceptible as the great events passed by their immediate world.

The purpose of this chapter is not to give exhaustive historical or social background, but to provide the reader with adequate information to understand the drama and intensity of the time in which these women were raised and the traditional limitations that circumscribed their lives.

Historical Background

Albania's history is characterized by constant struggles to maintain the country's independence in the face of invaders. The existence of a sense of nationalism is alternatively clear and vague, depending on the phase of this historical cycle.

Present-day Albanians trace their lineage to the ancient Illyrians whose empire reached its zenith early in the fourth century B.C. At that time, under the rule of King Bardhyllus, the Illyrian kingdom extended from Trieste to the Gulf of Arta in Epirus.* From the time that the kingdom fell to Philip II of Macedonia (father of Alexander the Great) in the late fourth century, Illyria experienced alternating periods of independence and occupation, including almost 500 years of occupation by the Roman Empire. During this time, around A.D. 50, Christianity was introduced.† Then, during the division of the Roman Empire between East (Constantinople) and West (Rome) Illyria was also divided, thereby sewing seeds of later disunity, both political and religious.

During the Crusades, when Albania served as a thoroughfare to the Middle East, feudalism was introduced into the country, which was broken up into principalities. From time to time these principalities joined and declared themselves independent Albanian states. However, unity and independence were achieved and maintained for a time only in the mid-fifteenth century when the various principalities joined in their resistance to the Ottoman Empire's invasion. In 1444 Gjergj (George) Kastrioti (later known as Skanderbeg, a term of honor associating him with Alexander the Great) returned from Turkey, where he had been educated and held a high position in the military. Upon his return to Albania, he claimed his father's chieftain position, renounced the Muslim faith in favor of Roman Catholicism, and gathered the Albanian chieftains at the Congress of Lezhë. At this congress, they proclaimed him "Chief of the League of the Albanian People," thereby uniting all of their areas under his leadership against the Turks. Under Skanderbeg the united forces successfully resisted the attacks of the Ottoman army. Skanderbeg died in Lezhë in 1468 and the Albanians were defeated by the Turks in 1479 after a 15-month siege of the city of Shkodër, during which women played an important role in the defense of the city.

Ottoman rule of Albania continued for almost 500 years until 1912 and was characterized by: burdensome taxes that were used for the enrichment of the government in Turkey, not for the needs of the Albanian people; suppression of the Albanian culture through the use of the Turkish language; and strong pressure exerted on the people to convert from Christianity to Islam. This pressure on Christians was manifested in the following ways:

---

*Epirus is thought of in Albania as being a southern province of Albania due to the extent of the Illyrian kingdom and the number of ethnic Albanians living there. However, this area is also claimed by Greece and is now included within the borders of Greece.

†Edwin E. Jacques, The Albanians: An Ethnic History from Prehistoric Times to the Present, Jefferson, N.C.: McFarland, 1995, p. 139. It is possible that the Apostle Paul himself brought Christianity to Albania.

1. Lower taxes for Muslims;
2. Greater advantages (ownership of property, good education, and employment, especially in the government and military) for Muslims;
3. The taking of male children from Christian Albanian families for education in Islamic traditions and military training;
4. Social pressures that included requiring Christians to defer to Muslims in public places and in social situations; and later
5. Outright persecution of Christians and their priests and bishops.

To achieve the conversion of the Albanian people to Islam, the Turks also took advantage of the dissention and weakness in the Christian churches, both Catholic and Orthodox, the ignorance of the people regarding the tenets of the Christian and Muslim faiths, the simplicity of the conversion process, and the desire of the Albanian people for identification with the Turks, especially with their military power and culture. It should be noted as well that many Albanians, beginning with those who served as janissaries* in the Ottoman capital, were attracted by the mystical aspects of the more tolerant Bektashi form of Islam.† In all, fully 70 percent of the population was converted to Islam.

The effect of the Turkish occupation of Albania was economic and developmental stagnation. No schools, roads, or railroads were built nor were industrial improvements made. At the time of its independence in 1912, Albania was essentially as the Turks had found it in 1447. Albania had effectively been isolated from the world and left out of the industrial era. As a result, the country was characterized by illiteracy, ignorance, and lack of development and progress.

From the beginning of the Ottoman rule there were uprisings and alliances of certain regions—predominantly Christian—with foreign powers, designed to remove the heavy yoke of Turkish subjugation. As the power and influence of the Ottoman Empire began to wane in the eighteenth century, there were several efforts made to unite the country and to

*The high-ranking soldiers who protected the sultan. This group was composed primarily of men from the countries outside of Turkey that composed the Ottoman Empire. Through these men, the Bektashi faith was brought to Albania.

†Jacques, The Albanians, pp. 200–240. Two forms of Islam were introduced into Albania. The first, the Sunni-Anafit sect, is the oldest and most liberal juridical system for the application of the laws. This reflects the Turks' attention to the administration of justice. In this system, for example, there was significant bureaucratization of the ecclesiastical levels that proved to be a way for the sultan to control the people. The other, Bektashi, is a mystical order of the Shi'ite branch founded in the 13th century by Agi Bektash Veli. This sect emphasizes personal knowledge of God and is also among the more liberal sects in its views regarding laws. It even incorporates some elements of Christianity.

liberate Albania from the empire. Although periods of suppression of the Albanians and their culture alternated with periods of leniency throughout the remaining period of Ottoman rule, it became increasingly clear, even to the Turks, that the periods of suppression led to increased rather than lessened nationalist feeling.

As time passed and the Albanians saw the successful independence and unification movements in other countries, the zeal for independence grew. At the same time its national existence was ignored by the major European powers and its neighbors. In 1877, for example, in an effort to stabilize Europe politically, and in an unsuccessful attempt to avert a war between Turkey and Russia, the European powers signed the Protocol of London under which regions containing significant Albanian populations were given to Bulgaria. This offense was compounded by the Treaty of San Stefano, signed in 1878 at the end of the Russo-Turkish War, which gave significant portions of Albanian territory to its neighbors.

In response to the threat of Russian influence in the Balkans, the Congress of Berlin was called. In anticipation of this Congress, Albanian patriots organized "The Committee for the Defense of the Rights of the Albanian People" in Prizren in June 1878 to formulate fully their position. The League of Prizren, as it is known, called for recognition of the territorial rights of Albania and the formation of an autonomous self-governing body. Despite these efforts, the Congress of Berlin failed to recognize the existence of an Albanian nationality, whilst giving independence and Albanian territories to its neighbors. To support the nationalist claims of Albania and thereby retain some of the Albanian territories within the empire, Turkey sought to demonstrate the existence of an Albanian nationality by lifting restrictions that had prevented national unity, including allowing the use of the Albanian language in schools and publications. This, along with the establishment of the League of Prizren, resulted in the rapid spread of patriotism and the foundation of nationalist organizations. Although fear of the rise of nationalism later led to the reimposition of restrictions, this was the first time since Skanderbeg that Albanians from Ioannina to Shkodër were united in the cause of nationhood.

The Historical Moment

It was into this period of intense nationalism that the women of the older generation were born. It was a time of passion and change. The old order was passing, although not without a struggle, and a new, as yet unformed nation was rising.

In the early 1900s there were a number of uprisings throughout the country, signaling the impatience of the people with Turkish rule. In 1908, in response to pressures from Western powers, the Young Turks movement was founded within the Ottoman leadership with extravagant promises for reforms. However, when the nationalist fervor of the Albanians was recognized, these policies were followed in the same year by a new policy of Ottomanization, resulting in punitive measures against Albania. Predictably, this policy had the opposite effect from what was intended and nationalism grew. The Turks tried to divert this sentiment and then, since diversion wasn't effective, they went back to suppression and nationalists were imprisoned or obliged to flee the country.

During this same time, there was a cultural revolution taking place. The period after the Congress of Berlin brought recognition on the part of the Albanian patriots that a critical unifying factor among Albanians was their language.* To propagate and encourage the use of the language in written form as a tool for rousing national feeling among the people, a uniform alphabet was agreed to in 1908 and literary and patriotic writings of the Fraseri brothers as well as the writings of other patriots and portions of the Bible were published in Albanian.† In addition, nationalist activities were carried on from abroad by Albanians living in Bulgaria, Egypt, Romania, Italy, and United States, including the publication of Albanian-language newspapers that were smuggled into Albania and eagerly read.

Two particularly significant events in the rise of Albanian nationalism occurred outside Albania at this time. First, at the 1908 Convention of Boston, the Albanian church led by the Rev. Fan Noli declared its independence from the Greek church. This gave great impetus to the nationalist cause in Albania because it allowed Orthodox Christians to participate in the nationalist movement without the risk of excommunication. The Muslims followed suit by separating themselves from Constantinople. The second event was the founding in 1912 of VATRA, the Pan-Albanian Federation, by Fan Noli and Faik Bej Koniza and others. This organization united all the Albanian nationalist associations.

A series of primarily local uprisings led to a general uprising in 1912.

---

*This realization and the subsequent emphasis on establishing Albanian as a written as well as a spoken language may have been in response to the frequently voiced opinion of other countries represented at the Congress of Berlin that "There is no such thing as a nation without a written language." Jacques, The Albanians, p. 237.
†The period of time between the latter part of the 19th century and the first part of the 20th century is referred to as the Albanian Renaissance in recognition of the vigor of this movement toward a written language and its use as a literary language for the first time.

At this time, Ismail Qemali, a diplomat and an Albanian political figure in the Turkish Parliament, returned to Albania to assist the nationalist cause by attending the National Congress at Vlorë on November 25, 1912. On November 28, as the elected president in the newly formed Albanian Assembly, he proclaimed Albanian independence. Although the Conference of Ambassadors in London recognized the creation of the Albanian state, disagreements continued over the national borders of Albania, and its neighbors pressed for portions of its territory. At the Congress of Lushnje in January 1920, the sovereignty of Albania was declared, along with the establishment of diplomatic relations with those neighboring states that respected the territorial integrity of Albania.

The period that followed independence was one of great political activity in which many new ideas were offered and tried and in which nationalist sentiments were strong. But the ability of the politicians and rulers to lead and administer the country as a whole was limited. National unity was illusive until a democratic government was established briefly under the leadership of Fan Noli in 1924. However, it wasn't until a young military man, Ahmed Zog (Ahmed Bey Zogu), began his climb to power by leading the military against the invading neighbors that the country's unity and independence became a reality, at least for a time. Zog's military forces overthrew the democratic government of Fan Noli just six months after its establishment, and Zog was proclaimed president in January 1925. Zog, who in September 1928 proclaimed himself King Zog I, relied upon close economic and political ties with Italy to achieve his political goals in Albania. During the next few years, the Italian government provided significant aid and support to Albania, assisting in the building of roads, rail lines, and buildings. However, on April 7, 1939, the Italians, under the leadership of Count Galeazzo Ciano, Mussolini's son-in-law, invaded Albania and King Zog was forced to flee. There followed a period of occupation by the fascists that lasted until the Albanian partisans expelled them, along with the Germans and others, at the end of the War of Liberation in 1944, following which the communist regime was ruthlessly established by Enver Hoxha as a People's Republic.

Societal Issues

In addition to the momentous changes that were occurring in the political sphere, there were radical changes occurring in society, including the liberation of women of this generation from some of the societal strictures of the past. Again, this section does not serve as a comprehensive historical study of the Albanian society. Rather, it seeks to explain the social context into which the women of different regions and different classes were born.

In addition to the mountainous and rough terrain and the dialectical differences, one tradition that separated the northern Albanian people from those in the south was that of the north's adherence to the Code of Lekë Dukagjini, referred to simply as the Kanun. These laws and customs evolved over many centuries and served as the foundation for social behavior and self-government of the peoples of the region.* Although some precedents for these laws may date back as far as ancient Illyrian law, this code is named for Lekë Dukagjini, who lived from 1410 to 1481 and fought with Skanderbeg. The Kanun has had a powerful impact on the lives of the people of the north for centuries and, along with the remoteness of the region, has allowed the northern peoples to maintain a certain amount of independence during Ottoman rule and in more recent times as well.

The primary elements of the Kanun that have had an influence on the women for these centuries include the following:

1. *Patriarchy is assumed.* The eldest male is designated as the head of the household with many rights, in return for which he is obliged to care for the other members of his family in a wise and equitable manner. The mistress of the house has rights and obligations relating exclusively to housework and cooking.†

2. *Marriage is "for the purpose of adding to the workforce and increasing the number of children."*§ Neither young men nor young women have any say in whom they are to marry. A woman may not reject the man chosen without dishonoring the family. A young man may reject the woman, but forfeits any gifts or money exchanged with the parents of the woman. Only widows and widowers can speak for themselves in the matter of marriage.

3. *The family of the man must pay a certain amount to the family of the woman: the "Bride Price."* This was originally thought to be the value of the blood of the woman.**

4. *The rights and duties of husbands and wives are clearly delineated.* A

---

*Kanuni i Lekë Dukagjinit (The Code of Lekë Dukagjini); *Albanian text collected and arranged by Shtefen Gjeçov, translated by Leonard Fox, New York: Gjonlekaj Publishing, 1989.*
†*Ibid., pp. 14–15.*
§*Ibid., p. 20.*
**Ibid., p. 28.*

husband is to ensure that his wife has shoes and clothing and he is to protect her honor, while the wife is to maintain the house, raise the children, and serve her husband. Further, the wife is "not to interfere in the betrothals of her sons and daughters."*

5. *The woman may not inherit from her parents.* This is mainly because she was considered to be superfluous in their household.†

6. *Women are not involved in blood feuds (although they may be killed in the course of one) because a woman's blood is not equal to a man's.* If she should kill someone, her parents incur the obligation to the person's family.§

7. *"A woman is a sack, made to endure."* This is the view of the woman's position in her husband's home.**

8. *A woman may be shot for adultery or for betrayal of hospitality.* These are both considered to be acts of infidelity.†† The woman's parents would have given her husband a bullet at the time of the marriage as a guarantee of her behavior. It was to be used to kill her should she dishonor her husband and family.

Clearly, under this law women were treated more as chattel than as people and their role was both prescribed and circumscribed. The effect of these laws was to place the woman in an inferior social position to her husband and other men and to limit her educational and economic opportunities. The only exceptions to the rules regarding marriage and inheritance related to the declarations of some women to remain virgins and not marry. In the event that the woman did not wish to marry the man chosen for her, the only way that she could avoid "incurring blood" in a blood feud was to become a virgin for life. Likewise, if a woman had no brother, she could declare that she would remain a virgin and take over as the "man of the house" when her parents became too elderly to meet the requirements of the code of hospitality. By so doing, she could inherit the home of the family for her use during her life. If a woman declared that she would remain a virgin, she would take on a masculine name, wear masculine clothes, do men's work rather than work in the fields, and keep the company of men. She could also "take blood" for her brothers or other male family members killed in a blood feud.§§

*Ibid., p. 22.
†Ibid., p. 28.
§Ibid., p. 38.
**Ibid.
††Ibid., p. 40.
§§The phenomenon of Albanian virgins continued through the middle of this century, but has now disappeared along with strict adherence to the laws of the Kanun.

While the laws of the Kanun have lost much of their meaning and force today, they were still adhered to in the early part of the twentieth century, as evidenced in the writings of Edith Durham.* Therefore, when the older generation of women was born, the women of the north continued to be under the rule of this law. There is also evidence to suggest that its influence was felt, to a greater or lesser extent, throughout Albania.†

Due to Turkish and Muslim influences, women wore veils in the early part of this century. This was true in all regions of Albania, but primarily in the cities and their peripheries, as well as in the region bordering Serbia. These veils consisted of a cotton cloth headpiece that went across the forehead and down the sides of the face with a rectangle of thin material that actually covered the face. This practice continued until 1912, when there was a softening of the Albanian people's faith in favor of expressing their national unity. However, the practice persisted among the older and more conservative women, despite the laws passed under the Zog regime and the propaganda of the communist regime. Remnants of the practice continue today with older Muslim women in the cities wearing the cotton forehead and hair piece without the thin face veiling. In addition, married village women of all faiths have traditionally been expected to wear white or black cotton scarves tied around their hair and heads to hide their beauty from men other than their husbands. Since this tradition still exists in the villages and among older women in some cities, the majority of the older women whom we interviewed wore such scarves.

It should, however, also be considered that there were not only regional social differences, but also socioeconomic differences among the Albanians. The women born to families of different classes had radically different opportunities and perspectives. During the Ottoman rule, there arose an upper class with education and a certain amount of wealth from the ranks of men who were favored by the government. Then, in the period following the independence, there were families that were successful in trade and commerce and those who held high governmental positions in the Zog regime. These two groups formed an upper class whose children, even the girls, went abroad to Italy, Austria, France and, in a few rare cases, the United States to study. These girls returned to Albania imbued with the culture and language of the countries in which they studied. Many of them also brought back radical political and social ideas as well.

*See, for example, Edith Durham, High Albania, London: Virago, reprinted 1985.
†The personal histories included in the interviews that follow give evidence to this fact in the preponderance of arranged marriages and force of parental discretion exercised over the lives of the young women as well as the adult women's roles within their marital families.

The Role of Legend and History

The stories and legends that have shaped the lives of these and all Albanian women, including those of later generations, tell of self-sacrifice, strength, and honor. Noteworthy among these is the legend of Rosafa.

In what is now the city of Shkodër in the northern part of Albania near the border with Montenegro, three brothers started to build a castle to protect themselves and their kinsmen. Each day for three days they labored long hours to build up the wall and each night

Above and opposite: Sketches by Albanian artist Pjerin Sheldia of women in the traditional dress of the Shkodër area (courtesy Pjerin Sheldia).

the wall fell. A good man (a man of God) happened to pass by and greeted them, wishing them good work. The brothers thanked the man for his greeting, told him their troubles, and then asked for his advice. The man asked if the three brothers were married and if their wives were alive. When they responded "yes" to both questions, the man said, "To be successful in building the castle you should not work on Sunday. Also, before going home you'll swear to keep faith with each other and you won't speak to your wives of what I will tell you to do. Tomorrow one of your three wives will bring you your breakfast and lunch. You will bury that one in the foundation of the castle and then the walls will not fall again."

The brothers agreed, but the two older brothers broke their promise. They told their wives not to come to them where they worked. The youngest brother did keep his promise. Therefore, the next day the wives of the two older brothers made excuses not to take lunch to the men, but the wife of the youngest brother, Rosafa, agreed to go.

When Rosafa arrived her husband was heartbroken. He and his brothers explained to her the advice they had received. She agreed to be buried in the wall of the castle. However, she had a young son and so she added, "I only want you to listen to my last will: when you put me in the wall, please leave out my right eye, my right hand, my right leg and my right breast because I have left my little son. When he starts crying I will see him with one of my eyes, I will pat him with one of my hands, I will cradle him with one of my legs and suckle my little son with my right breast. Then let my breast be dried and become stone and let the castle rise up strong. Let my son enjoy the castle, and let him grow up to be a brave man and fight courageously in the castle."

The young woman was killed and placed as she requested in the wall of the fortress, and the walls stood from that day on.

For the sake of her kinsmen, Rosafa had agreed to the sacrifice of her life. Yet even in the face of death she thought of the needs of her child and her dedication to him. This story idealizes the sacrifice that each Albanian woman is expected to make to and for her family.

The legends of historical women have also been repeated often and the women of this and more recent generations have grown up with them. The stories of the historical figures of Teuta and of Mamica Kastrioti, for example, have been taught to children for centuries.

Teuta was the Queen of the Illyrian kingdom from 230–28 B.C. after the death of her husband King Agron. She continued the aggressive policy of domination of neighboring tribes and defending her lands and conquests. She led the Illyrian kingdom, inspiring her followers and soldiers with her own brave fighting against the Roman army.

Mamica Kastrioti was Skanderbeg's youngest sister. She was married to Muzak Topia, one of the princes of Albania in 1445. After her husband was killed in the Battle of Berat, Mamica became the head of the Topia princedom. She herself led her people in the fight against the Turks and served as an adviser to her brother, who valued her opinion and sought her advice.

In these and in the majority of Albanian stories—both fiction and nonfiction—the women are portrayed as strong, as strong as men, in their commitment to their country and in their willingness to sacrifice all for their families and homeland. This has been translated into action time and again, with women taking up arms or providing active support to the troops who were engaged in the defense of the country. It is also part of everyday life; women have learned to see themselves as being as strong as men and to encourage each other to live up to this image. While this is clear in the stories the women told us, it is especially evident in a greeting between women that we heard in the northern part of Albania, "*A je burrnesh?*" literally meaning "Are you a man-woman?" but understood as "Are you as strong as a man?"

The Influence of History and Society

Many of the women of all social classes whose formative years occurred during this period felt the societal restrictions. Yet, because it was a relatively open and tumultuous period, many of them heard politics and ideas discussed everywhere: in their families, in the fields, and in the city streets. These women saw their parents or others of the older generation taking part in political activities, and these events shaped their own ideas and ideals. They learned, along with their brothers, to have a love for their country and a hatred for the occupiers and others who threatened their independence. They learned that other women in the world were not treated as they were and heard the words that represented the communist ideal of equality, not only among men, but also between men and women. Some of them even became ready to fight for their country and their ideals. With great courage these women broke the social strictures and codes of conduct and did in fact fight with their brothers in the War of Liberation. Others, many hundreds and thousands of women, worked behind the lines supporting the war materially and morally.

Yet the majority of women did not fight, but remained bound by social strictures. They remained in their families and in the society that had existed for centuries. Some of them may have suffered consequences later for who their parents were and the positions their families held, either social or political, in those years.

The lives of the women of this older generation have been characterized by hard work and self-sacrifice for family and community, in spite of limitations such as lack of education and self-determination. Their stories are an inspiration to their daughters and their grand-daughters. In the next two chapters the village and city women of northern, central and southern Albania tell their stories. This is followed by more detailed stories told by well-known women of the older generation.

Chapter 4

The Lives of
the Village Women

Since the vast majority of the older generation of women were born and raised in rural areas and were engaged primarily in agriculture, the primary focus of this chapter is on the village women. While their lives were restricted by social conventions, many of the women's lives were also touched at some point by the political events of the times.

In the North: Homesh

THE ROAD TO HOMESH

Our trip to the Peshkopijë region was exhausting both physically and emotionally. Ksanthi and I went by taxi to a relatively accessible village called Homesh with a young lady, Anita Jella, who was one of Ksanthi's students and whose family had agreed to host us during our stay. To get to the village the roads lead in almost a complete circle: east from Tiranë to Frushë-Krujë, north to Burrel, and then west to Klos to avoid a mountain range. Then the road turns north again toward the city of Peshkopi. The segment going north to Burrel goes through a section called Liqeni e Ulzës with vast and beautiful hydroelectric lakes that are pale green with a bit of blue, appearing almost glacial. At the narrowest points of the lakes there are primitive rope bridges strung across and small villages on the other side. The road twists and turns, but is generally quite good. Burrel is a wasteland of a city with only one noteworthy sight: one of the most terrible of Enver Hoxha's prisons for political prisoners. There is a single building above ground that was used for receiving people, and the remainder of the prison was built underground.

It took only about three hours to get to the village of Shupenzë, which is where we originally thought we were going. However, Anita instructed the taxi driver farther down the road and then down a narrow dirt road to the school (built by the Italians before the war and now in a state of disrepair). It wasn't far from her house, Anita told us, and we would walk the rest of the way. We all shouldered our bags and took off down the road with two of us thinking that our destination was close at hand. Then, as we walked down a rough path that was mostly a washed-out gully of rocks, Anita waved to her parents on the other side of a valley. Although we understood that we were not exactly on top of our destination, Ksanthi and I still did not realize how far we had to go. The trail got steeper. We slid down to the bottom in our city shoes, arriving at a rickety wooden bridge over a stream. We crossed successfully, still carrying our bags and boasting of our ability to master the tough path and carry our suitcases too. The path then began to climb, and halfway up the hill it became a stream as well. At this point, Anita's 15-year-old brother met us to help with the bags. Ksanthi and I nearly threw them at him in our haste to be rid of them. (So much for our efforts to show how strong we were.) We climbed the rest of the way balancing in the running water (which became much simpler when I just gave up trying to keep my shoes dry) and grasping at twigs and grass to steady ourselves. When we finally arrived on dry land again, we proceeded toward the family's house. The last remaining obstacle was a small stream with muddy banks that we could jump across. Needless to say, we arrived at the Jellas' house with mud-spattered legs and soggy, muddy feet. Anita's father, mother and grandmother greeted us warmly and showed us where to leave our shoes: outside.

We took time to rest only briefly and have lunch and then we started the interviews. We found the women to be attractive, eager to talk, and full of life and humor. It was 8:30 P.M. when we started back to the house, and it was beginning to get quite dark. As we were leaving the last house, one of the men told us to watch out for the goats returning from pasture. No sooner did we get around the first bend in the road when we heard a small roar behind us. We turned to see a large herd of goats heading down the narrow road toward us. We stepped aside to let them pass: which they did with curious looks at us. It also turned out that the path was a superhighway for drag-racing horses, mules, and donkeys at that hour of the evening.

Dinner followed with an abundance of food, including homemade bread baked in the *saç* (pronounced "such"),* and we were more than ready

Later in our stay we were shown the saç in a small building behind the house and across from the outhouse. The base sat on a mound and the iron lid was heated over an open fire burning on the hearth beside the saç. The lid was heated until it glowed red and then was placed over the food in the pan on the base.

to sleep when the time came. Our beds were the ingenious Albanian-manufactured sofabeds where the back lies down flat and forms half of the bed. They are not especially comfortable as either sofas or beds, but they are necessary equipment in a country where hospitality is so esteemed and lodging is mostly unavailable. We were given thick quilts to put over us (in the height of the Albanian summer) and were very glad to have them as the night became quite cold. We also left our last visit to the toilet until late, to avoid having to go out of the door through the farmyard to the outhouse (with its hole carved out of the rock and rough Turkish toilet–style foot pads on either side) in the total dark.

The next day started with a hearty breakfast, which included leftover bread and yogurt, and I quickly began to understand that we would be doing a great deal of hiking. Unfortunately, I had asked Anita before we went to the village what the appropriate attire for women was and she had replied that the women of the village all wore dresses. Not wanting to either offend or to imperil the interview results, I had opted to also wear a dress—bad decision! We had to walk about 30 minutes to get from one house to the next and always over rough, wet, and muddy terrain. It had rained shortly after we arrived and it rained again in the middle of this first day, so the mud quotient was quite high. Fortunately, we were expected to leave our shoes at the entrance to each house, so I had an opportunity to get my feet out of wet shoes for the length of the interviews. I spent most of the interview time with my feet and legs curled up under me to get my feet warm and to keep the hordes of flies off my legs.

As we made our way to the first interview, we met Besniku riding on his tractor pulling a tractor cart. He invited us to hop aboard and gave us a short and very bumpy ride. He said he had heard that we were there to interview the women who were going to die soon and proceeded to tell everyone we met that this was what we were doing.

After the first set of interviews, we had a relatively mud-free walk to the next house, access to which was under the ruins of an ancient stone archway. The house itself was a traditional northern Albanian style and had at one time been a kulla, a fortified tower for defense, mostly against neighbors with whom one was engaged in a blood feud. The living room was an enormous hall with sofas along the outside wall. The family had been one of the wealthiest in the region, the Dema family.

My general impressions of Homesh were paradoxical. It is a place of great beauty with the houses and farms placed on foothills and surrounded by high mountains. The views of Dibër in the Serbian portion of former Yugoslavia with the myriad lights at night and its mountains by day are stunning. But I also saw a place of great misery as the lives of the people were hard, unrelentingly so. Homesh also symbolized for me the paradox of life and death. There was a great beauty and vitality in the people in general and yet many of the women, especially the young girls, seemed to have death lurking beneath the surface: a kind of death of the spirit. There were also many stories of the excruciating pain of loss: loss of economic status, loss of a child, loss of community with others, and loss of opportunity and selfhood. Monotony was also palpable: the monotony of hard work and societal expectations.

SHYQYRIE'S STORY

It was in Homesh that we found Shyqyrie, the oldest woman we had an opportunity to interview. This lady was 98 years old, hard of hearing, and a bit senile, so her stories were told to us by her son who had been an actor, evidently of the vaudevillian type. As he told his mother's stories so vividly, I am reporting them in the first person.

I was born in a very poor family in a village called Gjaritë, near the border with Yugoslavia, and was orphaned early in my life. All I remember of my family is that my father was exceptionally fanatical and conservative. Because I was an orphan no one wanted to marry me, but a marriage was arranged for me when I was 13 years of age to a man who was 22 years older than I. Because I was young and short, my people asked me to stand on a stool when my husband came to take me. I was so young that I had not yet reached puberty and could not yet sleep with my husband. So for two years I slept in the same bed with my husband having no sexual relations. He turned his back to me and I turned my back to him for two years.

My husband helped me to grow up, but he beat me when I played with other girls my own age. He had to take care of me, but he was fanatical. He told me not to raise my head up while walking to the field or going to the mountain to cut wood. I had to look down and fix my gaze on the tips of my shoes. If I dared to do something different, my husband had threatened to cut my head off and he often beat me for nothing serious. Once my husband threatened to shoot me dead for asking my sister-in-law for some thread.

Ours was a typical patriarchal family. We (the women of the family) never had the right to speak to our husbands in front of others. It was considered to be shameful to do that. The women in our house never entered a room where the men were gathered to talk, drink coffee, or eat lunch. It was the duty of the women to prepare and bring coffee, food, etc., to the room—to the door of the room. We had to work and bear children.

When I joined the family there were 20 people in the house and they said that I brought them good luck. I gave birth to a total of 11 children, 3 of whom died. The first 8 children were born one and a half years apart. The last child, a boy, was born when I was 50. All of the children were born at home with the help of old women, not midwives. When I was pregnant I had to keep my pregnancy secret from the people in the house and from my husband, although the secret didn't last long since after 4 or 5 months the secret was revealed. [Shyqyrie laughed at this recollection.] It was considered shameful to be pregnant. I did hard work until the eighth month of my pregnancy and returned to work just 3 days after the birth of each child, leaving the baby at home alone or in the care of someone else. The young parents of the time never patted, kissed, or hugged their children in the presence of others. It was considered shameful for the son and daughter-in-law to do such things (or even speak) in front of the father or father-in-law.

Although the family was not wealthy it was declassed* because of envy of my husband's father who was a good and nice man. As a result, the family was extremely poor. I had no clothes for my children. I collected leaves in the snow and used them as a mattress in their cradles. This also saved washing.

The oldest interviewee, Shyqyrie, at her home in Homesh.

I now have three sons and five daughters and very good daughters-in-law. When our daughters grew up and the time to marry them came, only my husband had the right to decide on such a problem. I was not asked at all to give my opinion about my daughter's marriage.

Shyqyrie's son added that his mother was always nice to his wife. Shyqyrie didn't want her to suffer as she herself had suffered. He also said that during the last period of their marriage—that is when Shyqyrie's husband was about 100 years old, his parents lived a happy life because there were no more problems between them. When asked if her marriage had been successful, Shyqyrie gave a wonderfully ambiguous answer: "I loved my husband as much as he loved me."

As her son spoke, Shyqyrie sat with a smile on her face and laughed. Every so often she talked at the top of her lungs. Her face was leathered and lined. She seemed to be totally unaware of the flies that landed on her face as she sat there. It was almost as if part of her had already died and

*Declassed families were primarily those with a certain amount of wealth in land or other property whose property was expropriated by the state.

only the spark of life remained. At the end I asked her, "In all of your difficult life what was the source of your strength?" She responded simply, "God helped us in everything."

OTHER OLDER WOMEN IN HOMESH

All of the women in Homesh, a Muslim village, gave us a special perspective on the lives of women in their respective generations. The insights that the older generation of women were able to give us about their society prior to the War of Liberation and throughout more recent history were remarkable. It is better, however, to hear the stories of arranged marriages, polygamy, hardship, and strength told in their own words with both humor and pain.

Hide is 76 years of age and was born in another village in the Peshkopijë region. She has had no education and cannot write her own name.

I was born to a well-to-do family: one of four children and the only girl. I never suffered as a child. My father worked the land and my mother was at home. I remember them as a happy couple who liked to drink coffee together on the verandah.

In 1936 when I was 17, I was married as the second wife of a man who already had a wife, Turkish style. This man wanted a child and his first wife was unable to have children. I saw him and liked him, but the marriage was arranged. My earliest childhood memory was the moment before I got engaged. My mother said to me, "Think before you speak. He already has a wife." I responded, "I don't care. Let him take two more wives." After our marriage I came to live in the house with just him and his other wife. It was difficult at first, but we got used to it. The first wife was more like a mother-in-law since she was older, but she was not a burden. We lived happily together until the moment he died 15 years ago. My husband was a traffic supervisor and I worked one year in the cooperative and then as a dressmaker in Shupenzë.

My husband's family was poorer than my own, but we bought some land and did well. However, our family was declassed in the communist regime. We became what were known as *Kulaks** and our land was taken away.

I also had no children. So once we were invited by a friend of my husband's to visit an Italian doctor in Tiranë to see if I could give birth to a child. He said that I was okay, but he wanted to test my husband. My husband probably already understood that he had a problem and never followed through on the testing. Even so, we never spoke of this again and I maintained my great respect for him.

However, we still wanted a child. Later, when my husband worked at an important religious institution of the Bektash faith, there was a driver there who had divorced his wife. They had a son, eight months of age, and they left him in

*This is the Russian word used by Stalin to describe landowning people whom he declassed in order to expropriate their wealth and punish them for their bourgeois attitudes. The same word was used by the communist regime in Albania for this class of people.

the road. My husband took the child and we raised him as our own until he was five and a half. The parents came to us then and asked that we return him to them. According to the law they had the right to take the child. Although this was a very difficult time, it made me stronger. When the village people came to my house to express their condolences I served them coffee with sugar, rather than without sugar as is the custom in mourning, because I decided not to mourn, but to get another child.

We then adopted a son from the orphanage at the age of three months. It was very difficult at the time because of societal problems. People didn't like children left at orphanages.*

I found strength in myself. It's just like me that when I am confronted by lies, falsehoods, it makes me strong. I learned to be strong from my mother. She never gave in when facing difficulties. I don't agree at all that a hard life makes people hard. Wicked people have been bad to me, but although I don't forget, I don't seek revenge.

Our tradition of hospitality has helped me to keep my good-heartedness, but faith has played no role in my life. I forgot everything because of Enver Hoxha's actions.

Qamile is 64 years of age. She was originally from the village of Boçevë near Shupenzë, but married a man from Homesh and, of course, moved there.

My father worked in the fields and was good at agriculture. I was an only child. My mother died when I was one year old and my father remarried. My grandmother (my father's mother) raised me. I remember having great love for my grandmother. For a long time I thought she was my mother and only learned later that I was motherless. I admired her because she was clever, hard-working and cared for me well.

My childhood was a difficult time. We had wealth, but we didn't know how to live. We had a lot of land and animals, but we didn't know how to make use of them.

I was married at 14 years of age, before the Liberation. It was an arranged marriage and a damned time when I got married. The people lived a hard life and the fanatical views and backward customs added to the difficulty of life. The girl often had to marry the man she was told to marry, not the one she might have fallen in love with. Although the circumstances were awful, I was lucky. I married a man with whom I led a happy life. We were second to none as a couple. We lived together in Homesh with my in-laws for 17 years, then we moved to Peshkopi and lived on our own.

We had four children: three boys and a girl. They all went to school through high school and two of my sons are now drivers and one is a carpenter. My daughter is an economist. We sacrificed for them. We had poor salaries, but our concern was only to raise healthy children. I live well now because my children all work and I have a pension.

I recall a time of great difficulty when a voluntary action was called to build

People were prejudiced against illegitimate children as the offspring of people who had violated the societal rules.

The three sisters in Homesh: Hatixhe, Vahide, and Sulbie.

the bunkers. I worked an eight-hour shift at the hospital and then worked eight more hours on the construction of the bunkers. We suffered quite a lot: no food or coffee. It was my fortune to have good health and to work side by side with my husband. I also had faith but couldn't worship, so I just believed with my heart.

Three sisters, Vahide (63), Hatixhe (60), and Sulbie (55), told a poignant story of the hardship of isolation from family, which exacerbated other hardships that each experienced. The sisters were born in Homesh into a family of 5, including 2 brothers. Hatixhe told us: "We didn't suffer much in childhood. Our family had a plot of land during the Zog regime and we lived on our own. No one troubled us at that time. Our mother was hard-working, especially since our father died young. She told us how to become good wives and daughters-in-law. We had to learn how to take care of domestic animals, fields, and guests. We also learned good behavior."

None of the sisters received any education. It was Vahide, the eldest, who assisted their mother by caring for their father while their mother worked. It was after their marriages, and later as a result of the persons they married, that their lives diverged. Vahide told of her married life:

I married in 1946 at the age of 14 under an arrangement with a scarf over my face. I saw my husband for the first time at the wedding. I moved with my husband to the village of Bllacë to my husband's family. There were 30 people in the family and I had to take care of all those people. The burden of housework was mostly on my shoulders.

Later my husband was paralyzed for a year and then died three months after being diagnosed with cancer. At the time of his death, I had 5 children ranging from 3 to 20. A sixth child, a son, we gave in adoption to my brother-in-law.

I also spent many months in the hospital and only worked for six months in the cooperative. I was too sick with thyroid and kidney problems to work in the fields. The oldest children helped me. My son and I know how difficult it was to care for the family after the death of my husband and with the health problems I had.

Hatixhe and Sulbie were also married under arrangements that at the time appeared to be fortuitous. Both were married into the Dema family, a wealthy family in which the father was a major in the reserves in Zog's government. Hatixhe said this of her in-laws and her married life:

I was married into the Dema family under an arrangement when I was 17 years old. My father-in-law had 5 wives. The 9 children born of the first wife died; 2 born of the second wife also died. There were no children born to either the third or fourth wives, but a boy born to the fifth wife lived and became my husband. My father-in-law didn't like the occupation of the Italians although he was in the government of Zog. The family later suffered consequences because of his association with the Zog government.

My husband was a good man and we had seven children, three boys and four girls. However, when the communists came into power we were forbidden any contact with my mother's family because my husband's family had been anticommunist. We had a bad biography. We are just now meeting our cousins and other relatives for the first time in almost 50 years. Sulbie and I experienced intense loneliness throughout this separation from our sister, Vahide, and her family. I even had to leave my children in the house alone when I went to work in the fields. The Party of Labor separated our families, and my most challenging moment came when my daughter died. No one came to express their condolences for fear of suffering the consequences. I understood that they had to protect themselves and didn't blame them, but it caused a pain deep in my heart. You could debate with each other, but not with the government.

Later our family suffered other consequences. For example, my husband was not allowed to work in the village and was sent to Bajram Curri as a form of exile and my son, Besniku* was sent to prison because of our family's biography, but the pretext was that it was because he didn't want to work in the village. He wanted to go to Tiranë to learn to play an instrument. The Hoxha regime imprisoned him for a term of ten years, although he only served four years because democracy came along.

Sulbie was married into the same family under an arrangement when she was 17 years of age as well. She and her husband worked on the cooperative as well and they had 6 children, 2 boys and 4 girls. "I was as isolated

---

The man we met earlier driving the tractor.

from my people as my sister was. When my son was married, even my uncle couldn't come. My father-in-law was imprisoned for eight years by Hoxha, but my husband and children were not imprisoned. My children were given the right to attend the village agricultural school, but no more."

What gave these women the strength to survive the hardships, the uncertainty and the separation and isolation?

Vahide answered this question, "I have believed in God and my faith has been rewarded. For example, once when my granddaughter was a little child she got very sick. I went to a sacred place with her. There I prayed to God and her health improved."

Hatixhe's response was, "My sister, Sulbie, was close and supportive. She kept me from going mad, but God gave me the strength to survive. People say that there is no God, but I believe. We respected religion even when it was suppressed. I also think of the good things, not just the bad things, that came out of the communist regime. It was a quiet and safe life, there were hospitals and the midwife came to your house, both free of charge. Despite all the sufferings I have had, there is really only one thing I don't forgive. That is that my children were not able to get an education. When I die, I won't be quiet because of this great suffering."

Sulbie said simply, "We had to find the force somewhere ... only in God and no one else."

In the South: Vithkuq

Vithkuq is a clean and well-constructed village with stone houses and roads set on three hills in a mountainous area near Korçë. There are 250 families living in 3 distinct and physically separated neighborhoods. Most of the families marry their children within the village and have done so for generations. Therefore, the family relationships are complicated. There are 13 Orthodox churches here, all built on the tops of the hills with splendid views of the surrounding area and the village population is entirely Orthodox.

Since Korçë and the villages around it were among the first to have emigrants go to the United States, one of the themes we heard in this village, especially from the older women, was that of loss of a parent, generally the father, who left during their infancy to seek opportunity in the United States. Also, for this reason, the villagers of Vithkuq are relatively prosperous. The tradition of emigration continues today as there are now about 50 young boys from the village working in Greece.

During the War of Liberation, Vithkuq was in the center of intense fighting between the Albanian partisans and the Germans, and it served as a headquarters for the partisans. We heard many stories of the burning of the village and the time that the villagers were obliged to spend in the mountains to escape from the Germans. All of the families of the village are reported to have been idealistic communists.

PANDORA'S STORY

We met Pandora, 70, living in a house that had been a center of national liberation activity and was visited by many prominent partisans during the war, including Dhora Leka.* The partisans came to the house to be clothed and fed. The Germans destroyed the house for this reason, and now the house is only two stories instead of the original four. As the daughter of an Orthodox priest, Pandora incorporates in her story many of the elements that distinguish Vithkuq and its women, as well as elements of her faith.

My father was a priest and my mother was an orphan, because her parents had gone to America without her and had died there. What I remember of my childhood is that we all worked in the fields. My mother taught us everything, inside and outside the house. We were very close to her. Our father worked hard in the church and religion was in our blood. He was alive when the churches were closed, and they made him shave his beard. At first, he closed himself in the house for a month, but then he went on with his activities—secretly, of course.

At 17 I married under an arrangement. My husband was a partisan. I had known him as a boy, but had not met him as a man. One day when the partisans were returning from the war, I went out to see them. The brother of my husband saw me and suggested that he marry me. We girls couldn't say yes or no, we just had to accept the arrangement. We were engaged while he was still a partisan and were married in 1946.

We had six children, four boys and two girls. I worked in the fields and had no one to help with the children. I have suffered a lot to raise my family because my husband was wounded in the war and couldn't work. I had to work extra to make up for this. For example, I used to pick medicinal flowers to sell.

I found strength in my love for life and a desire to lead a better life. I remember that many times I put my children to bed with no food. Now that we can live better we are old, but I am happy to see my children living better because they have suffered so much.

When asked about the role of faith in her life, Pandora added with an expression as if it should have been self-evident, "I had religious belief in

*Dhora Leka was a well-known partisan who also wrote the songs that inspired the partisans in their fight. Her story is presented below in chapter 6.

my blood. I did everything in secret. It was foolish of *him* [Enver Hoxha] to close the churches. Sometimes we didn't even tell our husbands or other relatives about lighting the candles or keeping the religious feasts. Because of my faith, I do not fear death. When I die, I want everyone to sing and dance."

OTHER OLDER WOMEN OF VITHKUQ

Two other women particularly spoke of the lives of the villagers in the period of the War of Liberation and of their lives thereafter.

Jorgjia, aged 72, reminisced,

I was the only daughter in the family and we lived a good life. Before the Liberation, my father was a tradesman and later he was an elementary school teacher. My mother was a housewife.

I was engaged at 18 and married 3 years later at the age of 21. It was an arranged marriage. My husband used to do business with my father and wanted to marry me. We were married in December 1944. The Germans had burned all our houses, so my parents built another small one where we had our wedding dinner. Because my husband came from a family of partisans, they wanted me to dress as a partisan for my marriage. (My eldest brother-in-law had married a partisan girl. That was an honor!) Yet I didn't dress in partisan clothes—just a pair of partisan shoes with my dress.

I had a good life after my marriage, but we had very little money as the salaries were so low. My husband and I worked hard, however, and we got along. Our income was only 4,000 old lekë [about $4.00] per month so I had to sacrifice much to marry my daughter with a dowry. The rule was that the dowry was to consist of at least one *qilim* [carpet], two blankets, linens for the house, and mattresses. To come with less of a dowry was a disgrace.

There was also a difficult time when my husband was imprisoned early in our marriage. He was accused of profiting in his trade. It was really a problem of not keeping good books, but he was imprisoned anyway. One day his brother who was the head of the prison system came by chance to inspect the prison that my husband was in. As he was looking at the prisoners he saw his own brother and went and embraced him. "This is surely a first," people remarked, "the senior prison official embracing a prisoner." Later my husband was released because they understood that he had done no wrong.

Violetta, 65, also spoke of this period,

I was the youngest of a family of three girls and one boy. My mother worked in the fields. I never knew my father because he left for America in 1930 before I was born and never returned. He died there at the age of 72. We were also planning to go to America to join him, but in 1938 when we were trying to go the roads were blocked because of the fear of invasion. We could not get out. I remember my mother being desperate because she was married and not married at the same time. That is, she was considered to be married, yet she had no husband. No one to help her.

Jorgjia in Vithkuq.

I remember especially the time of the war. I was 12 when the Germans came. They told us to leave the village and go up the mountain. We all left and left everything behind. We thought only of our lives. In 1943 the village was burned, but we had built huts up in the mountains where we could live. Time and again when the Germans occupied our village, the people were told to leave. We always returned after the Germans left. Sometimes we stayed away longer than other times, but all in all we lived about two and a half years in the mountains.

Both of these women replied that their source of strength came from their children and their desire to give them a good life. Jorgjia said, "We tried to do everything to give our daughters enough so that we would not be ashamed." Violetta told us, "I wanted to help my children grow up." She added, "I have also enjoyed having many guests."

Although neither of these women identified faith as a primary source of strength, both responded eagerly when asked what role faith had played in their lives, saying,

"I never stopped being religious. I have a boundless faith in God."

"When the churches were closed, I didn't give them my icons, but kept them in a secret place and found a place to light a candle."

"I lied to my husband who was a party man. 'I'm going to pick vegetables,' I would say when I went to church."

Katrina in Himarë.

HIMARË

On a brief visit to Himarë I met Anastasia and her daughter Katrina. Anastasia was a wizened little woman, crippled and wrapped in a coat and many blankets, lying on a sofa in a dingy and smelly kitchen. She spoke in Greek and crossed herself almost continually as she told of a more desperate existence. "I don't know how old I am—maybe 99 or 100 ['93,' interjected her daughter]. I was born in Himarë and lived in the castle on the hill because I was from one of the oldest families in Himarë, but don't ask me about the life I have had. I feel ashamed. I grew up when we had no roads and we used animals to go to other villages. We lived a life like a dog's when I was young. We were far back behind the world in those days. I have lived a black life. We were the same as animals and we have even lived with them under the same roof.

When I asked about where she had found the force to overcome her difficulties, she said, "We had no force. We just had to live life as it was. My husband didn't help me, in fact, he beat me. I have raised seven children, but with what? Hunger."

In answering my question about what role faith had played in her life, she responded in short thoughts interspersed with her prayers, "I believe in God. God has brought us such good changes. Before when we washed our clothes we used ash, now we use soap."

Her daughter, Katrina aged 67, added,

Growing up we had no electric light and our mother made fire with sticks. We had no hospitals when I was young and my mother gave birth to all her children at home without the help of a nurse or midwife. When I was a girl, we had our property and we worked the land with a plow pulled by oxen. I remember that we always felt hungry because we never had enough food.

If you are looking for the woman who has survived the hardest life of all, I am she. I am the hardest-working woman in the area. This was true when I worked in the cooperative and now. I spend so much time with my donkey that he is my friend! All the women of my age have worked hard to survive—even carrying heavy loads on our backs—water from far away.

Like the other women I found strength in caring for my children. Believing in God in our country was not allowed. I had God inside of me because if I spoke out loud I would be punished. We were not free to talk to our people and didn't speak openly because we were always afraid of betrayal. We lived in great fear: even of our husbands and children. Now I believe whatever I want. I say it loudly and am free: no one punishes me.

In Central Albania: Perondi

In the village of Perondi, a predominantly Muslim village 30 minutes by foot from the center of the city of Kuçovë, we met Urani (Orthodox) aged 60, Nadire aged 65, and Sadije aged 69. They told us about the difficulties of their lives and the problems they had faced.

Urani told us, "I lived with a blind mother-in-law who was good to me. I had six children and a total of nine people to take care of with very little money. We had no clothes except the ones we wore, so I had to wash the clothes at night to get them dry by morning. We could hardly buy our daily food with the little money we were paid for our work."

The story Nadire told us was unique for us, but repeated in many lives in Albania,

I was born in the village of Lapardhë in the time of King Zog's rule. When I was just 7 years old my mother died, and when I was 8 years old my father died. They were both killed in a blood feud. At the age of 10, as the eldest of 5 children, I had the whole burden of the family on my shoulders. My uncle took care of us, although his wife divorced him because she didn't agree to have us. There were 19 people in the combined family, and for 6 or 7 years I worked hard for them all. When I was 17 years old, my uncle remarried a girl younger than I. In 1948 I married at the age of 18 under an arrangement. My husband was 3 years older than I and was a hard-working and honorable man. We have been much in love. We had 6 children because we didn't know you could keep from having children. I lived happily with my husband's family because I found both warmth and love there. When the cooperative started, I worked hard and was given much responsibility.

Sadije said, "I was born in a village of Fieri. At 18 years of age I was married under an arrangement and had six children. My husband and I worked in the cooperative as did all of the other villagers. It was difficult to raise children with no kindergartens, and life was hard. Now I can find things to buy, but I have no money. Although I worked on the cooperative, I didn't have enough years working to get a pension. I sold my cow to pay for higher education for my son, who is now a teacher."

Hard work and deprivation have figured strongly in the lives of these village women. What has given them the strength to overcome these difficulties? Nadire and Sadije summed it up.

Nadire said, "I grew up thinking that I would have to take revenge for the deaths of my parents. Life and necessity have made me strong. I had to think of my brothers and sisters. My mother's deathbed words were 'My dear daughter, take care of the children.' Hard work has been most important to me. I couldn't have brought up children and raised a family if I didn't work hard. We believed much in God earlier, then the religious institutions were abolished. We had to do what the party said. Now I believe again. I don't believe in the priests and hoxhas, but in God. I frequently pray 'Oh God, I am always tired, but I hope to be better.'"

Sadije explained, "God and hope for a better life have given me strength. Although we had no religious institutions, we kept God in our hearts."

Chapter 5

The Lives of
the City Women

While conditions in the village were difficult and the work was hard, the city people and intellectuals suffered as well.

Shkodër

When we visited the northern city of Shkodër, which is dominated by Rosafa Castle and located on the edge of the Lake of Shkodër near the border with Montenegro, the women, all Catholics, told us of hardships related primarily to persecution of intellectuals and those who professed their faith.

Çiçilja, a small woman of 73 with age and troubles physically weighing down her shoulders and back, told us,

When I was young, I lived in Tiranë. My father, Rrok Kiçi, was one of the founders and head of the Albanian Red Cross before the war. As was the case with many people who had studied abroad or worked with international organizations before and during the war, he was suspected by the communist regime. Also, two of his children had gone to America, which compounded their suspicions. Therefore, in 1944 my father was arrested. Even though he was later released to serve in the army, we were told to leave Tiranë at a time when many families were being sent out of the city. Everything was left on the streets as only one truck was sent for two families. We really didn't have time to collect our things so we had to leave them.

When we first arrived in Shkodër, our aunt gave us shelter. Later, our aunt's house was destroyed and we went to share an apartment, with only one bathroom, with another family.

We found strength only in God and in our close family relationships. I have had many problems—too many to recount—but God has given me strength. It was a joyous day for us when the churches were reopened.

It was late one sweltering summer evening when we met Maria and we were exhausted as we stumbled though the dark streets to her house.

The house itself was well lit and located in a pretty garden behind a grill-work gate. We were shown into a breathlessly hot room adorned with pictures of Christ, the Last Supper, and Maria's sons who had died. Maria herself is a strong, straight, and solid 72-year-old woman of clear conviction and faith. We found it unnecessary to ask what her source of strength had been.

I have suffered a great deal, but my strong faith in God has helped me overcome my sufferings, my pain. I have had in my life both bad consequences and the touch of God. I come from a family with strong faith and my brother was a priest. We were always looked down upon by the communist regime because we were the family of a priest who had been imprisoned.

My brother, the priest, was imprisoned by the Italians before the war because he wrote a book in defense of the country, against the Italian occupation. Then, he was arrested by the communists just two months after my other brother was arrested and sentenced to five years in prison, accused of organizing a protest against the communists. This second arrest came right after the Liberation when he was just 28 years of age. Someone had set fire to a warehouse and my brother was accused and shot dead on Christmas Day. I heard the rifle shot and ran to the place where it had happened. I saw my brother there still with the handcuffs on and with blood all over the place. I paid two villagers to follow the police to see where my brother was buried. Sometime later I asked them to show me the place where they had buried him. It was camouflaged, but after 41 years (after the democratic reform) we found his skeleton. He still had the handcuffs on.

I accepted an arranged marriage—a villager in Kryezi, a village in the Pukë district. He was a good man, but ignorant. We had two children. Later, my husband suffered two years in prison simply because he married me, a woman who came from the family of a priest.

After 15 years I returned to Shkodër, but I kept on keeping the church in Kryezi open. It was difficult to get the right to work when we came back, but we got jobs in the sawmill. God knows how much I suffered and how many suffering and tortured people I've seen. The term genocide is correctly applied, based on the cruel tortures I have seen. I remember the body of a young man tortured and dragged along the road. Such scenes terrified us.

Another personal sadness I had was that my son drowned while he was a soldier. One day I was sick and couldn't go to his grave. That day I put down on paper what came into my mind. It turned out that I started writing a book. Lot Nënë [Tears of a Mother] it was titled by the publisher. I am not a writer and have had only four classes and no other education. I just wrote what came out of my heart.

Through all my life I have preserved my faith in God. It is not for the state or an ideology to forbid religion. We were not the first country in history to persecute faith. People keep these things deep in their hearts. God has been more helpful when we were forbidden to believe. I have never been tempted by the hardships to give up my belief. God hasn't done anything wrong. He has his own plan. I have a stronger faith and have done the work of the priests, including baptisms. Faith survives in the hearts of the people. As for me, I have felt the miracles of God whenever I've found myself in difficult situations.

Terezina, at right, with her friend Ana Daja.

TEREZINA'S STORY:
CIGARETTES AND TEARS

Terezina, 69, is broken in body and spoke with her hands, feet, and voice trembling—cracking with recollected pain. She smoked cigarettes and wept quietly throughout the interview.

I was born in Shkodër in 1927 and had a nice childhood. There were no economic problems and my father worked in the Italian consulate here. Hell began for me when *they* came into power in 1944. My uncle was imprisoned soon after the Liberation for trying to leave the country.

In 1946 I was expelled from school and arrested. I was sentenced at first to two years of house arrest. In 1946 came the Postribe Revolt, the first and most important revolt against the communist regime. As a result, I never served the house-arrest sentence, I was imprisoned waiting for my trial for 14 months in a cell with men and no water for bathing, which was particularly difficult when I had my period. I was allowed to drink water once a day and go to the bathroom twice a day. The most difficult part of this time was hearing others tortured: their cries of pain and anger at their torturers. It was worse than being tortured yourself. I particularly remember when my 21-year-old cousin, the son of my uncle who had tried to escape, was shot dead in September 1947. Also, the voice my uncle is still echoing in my ears as he died while being tortured. At the end of 14 months the man who later became my husband and I were sentenced to 5 years' imprisonment.

At the end of our term in prison, the real moral torture began. The only thing that could get you out of that life was to spy: we refused. My husband and I got out of prison, married, and had children. My husband was a painter, writer, and translator, but neither of us were given work. When I did get work, it was cleaning toilets. A further torture was to see our children who were bright and good students not be given the right to attend high studies.

I personally did nothing, but my attitude meant much to people. I was and am against oppression from either the left or the right. If someone asks to be forgiven in the name of Jesus Christ, I will forgive them even *them*, but they have never asked. Nexhmije Hoxha said recently [in 1991] that *they* had made some mistakes, as if they were mere mistakes.

When asked about what had given her strength, she replied simply, "My faith in God."

THE WOMAN IN THE CHURCH

After talking with these faith-filled women, I went to visit the recently remodeled cathedral that had been used as a sports complex during the communist regime. It was a moving and yet curious place. There had been an obvious attempt to create a modern-looking church with spare lines and a sleek grey granite altar. The only vivid ornamentation that was originally envisioned was the placement of brightly and dramatically depicted stations of the cross on the walls around the church. However, the people wanted a restoration of the sanctuary as it had been, including a copy of the original ornate altar. Since the granite altar is now covered with a cloth, the overall effect is one which complements the ornately carved original wood ceiling.

There were many people, young and old, men and women, in the church praying in the middle of the day when there was no service in progress. Some of the women there wore the traditional costumes of the area. One in particular caught my attention. She not only had on the traditional costume, but she also had a cross tattooed on her forearm. I asked if we could talk with her and she replied enthusiastically.

My name is Drane, I am 62 years of age and I am from the village of Shelqet. I was born into a wealthy family, but everything was taken away from us when my father was asked to join the party and refused. He said, "If my body were to be cut to pieces I would not join the Communist Party." After this, he was shot dead as he worshipped in church one day. We did not know where he was buried, but four years ago we were able to find his grave and reburied him where we wanted him.

Despite all our troubles, our faith in God got us through. I always kept my rosary with me in special pockets that I sewed into my clothes. I used to work on a pig farm. It was hard and dirty work. I used to wear this pendant. [She showed it to us. It had the image of Saint Anthony on one side and flowers on the other.] When my boss saw it, he told me not to wear it there again. I kept it in a safe place in my house until I could wear it publicly again. Each night I said my prayers and the rosary in the dark. The tattoo was placed on my arm when I was five years old. This was a common practice in the villages of this area. Throughout the communist period I was told to keep it covered, summer and winter.

In the South: Korçë

Korçë is a gracious city in the southern part of Albania, not far from the Greek border, known for centuries as a center of learning and culture. It is located on a plain and surrounded by mountains. There is an old town of lovely homes, and the city is generally cleaner and more picturesque than most cities in Albania.

Evanthi, aged 76, and Krisanthi, aged 68, were typical of the older women in Korçë. There lives have been relatively placid and the difficulties encountered have been nothing extraordinary.

Evanthi told us,

I was born and raised in Korçë, the fourth girl in a family of five girls and one boy. My mother was a housewife and my father was engaged in trade, transporting goods by mule between Albania and Romania. Although it was dangerous work and he had bodyguards to protect him, we were a well-to-do family due to his hard work.

I finished my secondary school in Korçë and then went to study home economics in Athens. My father wanted me to have education outside the country. He understood that there was something in me that would make me successful. I was the only one of the girls in my family that had education beyond high school.

I married my history and geography teacher. It was an arrangement, of course, but I liked him and was happy to marry him. He was a good teacher and I was a good student. We were happy in our 27-year marriage and had one son who was educated in geography and history and has now graduated in law.

I studied, but I didn't start work in my field. When my brother studied we all had to contribute for his studies. However, my brother died while he was studying in Italy. When he died my husband was a great moral support. When he saw me desperate, he comforted me.

What has given me strength is happiness in life, especially in my marriage. My husband appreciated me and my care of his mother as well as my housework. It made for a happy life.

Krisanthi told us,

I am from the village of Polenë where my father was from, and I was married there. My mother did sewing and embroidering, especially preparing brides for their weddings, and my father worked in the fields. I married for love and my parents approved. It has worked out very well and we have three children.

Our village was burned during the war and we came to Korçë in 1946. Now I am happy because my children are grown and married. Everything has gone well.

A unique story was told by Hava, a 62-year-old woman originally from a nearby village, who just happened to be in the building where we were interviewing and asked if she could join us.

I am from the village of Gjonomath, a remote village in the mountains near Korçë. I was born in another village in the plain, Gjergjevic, but was married to a man in Gjonomath. I was married under an arrangement and met my husband the day of the marriage. I feel so sorry that at the age of 17 I was engaged without knowing the man. I could have been in love and walked with a boy. Why did I have to be engaged and go to the mountains from the plain? Before my engagement, my eyes had fallen upon another boy, but I dare not talk about it even now. I was engaged for 3 years because my family needed me to work in the fields for that time. I longed to see the man I was engaged to, but I dared not ask. Once I was told that he was coming to the village to make preparations for the wedding and I tried to see him secretly, but I couldn't. It was a custom at the time that 25 groomsmen came with the bridegroom to take the bride away. First, they sang and danced in front of the haystacks while the groom was shaved; then they came on horseback to get me. One groomsman put a red veil on my face and another led my horse back to the groom's house. Fortunately, when I saw my husband I found that he was good-looking, far better than I. He was always good to me. His family was not poor, but we worked hard and reared 6 honest children.

Through all the hard work I have done, I found my source of strength in my family. I was a happy wife and had a happy family.

Although Hava, a Muslim, had not mentioned faith as a primary source of strength, when asked if faith had played any role in her life, she responded with sincerity and feeling, "I believe. My husband and I don't eat without praying to God. We say 'God before—we after.' God protects us."

In Central Albania: Tiranë

Tiranë is like other large cities in the world where the population frequently comes from elsewhere. However, the women included in this section are primarily those who have lived a significant portion of their lives in Tiranë and are currently living here. In many cases, though, it is clear that the region of their origin has had an impact on the formation of their ideas and the source of their strength.

Terezina (61), a Catholic, told us of her life and of her faith in Tiranë.

My family was involved in the founding of Tiranë in the 1920s and my father was a high officer in the army of King Zog. My entire family was anticommunist.

In 1945 the family was expelled from Tiranë and my father was imprisoned. I was expelled from the school in Shkodër for anticommunist activities in 1950 and was unable to receive further education or to hold a job for the rest of my life because of my beliefs. I just could not reconcile myself to the new ideology. However, I never felt inferior to other people because I received education from my father.

I married a composer who came from a famous family in Shkodër. My father-in-law had sacrificed his life in 1912 in the struggle against the Turks, and my husband and his family were also anticommunists. Although I feel that I have lived only ten years of my life, as I only survived under communism, my husband and I were fortunate not to have more serious consequences than we did. He was a very talented and kind man, and I believe that the regime's recognition of his talent was what kept us from having more serious consequences for our beliefs.

Because I couldn't go to school or find work, I stayed with my mother all the time and she helped me to be content with life. She taught me the sacredness of simple work, and her strong will and desire to work inspired me. I also learned that all life is sacrifice. Even more, my faith in Jesus and my love of life, my husband, and my children have given me the strength I needed to overcome the difficulties of my life. I have kept my faith alive within myself and believed that one day providence would come and make a change in my life.

Andromaqi Gjergji, a well-known and well-respected ethnologist, whom we interviewed in Tiranë, told us:

I am from Korçë which is a town known for its cultural traditions. I had a great zeal for learning. I received an excellent education at the Lyceum there, and so when I came to Tiranë I found myself head and shoulders above the others. I attended the university here and had high marks. I never married; I worked hard all the time and in 1980 I was given the scientific title, Doctor of Science, being the first Albanian woman to be given such a title. I was not a member of the Party of Labor of Albania and I've joined none of the parties now. Science has always been enough for me. I didn't want to have myself and my work linked with party problems. I felt free. If I were a member of the party I would have been obliged to do things that I didn't feel. I have published many articles in my field, and many of those have been translated and published in other countries, including those in Western Europe.

My work has required me to travel all over Albania and in the early days travel was very difficult. The work outside of Tiranë, mostly in villages in different parts of Albania, made me know the life of the people concretely. There are very few villages I have not been in Albania. It was tiring, but it gave me pleasure. The conditions were very difficult, especially transportation. I covered long distances on foot, going from one village to another. I remember the years from 1950 to 1960: very difficult conditions, no adequate roads for cars in most of Albania. I wonder how I did all the work I have done. I have worked hard, but my field work gave me pleasure. My parents, especially my mother, were worried about me because I didn't enjoy good health. I was thin and it was not easy to go from village to village.

I was inspired by my work and the scientists I worked with. My strength to overcome the challenges I faced came, however, from my family.

Ethnologist Andromaqi Gjergji.

THE SPORTS WOMEN

In Pogradec we had a unique opportunity to meet three trailblazers from Tiranë: three women of the older generation who had been among the first women to play sports and represent their cities and their country in athletics. Susana, Efigjeni, and Medi, all 62 years of age, played basketball, volleyball, and other sports with the Tiranë sports club in the 1950s and enjoyed a 17-year winning streak.

Since they were all born in 1934, they would have been born into the historical and social period of the other older women we interviewed, but it is clear that their lives were radically different from those of the majority of women of their generation. Even in the 1950s the popular opinion was that good girls did not play sports. Therefore, speculation, both public and private, about the morals of these women and their teammates was the rule rather than the exception. In addition, even though they played for their country here and abroad, they were unpaid (except for food provided to them during tournaments). As a result, they were required to work, often at manual labor, to earn a living while they were also playing on the team and leading the demanding life of an athlete.

Susana is a lithe and attractive woman with quick movements and a sparkle in her eyes. She told us,

I was born in 1934 in Elbasan to one of the richest families in the city. I wish I hadn't been the daughter of such a wealthy family because of all the suffering it has brought me. Both of my parents and their families were politically and economically persecuted. They had been nationalist families, but my father was never engaged in politics.

Our troubles began after the war. Everything was confiscated and we were

The sportswomen from Tiranë: Medi, Efigjeni and Susana.

left totally in the street in 1945. My father was imprisoned for 20 years only because he had been rich. He suffered 14 years and was released during one of the amnesties. My mother too was imprisoned because she did not accept to work for the Sigurimi. She suffered 5 months of a 5-year sentence.

We were two sisters in my family. My younger sister was taken in by another family, but I went to live with my aunt and uncle in Tiranë. Because I was talented in sports and emancipated by comparison with other women of my generation (due to my uncle's influence), I participated in the national sports teams for volleyball and basketball from 1948 to 1967. I represented my country, but was never allowed to go abroad because of my biography. The team was the champion for 17 years while I was playing on it and I deserved to be given the title of Master of Sports, but I wasn't given it until the coming of democracy, again because of my biography.

It was difficult for girls of my generation to participate in sports because of social opinion, but we were good girls and tried to show others that their prejudice was not warranted. The fact that I was a sportswoman had no impact on my marriage because my husband loved the fact that I was engaged in sports. He encouraged me and I did not have to give it up. Even though his family encouraged him to make me give up sports, still he supported me.

I have done very hard work to prove myself. All the time that I was a sportswoman and even after for 42 full years, I worked as a stone crusher. I had to work at hard physical labor on three shifts. I had to take my child with me when I worked the second and third shifts. When I left work at 11:30 at night I wrapped my son in a blanket filled with sawdust to make him comfortable for the trip home on my bicycle.

I found strength almost entirely in my desire to change the opinions of others about me. It is a problem of personal dignity. Also, I thank God that I have a very good son. It is a meaningful joy for me. I want him to have a better life. I want to forget the past—I don't like to think of it.

Efigjeni, who is known both as Geni and by her sports name Xheko, told us,

We have tried to be successful at a very difficult period of time, a time of fanaticism. When other girls our age were still wearing veils, we were wearing shorts! My father was emancipated in his views because he had spent ten years in America. All of the children in our family were involved in arts, music, and sports. We pursued the passions of youth.

All the while that I played in sports I worked as an economist, for the sports club and also for a while with a newspaper. I never married, not because of the societal prejudice against sportswomen, but because I have been a bit capricious. I cannot blame sports.

Many people have asked if playing sports negatively affects the morality of a girl. On the contrary, it makes a girl have good character and good morals. I have always been correct and set a good example. I have been a model and was treated equally with men. We were trailblazers and had to blaze the trail with sword in hand.*

*It is interesting to hear the unconscious paraphrasing of Enver Hoxha's words here: "Albania has blazed the trail of history with sword in hand."

I was also asked often "Why do you have friends like these (referring to Susana and Medi who had bad biographies)?" when I was considered to have a good biography. We played for the Tiranë team, which was nonpolitical. In fact, the team was made up primarily of declassed people. They were not privileged, but they were strong.

I have always believed that people should not give in easily. They should take life as it comes. We were and are patriots. We played for Albania and with the changes brought about by democracy we are optimistic for the future.

Medi, who also goes by her sports name Lali, added,

I liked sports. It was my passion and made up for what society would not give me. I was from a rich family and because of my biography it wasn't easy for me to find a job. While being in sports I had the right to work, and it wasn't physical work. First, I worked as a meat inspector and later I was an economist for the sports club. When the class struggle was more bitter, I was fired, but the sports club demanded me back. It was an advantage to be a sportswoman because sports people were not political. Despite this, I have a bitter memory from 1957 when the team was preparing to go to Moscow for the world championship. After intensive training with the team, I was told four hours before departure that I couldn't go: that there was no visa for me.

Despite the obstacles and challenges I found strength in being with other young people and in playing and working together with them.

When asked about the role of faith in their lives, Geni/Xheko, who is Orthodox, replied, "The greatest role in my life has been played by my family. They gave me the liberty to follow my passion. However, I believe in God and always have. Even when it was forbidden, I maintained my faith. As a club, we maintained our faith. I was always the one who agreed to clean the sports arena because it had been a church before. I respected all the rites and feasts. People knew I was very faithful and thought I was crazy. We continued our faith from generation to generation in my family. I have always had a picture of Christ in my home, even during communism."

Medi, who is a Muslim and wears a miniature Koran on a chain around her neck, answered by kissing her Koran.

Susana, who is also a Muslim, answered, "We were born with God and will die with God. God is first and we are second."

Summary

Raised in a period characterized by physically demanding work, strict societal limitations, and political and national instability, the women of this generation were prepared for the difficulties and challenges of life. Although their world was turned upside down by the political oppression of the communist regime, they drew strength from within themselves and their families, from the struggle itself, and from their faith to live and surmount their difficulties. These women exhibited an acceptance of their lot in life, combined with an intense desire to see their children and their grand-children enjoy a better life than they themselves had experienced.

The following chapters contain in-depth interviews with special women of this generation. They were chosen because they exemplified the characteristics of the women of this generation, because they are well known and respected, and because they have particularly compelling stories to relate.

Chapter 6

Dhora Leka:
I Have Remained
a Soldier All My Life

We were introduced to Dhora in May 1995 and met with her four times between then and October of the same year. In addition to the material Ksanthi and I gathered in the interviews, this section includes information that we were given from an interview that was given to the local radio station and from her own book about her mother, *Nëna Ime.** We found Dhora living in Tiranë in a very attractive apartment that is large and well furnished. She has had the good fortune of being able to live in an apartment owned by a German organization that is supporting the artists of Albania. The Germans use it for an office when they are in Tiranë, but they allow her to live in it when they are not. There is a wonderful oil painting over the piano showing Dhora as a partisan fighting in the mountains. We were told that Dhora's only other personal possessions are a blanket and her clothes.

We wanted to interview Dhora because she is an artist, a freedom fighter, and a woman who clearly exemplifies the spirit of the Albanian women. Dhora fought as a partisan in the War of Liberation of Albania from the fascists and was an early member of the Communist Party. She also wrote the songs that the freedom fighters sang. After the war she was sent to the Tchaikovsky Conservatory in Moscow to study music. When she returned, she learned that the ideals that she had fought for were not being realized and spoke out against Enver Hoxha. As a result, she was imprisoned and spent all of her life until the democratic reform in prison or exile. While in exile she wrote four operas, many songs, and much poetry. Now she is having the joy of seeing them published and performed.

*Dhora Leka, Nëna Ime (My Mother), Tiranë: Shtëpia botuese "Monroe," 1994. This was written to celebrate her mother's 100th birthday, May 15, 1982.

Dhora Leka in 1995.

Dhora is a lively woman with a warm and ready smile, a heart full of joy and optimism, and love for her country and its people. She has lived a difficult life and yet has retained a good heart and the joy of living. She epitomizes the Albanian woman of her generation. While she was talking, it seemed that her heart sang with love and life.

Formative Years: The Gun and the Song

I was born in February 1923 in the city of Korçë to a simple town family. I loved my mother and admired her. She was from a village in the Korçë area, Polenë, and was the third child in a large and very poor peasant family. My mother had a great desire for education, but it was not available to her. She could neither read nor write Albanian although she learned some Greek from a local priest. Although her life was a fight for survival, she lived life fully and remained sharp-witted to her death at the age of 94. She had a great desire to live, despite the fact that her life was an unceasing struggle.* It was, in fact, a struggle for existence. Hard times in poverty never lessened her desire to live.

I learned many lessons from my mother. She taught me that I could be strong and she taught me to hate injustice. She taught me not to accept things as they were. I remember some of the things she used to say:

"Ah, my dear daughter, man is strong. Stronger than stone, than iron, stronger than everything in the world. Look at me, at your mother. I've shouldered a very heavy burden. And do you see, my back is not bent.†

"How much work I had to do! The heaviest burden was on my shoulders. I had to get up before dawn to take care of the cow and sheep, to milk them.... I had to make and bake bread, I had to cook ... to go and work in the field ... either to sow or to harvest. Then I had to go to Korçë twice a week and it took me two hours on foot to go there and buy some oil, rice, sugar ... and to see the house in Korçë ... 24 hours were not enough for one to do so much work and to get up again before dawn. No. How could God tolerate this? How, didn't he see the injustice?§

"To whom are you going to complain, I said? When God didn't feel pity for us when He took away everything, who will you complain to? To the gendarmes of Zogu? No ... all the pigs are alike."**

My mother also characterized my father and his life in the following way: "Your father was a good man. He tried hard doing everything that came along just to provide food for the family. Yet, poverty followed him step by step.††

One of my early lessons and a significant event that shaped my life occurred when I was ten years of age. At that time I had my first confrontation with force. This was in 1933 or 1934. My brother had been studying agriculture in Greece. When he returned, my family bought a plot of land on which he could work. In

*Ibid., p. 5.
†Ibid., p. 14.
§Ibid., p. 17.
**Ibid., p. 20.
††Ibid., p. 13.

doing so they mortgaged the family's home and land. Since the land they purchased for my brother turned out to be nonproductive, we had no money with which to pay back the loan. We were very poor. Our only source of income was one cow. When the police came to take that cow, they acted with cruelty in not showing concern for our poverty or the disaster that was to be visited upon my family when they took the cow. To discourage them from taking it, my father came down the stairs with his gun on his shoulder, but did not use it. My mother said to him "What's the good of a gun if you don't shoot?" This moment left a strong impression on my mind with this lesson: it is not important only to discover evil, but to find it out and fight against it. I understood that if I had to carry a gun I was also going to have to use it. I believe that a fundamental characteristic of my personality was also formed in this minute. If I am confronted with evil, I must fight it. This incident and others in my life have taught me that evil should be fought against violently, otherwise evil will triumph. As a result, my life has been a constant confrontation between good and evil.

Later my family moved to Tiranë, where I attended Nënë Skanderbeu School and graduated in June 1942. I was expelled twice from school due to my participation in revolutionary activities. On April 2, 1939, a recital at my school turned into a political demonstration protesting the occupation of Albania by Italy. Although the news of the occupation turned out to be a rumor at that time, I took part in a real demonstration that occurred on April 5 at the gate of King Zog's palace. The people were singing and the crowd grew ever more impassioned. The gate was opened and the people went in, demanding to be given arms to protect the country against the Italians. Although they saw King Zog in the window, they were told to go away or they would be shot. Zog left Albania two days later and the Italian occupation began. I was, however, impressed by the power of the people and by the power of song to mobilize the people.

After I graduated from school, I was appointed to teach in a village called Plasë for the school year 1942–43. I returned to Korçë and there in August 1942 occurred a turning point in my personal history. I was actively involved in antifascist youth activities and distributing leaflets. As a result of the activities of this antifascist group, the headquarters of the fascists had suffered much. To punish the antifascist youth for their activities, the fascists caught two of my friends and fellow antifascists, Kiço Greço and Midhi Kostani, and hanged them. I saw the hanging and was both shocked and revolted. Afterward, I wrote my first song in their honor, "Kushtrimi" (a "Call to Arms"). It was my duty to translate my horror into song. This song became popular and was known all over Korçë in just one week. Since at that time I could not write music, I taught the song to my sister right away, then the next day we taught it to a group of young people who taught others in the city. Although I had sung with my father in the garden of our family's house in the evenings, I didn't know until this time that I could compose. I discovered at this moment that I was not just a fighter, but also a composer. For me the gun and the song were inseparable. Therefore, throughout the war I was engaged in active fighting and I wrote songs that described the life I led. Each song was dedicated to a significant event.

I joined the Communist Party in 1942 and fought with the partisans until the day of Liberation. During the War of Liberation, on January 7, 1944, there was a great battle. My fiancé, Jorgo, was sent to the top of a hill to observe the enemy (the Germans) and was followed by a group of partisans. He was ostensibly shot

Dhora Leka as a partisan in 1944 (photograph courtesy Dhora Leka).

and killed by the Germans in this mission. His diary was stolen and he was beaten as well. I thought that the report of his death was suspicious, but never knew the real story. My theory was that my fiancé, who was very intelligent and spoke English well, was a threat to Hoxha and that Hoxha wanted to eliminate him early in his struggle for political power. (Much later Enver Hoxha bragged publicly that it was actually he who had killed Jorgo, so my suspicions were justified.)

After the Liberation I went to Moscow from 1948 to 1953 to attend the Tchaikovsky Conservatory for music composition. When I came back to Albania I was appointed to teach at the Artistic Lyceum, Jordan Misja, in Tiranë and in 1954, at the Conference of the Artists I was elected general secretary of the Artists' League. However, I came back to Albania with new ideas regarding the personality cult of Stalin and wanted to analyze the situation in Albania in light of this. As a result, I found myself looking with a very critical eye at Hoxha. I was disappointed by the government and the manner in which it governed. I felt that the ideals for which I had fought and for which my friends and fiancé had died were not being realized by the government of Enver Hoxha. It was clear that my ideals, which included an intense desire to live in a better society where everyone was equal and free, were being undermined by Hoxha's dictatorship. I expressed my opinions and as a consequence was not allowed to take part in the Tiranë Conference on April 7, 1956. Until this time I had been well known as a heroine, but now I was known as a dissident.

The Turning Point—From Heroine to Traitor

In May 1956 I was expelled from the PLA (Albanian Communist Party) for my participation in the events surrounding the Tiranë Party Conference and I was discharged from my position as general secretary of the Artists' League. In July of the same year I was exiled to Gjirokastër. Officially I was sent to Gjirokastër to fill a position as a composer in the cultural center. Only the director there knew that I had to check in with the police twice a day at 7:00 A.M. and 5:00 P.M. I was not, however, asked to do anything. Young composers and others would come to me for advice and help and there was nothing I could do to help them. I had an intense need to work, to do something.

It was during this period of exile in Gjirokastër that I learned that everything bad has its good side. When a group of folk singers sang a folk song of the region in polyphony, I was impressed and sat down at once to start my work on the piano. I was inspired by their song and so I was eager to learn more about the folk songs of southern Albania. I used what I learned and composed a work based on the folk music of southern Albania that influenced many of my future compositions. Also, I used some of the music that I composed in this period in the opera I wrote later called "Zojna Çurre."* I consider this to be a very positive result of this otherwise

*Zojna Çurre was born in 1920 in the village of Tragjias, in the Vlorë District. She is remembered as a People's Hero for having fought bravely as a partisan in the War of Liberation, serving as both a team leader and a company leader. She died on the battlefield on July 22, 1944, while fighting against mercenaries in Klos, in the Mat district.

difficult time. Sadly, the music I wrote while I was in Gjirokastër was attributed to another composer who made the money for my songs.

In May of the following year, 1957, I was arrested and sentenced by the Military High Court to imprisonment for 25 years, to the confiscation of my property, to the abolition of my military decorative rank, to the deprivation of the right of authorship, and to the deprivation of voting rights after serving my time in prison. The accusation was: "for treason to the country and people as an antiparty element."*

The prisons for women at the time were different from the prisons for men. They were a special place with a workshop where we were deprived of the right to contact other people. I did sewing in shifts for 8 old lek per day (equivalent to 0.8 new lek or less than 1 cent). The guards checked on us regularly to make sure that we were there. We had no radio or newspapers. We were allowed only one meeting with our family per month, and we were allowed to send just one letter. There were also no mirrors in the prison, so I was unable to see what I looked like. I wrote the poem "What Will You Say Then?" about what I would say to myself when I saw what I really looked like after so many years in prison. After 1963 (after I was released from prison) I found out that there were prisons that were terrible even for women. The regime had begun following the Chinese example in this field.

There were some difficult moments while I was incarcerated. For example, if I or my friends didn't do what we were asked, we were put in an isolated cell, with no contact at all and with nothing but a blanket on the floor, for one month. We had little food there: just bread and water. I had this punishment two or three times.

I also couldn't do any of my own work—writing or composing—but I worked the compositions in my mind. I wrote many beautiful poems this way. Instead of saying prayers at night I repeated my poems and remembered them after my release. In addition, I worked in my mind my opera "A Stormy Autumn" about a young woman who was sentenced to death. It seemed to me that I was sentenced to death, too. I felt deep in my heart the painful moment when she sings an aria before the hangman. I formed the idea and worked it out in my mind. When I was released into exile and was working in the fields during the day, I wrote it down in the evenings in just three months.

Thanks to some amnesties in 1957, 1959, and 1962 (all in November), I was released from prison in November 1963 and sent to work in the area of Berat, but was limited in my movements. Then in February 1966 I was exiled once again to Semani, a village in Fier. I remember a moment when I worked there in a warehouse where corn was stored. I was amazed and delighted by the large number of beautiful butterflies in the place. It was only later that I learned that they were there because the corn was infested. Many people in the area suffered greatly from eating the products made with the corn.

In December 1970 I was allowed to work as a dressmaker in Fier. However, on January 13, 1983, for the third time, I was exiled to a village—Shen-Marinezë of Fier—where I stayed until June 1991. Only after the overthrow of the communist regime did I come back to Tiranë.

My goal while I was in prison and in exile was that I wanted to enjoy good physical and mental health. I didn't want to become pessimistic so I tried always to find something good and joyful, something that would help me not to feel

---

*The prosecutor also asked for the death sentence for Dhora.

depressed. One particularly joyful occasion was the birth of my sister's grandson, Lulzim (Luli).* We loved and cared for him so much and he was such a joy in an otherwise grim situation.

We were very isolated, however. I was cut off from much of my family. My sister Mita and her family were near me as they had also been exiled,† and my mother chose to stay with us and share our exile as well. It was a great sadness that I didn't see my brother for 35 years, and he was not allowed to come from Tiranë to see my mother when she died. The only interaction we had with the people of the village we were exiled to was when they abused us. My most difficult moment came when we found the village children trying to force my sister's three-year-old granddaughter to eat feces because they said they hated traitors. Another sad and ironic moment came when some schoolchildren threw stones at me as they were singing my songs.

My sister's children didn't understand why they were treated so badly by the village children and why I was called a traitor since they thought that I was a good person, a partisan and a heroine of the Liberation. In fact, we were not traitors to the country. We were simply against the regime of Enver Hoxha. Hoxha had created such a psychosis in the country that the villagers and even the children showed such hostility to those whom he considered traitors. Needless to say, it was this that helped his dictatorship survive for such a long time.

The Source of Dhora's Strength

For a true artist, and I believe that I am one, it is not difficult to find something to keep morale high. I always dreamed of change and believed in a better future. I also found strength to keep my morale high and help others—family and friends—by singing songs and telling jokes. During the period of my imprisonment and exile, I composed two operas and many dances, and I wrote many verses. I have to say that I've never had an emptiness in my life. My desire to write "a page that had not been written" by those who lived a good life, gave me force. To work in the field, to dig canals, to do the difficult physical labor all day long, and then to come home and settle down to write was not easy. Yet I couldn't have written more than I wrote during those years.§ I don't know what helped me—perhaps God, I don't know.

My mother's influence on me was also strong. She gave me everything. She gave me faith in the strength of the individual and in the value of suffering. My mother often reminded me, "If you don't suffer, you don't know what suffering means and you don't remember the needs of others." She raised her children to value honesty and truth and live with their conscience. She was a friend to us as well as our mother. She supported our activities, came to us when we fought in the mountains, hid the evidence of our activities from the police, and shared our exiles.

*Meaning the flowering of prosperity.
†They were exiled because her husband, Tuk Jakova, a member of the Political Bureau, was accused of being an antiparty element by Enver Hoxha. Mita, like Dhora, was a former partisan and member of the party.
§Radio interview with Kozeta Mamaqi.

Once my mother told me, "I was and still am your mother. I say this because I've made up my mind to follow you—as I did during the war, I'll do now—wherever you go I'll come with you and I'll keep my head high because I understand that you are not in the wrong way."*

My mother had a strong faith in the future and desire for freedom. She was always optimistic and frequently reminded us "even when you don't love life, life loves you."† She was proud of her children and taught us courage: "He who tells the truth never has to fear. I didn't fear either the fascists or the Nazis. I don't fear anyone. He who tells the truth, doesn't fear anyone or anything."§ The only thing she feared or refused to tolerate was injustice. She saw much injustice in the Hoxha regime and felt that if people didn't speak out against it, it would prevail and get worse. ("If you don't care for a wound, it will get worse and worse and it will poison the blood."**) I want to live, to live long like my mother, to tell the truth, being afraid of no one and of nothing, just like my mother.

Another source of my strength was my great hatred of the regime and especially of Enver Hoxha. I don't know if anyone has cursed him as my mother did or spoken as badly of him as I have in my poems. For example, I have described Hoxha as the embodiment of all men who exert oppression, take all the credit for accomplishments and terrorize others. Enver Hoxha claimed to be the creator of everything in our country. In 1963 I wrote this poem, "I and You," about my "relationship" with Hoxha.

> I and you a life or death struggle
> Since 1955 wage
> Neither I, nor you lay down our weapons
> You no, for you are the head of tyranny
> Neither do I, for I am the loyal soldier of the poor
> Well, who then?
> Let's leave it to history.

And history showed who of us, he or I, was right.

I especially shared my mother's passion when she spoke this deathbed curse on Enver Hoxha:

"Oh God! You are one and real, Listen to me: Let my curse fall on the head of him who caused me, an old mother, many sufferings, so much pain! Let his soul burn with the longing for his children, just like my soul. Let him long for his children and not have them at the last moment. Let him crawl along carrying a bag on his shoulder, barefooted, in rags and having no bread to eat just like me and other people like me! Let him see and feel what hunger and cold are!—Not to die. *No.* Death is a golden lid. Everybody will meet his death. But to wander, to crawl along the street while being mad and to be seen by all those he 'disappeared,' all those who want to take revenge on him. Let him hear the sigh of all those who have suffered, and let him squint and find no relief, no remedy ... to want water and find no water. Today ... tomorrow ... all life long."††

Leka, Nëna Ime, p. 58.
†*Ibid., p. 54.*
§*Ibid., p. 44.*
**Ibid., p. 46.*
††*Ibid., p. 82.*

The Role of Faith

When I wrote verses in prison, I did not say "God" as I say "God" today. We were brought up from our youth to be atheists; it was the way we were educated.* One poem I wrote when I was in prison was "Prayer," but I addressed it to "Mother" not to "God." Now I am old, and maybe old age creates new things. I look back over all this difficult life and the good comes into view. God may have been in my subconscious and I may have lived life as God wished. Although I am not a church-goer, I believe that there is a supernatural force that brings people into harmony and love.

The Intimate Hurt in My Soul

I wish to add something that I have not told any other interviewer. Although I seem to be enthusiastic, cheerful, and glad, inside of me there is a hole that hurts. One child was born to me and died at one week of age. I love children because of this, but nothing in my whole life could fill this empty place. My child didn't live to call me "mother" and I longed to call him "son." He was just a week old when he died, but he would have grown up one day. This is also why I hate wars that hurt children.

Dhora: Fighter and Woman

Dhora is clearly a woman of conscience and one who cares about the plight of the poor and helpless. Her own family's experiences taught her how precarious life is for poor people and that they have to act on their own behalf, even against the forces of what is called law and order: the right of the individual over the rule of law and confidence in that right. She is proud of her double contribution to her country's liberation: her revolutionary past and the role that she played in arousing and inspiring the Liberation forces through her songs. She experienced the horrors of war and personal tragedy and never lost her voice: her song and her dedication to the truth. It is astounding that someone who has been through as much as she has is still able to remark that everything bad has its good side.

Dhora exemplifies Albanian women of her generation, but yet her experience is not that of the average woman. I asked her what had made her different and she replied,

Her family, however, was nominally Orthodox.

I cannot explain. It would lack modesty if I told you something I remember well from my early past. At the age of 12 (1936) I sent my mother a photograph of myself. I wrote on the back "One day your Dhora will be a great woman and will honor the family name." This may suggest my difference, but also I had opportunity: my older brother was a good friend. At his invitation, well-known authors and composers came to our house and I listened and learned. It made me dream of doing something for my family and my country. This was a strong desire from the time I was very young. Then, fortunately, I happened to live my life in very important periods in the history of my country. I fought to give freedom to her people, I raised my voice against the person and his regime that stood against the principles I had fought for. I had the opportunity to fight for freedom and to fight against those who prevailed (as a result of my fighting) and who oppressed and persecuted me. Rarely do you find these extremes in one person as you find in me. I fought for what came into existence and then fought against the actuality that didn't match my vision. A fighter for freedom could not be reconciled with dictatorship. This makes me different. It seems that all of the turning points in my life are associated with significant political events in the life of my country. Even today in democracy, if I see that something doesn't go right, I have the courage to speak out. I won't give up my ideal. It is not enough to show the victory sign symbolizing democracy, I must fight for freedom and real democracy.

However, Dhora is not only an idealist and a fighter, but she is a woman with the pains of lost motherhood. She retains her love of children and is actively supporting the efforts of young artists to write and publish their works.* She also ended our time together with the following words: "This is the message I have for the coming generations: always live with great hope for freedom."

On the occasion of the eightieth anniversary of the proclamation of independence in November 1992, the president of the republic, Sali Berisha, awarded the title of "People's Artist" to Dhora Leka.

On February 23, 1996, Dhora's 73d birthday, the Dhora Leka Foundation was established as a nonprofit organization to motivate and support young artists (composers, performers, writers, and others) by encouraging them and providing financial support and prizes for their work and accomplishments.

Chapter 7

Margarita Xhepa: A Life Nourished by a Great Gift

Margarita Xhepa is a well-known and talented actress who exemplifies the women of her generation in a distinct way. She followed her heart into acting and succeeded in this field at a time when societal pressures made it difficult for women to excel. Her gift and her art set her apart and gave her a certain freedom to stand outside of the political realm. Margarita is handsome in the manner of Ingrid Bergman: a simple and unaffected woman of great beauty. She is also a woman of great passion for her art, her country, and her family. Margarita carries herself with dignity of bearing and yet is not aloof. She seems to burn with an intense energy.

The Nascency of Art

I was born in December 1934 in a small but famous Albanian city, Lushnjë, situated in Myzeqe region. I am happy that I was born in this area because it gave me much food for my future. It supplied me with my best memories and was helpful to me as an actress. As a child I didn't know my future, but I loved to learn poetry and recite.

My parents had three girls and one boy, but my mother was sick and died when I was nine years of age. When she died, my father was only 39 and married a woman who said she had one child. A few days after they were married, another child appeared and later another child came. My father's new wife actually had three children, not one. As a result, there were seven children living in complete poverty. Then my father and his wife had three more children. Despite the poverty, we all loved one another, and later when I was successful I tried to help them all with houses and education.

We lived in poverty, unspeakable poverty. I remember my mother asking me to recite poems. "The others don't say them as well as you," she said. It gave my mother great pleasure and her encouragement of my talent gave me confidence.

She helped me learn the beautiful mother tongue, not the dialect of the area, and taught me to love both music and poetry. When I was left motherless at nine years of age, I felt the absence of my mother very much. It is said that when you have your mother you are rich; when you have no mother, you are poor.

As a child, I recited poetry. I remember particularly one poem, written by Alex Caçi, about the girl who left the rope and spade and went on studying. This was in a period of emancipation of women. It was an important issue at the time. I thought that my performance would give something to women.

The people were poor, but they loved art. There were amateurs who gathered to perform one-act plays or recitations. Sometimes they asked me to perform with them.

I have been asked to play some roles that I have lived. I have portrayed them truthfully because I had the memories from my childhood deep in my heart. Once, I remember, when I was asked to play the role of a village woman, a young mother whose husband was killed, in the film *Pylli i Lirise* (*Forest of Freedom*), I told the director, "I don't need to study the role, I have lived it." I then took off my shoes and walked as a barefoot woman would in the fields. I knew how to do this because I walked barefoot until I was 12 years old. In addition, I have all the memories of the hospitable, noble women who would do everything for their families.

The Flowering of Art

I was a girl, not yet grown up, when I came to Tiranë from Lushnjë in 1950 and the doors of the theater were opened to me. It was a great opportunity and I had good fortune. I tried my best to justify the confidence that people had in me. Work became second nature to me; I worked hard. Even when I had three small boys, I still had to play leading roles almost every night, but I found the strength and reserves in myself to keep going.

When I was 15, I was asked to come to the Artistic Lyceum in Tiranë. There I met Pandi Stillu,* the head of the producers of theater. He helped me very much. When I entered the room for the tryout he said, "Margarita is a promising girl. I will ask her to work while she is studying." Therefore, I was given work as an apprentice with a small salary and I worked and studied at the same time. At one point I was given an opportunity to play a role and Pandi agreed, while another producer said, "No, Pandi. You are just agreeing because Margarita is beautiful." Pandi responded, "Her talent is even more beautiful than her face." His words were a great inspiration for me and raised my confidence and the confidence of others in my ability, including producers and other artists.

I was lucky because at that time the theater had a wide repertoire. I played in Shakespearean tragedies and Chekhov roles including Helen in *Uncle Vanya*. I have played in 35 films and performed 150 roles in the theater. All of my success has been based on hard work, devotion, and reading. I faced many challenges in performing. For example, I never saw performances outside of Albania, so I had no

*Pandi Stillu was born in Korçë in 1914 and died in 1970. From 1937–42 he studied at the Academy of Art in Bucharest, Romania. He returned to Albania in 1946 and worked as the producer at the People's Theater in Tiranë for the rest of his career.

idea of how the roles might be played differently. Also, society was so strict, so fanatical, that it was difficult to play the roles in which the woman was required to hug or kiss the man.

I was not paid much and did not have other compensations that actors in the Western countries have had, but the sympathy of the people has been important to me. Of course, there has been frustration because of low pay and the harshness of life. I am sorry that my house is falling apart. Yes, my house is badly furnished, but it is the same for my friends. All have felt the same poverty and consoled themselves that this was for all, not just for one. I have suffered much, but I have almost forgotten the poverty through the inspiration of my work. I forgot the poverty in my family when I had the admiration of the audience. I love my country, I love

Margarita Xhepa in 1995.

my people, and their admiration for me has been the greatest reward. Many journalists, especially critics of the art, have written articles about different roles I've played. What has really impressed me most is the respect of the people for artists. The actor is just like a flower being watered and fed with the inspiration of the people: the love of the people has helped me grow. I have never been a communist, although I was favored (by the Party leaders) to join because I belonged to a poor family. It has been said of me, "her work glorifies her, not party membership."

In the United States and England a book has been published about the well-known women of the world. My name is mentioned in this book among five distinguished Albanian women. This means much to me. In meeting foreign producers I have felt inferior, not because of my talent, but only because of my poverty.

The Actress as Woman

My life has been very complex: full of joys and sorrows. I always had a great belief in myself because the applause from the people of Lushnjë gave me much inspiration.

I was a poor girl and had the support of no one when I arrived in Tiranë. At that time fanaticism was very strong. In 1950 I married an army officer from

Shkodër, a handsome young man, a former partisan, who fell in love with me. My father agreed that I could marry him. My husband was not a fanatic and he didn't prevent me from continuing the career that I had chosen to follow. After my marriage my life changed in many ways, including the fact that we had more to eat. At that time rations were very small, but the army officers were given more. When I arrived in his house, a plate of food with a large piece of cheese was put in front of me. I exclaimed, "Is this all for me?!" I was happy in my marriage, but in 1954 my husband died of a brain tumor when he was not yet 30 years old, shortly after our son was born.

My second marriage was to a singer and actor who accepted me with my son. My second husband was extraordinarily good. He was a good artist and he understood me. He was a great man and supporter of me in my work and of my family. He never said a bad word. Now I feel his loss, but I have good memories of him.

Despite our love, life was still very difficult. My second child, a boy, was born in 1957; my third son was born in 1969. I had hoped for a daughter. My mother always said, "A daughter to a mother is the poetry of the house." I was, however, a very happy and proud mother. It was a great pleasure to be successful on stage and even a greater pleasure to be proud of my children. However, the Albanian mothers have shouldered the suffering of the people for centuries.

The Source of Her Strength

I have put all my sufferings into my work. It seems that my life has nourished my gift and has not impeded its progress. Neither poverty nor sufferings have made me give up work. I had to mend my underwear and had only two dresses, but I was accustomed to not being paid for what I did. Passion for work helps to overcome poverty. I worked hard and had money to buy good food, but not for new clothes.

Also, the spiritual world kept enriching me with every passing day. By the "spiritual world" I mean the inner world. That is what I have most appreciated. Each character represents an event in life. What I study most before I play a role is the inner world of the person. I don't care much how people dress or how they express themselves; it is the inner world that I kneel down to. This is my particularity. I don't care much for the externals, only for the inner person. I built up my characters from the inside out. For example, in *Pylli ë Lirise*, when I played the role of the young mother whose husband was killed, the producer wanted me to wear a beautiful new black dress, but I told him that would sabotage my role. I wanted to give the audience the portrait of the real woman of Myzeqe of that time. So I used an old dress that I borrowed from my aunt. A beautiful person is a person with a beautiful inner world. I love people and am ready to sacrifice for them. What I am saying is not just true of Margarita but of the Albanian women in general.

In my opinion, every woman does something in her life. If she is inspired by great patience and love for work, she does it well. The beauty of things has always inspired me. I didn't like to study inside when I was in school; I liked to study in the shade of a tree. I learned outside, in the beauty of nature. Also, my mother was a good housewife. She kept the house clean and did beautiful handwork. Even the dish towels were embroidered. Also, my mother was not only a hard-working woman but was also very intelligent. As a result we did not come from an empty world, but from a rich spiritual world. We children forgot that we were hungry because my mother told us stories so beautifully and with much love. She was full of poetry without having read anything. She was a woman with a world.

There has been something in the spirit of the Albanian women that makes them tireless in work. They are nourished by love of work. It is a tradition: part of their body and spirit. In great poverty women have worked harder than men. The personality of women has been created through hard work. They are artists at work and have a love for it. People here have always been poor, but have always had clean houses and been hospitable. These are the virtues of the Albanian people. Also, stories are important as are the songs and poetry of the Renaissance. The songs, stories, and poems convey messages that have influenced and supported me.

Memories are the food of my inspiration. They have always nourished me and fed me well. As I grew, I became richer and stronger. My memories helped me to overcome my difficulties.

I now live my life as a woman should live it. I receive a very good pension of $88 per month, the highest in the country. Now I can buy what I want and I don't have to ask my children to buy things for me.

The Role of Faith

I am positive about faith. When I was a child, I used to go to the Orthodox church. I joined the church choir and sang the songs well. I remember it as a beautiful time in my life. Easter was an especially great day because in the name of God we had new dresses and sandals. We looked like butterflies. I learned the liturgy and I think religion has played a good role in my life. The fact that I had been to church as a child even had a great influence on my art. For example, when I played Ophelia I knew how to pray. The teachings of the church to love people, to help the poor, and to be just to everyone are a positive influence. Religion has its own philosophy, which is good even though some people have used religion for their own purposes.

In retrospect, I have three serious criticisms of Hoxha: isolationism, the class struggle, and his destruction of religious institutions. For a long time it was against the law to think of God or go to church. In the 50 years of communism there was a change in me, as there was in many other people, but after the coming of democracy I went to church again for the first time. Tears rolled down my face and I was sorry to think about all the churches that had been turned into sports arenas and all the icons that had been broken. I was also sad for the fate of the old religious leaders. The smell and everything about the experience made me remember.

Now I am a churchgoer. I feel relaxed and quiet in spirit in church. I don't go so frequently, but I go with a desire to believe and feel good, admiring the decorations and listening to the priest. My children love the Orthodox religion, even though my husband was a Muslim, because it is more flexible and open.

I have also become attracted to the Baha'i religion. Learning something about the programs and activities of this religion made me think that I was dealing with a scientific approach to faith and I like the broad way it approaches belief. I have read some books on Baha'i and find the teachings both interesting and convincing. Many young boys and girls are embracing this religion enthusiastically and I am drawn by this. So, I attend all of their activities and am frequently asked to read or recite poetry. I love trying to find appropriate verses that fit this spacious religion.

Conclusion

In addition to interviewing Margarita, Ksanthi and I also arranged to go to the Kinostudio (the Albanian version of Hollywood) to see some of Margarita's films. The Kinostudio is on what used to be the outskirts of Tiranë and is now surrounded by new construction, both legal and illegal. The crumbling main structure is outrageously grand and tawdry. It is surrounded by a high iron fence and grass and shrubs that are growing wild. There are other buildings on the grounds that are in worse repair and apparently vacant. We saw the films in a movie theater that was dank and disreputable with a high mosquito quotient. The films, however, were striking. The Margarita we saw captured and held us. It was her tone of voice and her actions, in fact her very presence on the screen, that affected us this way. It was also, however, the genuineness of her performance and the realism of the film. My heart broke when I saw the village scene in *Pylli ¿ Lirise*, when the young mother learns that her husband has been killed. It was not just the intensity of Margarita's performance, but also the scenes of the village itself. This film was produced in 1977 and portrayed an event occurring in the early 1940s, yet the village pictured could be any village in Albania today and the women were indistinguishable from the village women today. Life has not changed for these women in any significant way in all that time.

Our last meeting with Margarita took place on a chilly and damp fall day at the National Theater, found behind some ministry buildings off Skanderbeg Square in Tiranë. The theater is shabby from the outside and even shabbier inside. We followed in Margarita's wake as she swept through to the stage entrance. She greeted the guards familiarly and led us directly into the theater, where we found darkness. Only a single light illuminated the stage. It was set up with a gazebo and the form of a bunker for a current production (a comedy in which a small child urinates on the bunker in a symbolic comment on the former communist regime). Margarita asked that the house lights be turned on, and we waited for 45 minutes in the damp,

Margarita Xhepa in one of her film roles (photograph courtesy Margarita Xhepa).

unheated theater on hard, wobbly seats for someone to come. During this time, Margarita reminisced about the roles she had played on this stage: her major theatrical successes and some of the people with whom she had acted. She told us also with sadness: "My generation of actors has been called the 'lost generation' of artists, because the coming generations will see nothing of us because there are no films of our early performances."

She also spoke of the discomfort of acting in an unheated building with many other physical limitations. When no one came to turn on the lights, we went up onto the stage to take her photograph. Slowly she turned to the "audience" and began to recite. I almost forgot to take the photograph, so quickly did she grab my total attention. The cold and shabbiness faded as the glory of her performance shone on stage.

Margarita is truly a national treasure and a woman with a great spirit who has portrayed the essence and ideal of the Albanian woman throughout her career.

Chapter 8

Drita Kosturi: Broken but Not Bent

Ksanthi and I had heard the name Drita Kosturi everywhere we went. It was the most frequently mentioned name when we asked people for suggestions of women to interview. She is held in esteem by many for her partisan activities during the War of Liberation and for the sacrifices she made for her country then and throughout her life. People admire the spirit of sacrifice that she represents, her profound respect for the rights of others, her loyalty to her family and her country, and her generous nature.

She came to my house for the interview because she has no home of her own. She is now living in her niece's apartment, which is up several very difficult flights of stairs, and she did not feel comfortable meeting and talking to us in that place.

In a land that has an abundance of broken and hunched old women, my first impression was that Drita was one of these. As I looked at her more carefully, I found a totally modern woman with style, giving the impression of sophistication and a more privileged upbringing. Unlike her peers who dress in widow's black, many of whom wrap their heads in white or black cloths, Drita had on a smart dress with brass buttons and her hair beautifully done—loose and curly, but contained by a hair band. Although she walked with difficulty using a cane and was stooped, she had a dignity about her that belied the broken body. It seemed that as she talked her body straightened and the years rolled back. A more youthful woman of strong purpose and determination was clearly visible in her face and frame.

We spent many hours with Drita listening to her story, and there were times when I was horrified at the thought of going on. I didn't want to cause her pain and was not sure that I could bear to hear the details of her torture and persecution. While Drita was not eager to talk about herself initially, she finally recounted her story, leaving nothing aside, assuring us that she was not suffering by doing so. "Physical pain one can forget, but moral

107

pain is indelible," she told us. At the time it seemed a blessing that she was able to give the details of even the most difficult of times in a dispassionate and even remote manner, almost as if these events belonged to someone else's life. The only times she cried or lost her composure at all were when she spoke of the sufferings of others. Her own sufferings she considered to be so much less than theirs. In retrospect, however, I have felt that the very calmness and detachment with which she told her story makes the horror of Drita's story all the more tangible.

The Making of a Revolutionary

I was born in Lezhë, where my father was working in the military police, in August 1920, which makes me 76 years of age now. My parents had many children—12—although only 6 lived, 4 boys and 2 girls. Our mother died when I was 4 years of age, and we were raised by our father with the help of a housekeeper. For that reason, my father had a very great influence on my life.

My father, Ali Fehmi Kosturi, was born in 1879, was educated in the military academy in Turkey, and fought as a Turkish officer. His family lived in Kostur, a part of Albania that was later given to Greece, and he had the right to go either to Turkey or to Albania. Because he loved his country, he chose to live here rather than go to Turkey as his brothers did. He served his country well and was promoted to the position of the general commander of the Albanian Gendarmerie in 1922. He was later a supporter of Fan Noli and participated in the 1935 rebellion against King Zog. As a result of my father's influence, I was born and brought up in a family with patriotic feelings in which our people worked for the good of the country. Intellectual, patriotic, and democratic ideals were instilled in us.

In 1936 when I was 16 years old, I spent a great deal of time in the library. One time I had a project for school to copy the design on an Illyrian coin. At the library I met Qemal Stafa* who laughed when he heard what project I was working on. "Is this the time to spend on projects like this? Let the historians do it!" At the same time, he gave me a book entitled *Les Garçons*, from which I learned the idea that women should fight for their country and for their own freedom. I had already heard about the women who fought in the Spanish Civil War and the impact that Dolores Ibaruri† had in that struggle and therefore was receptive to the message of the book. The words of the heroine, Margarite, echoed in my ears "Shame is yours (if you do not fight), blessed water will not wash away any of it."

*Qemal Stafa was a talented literary man who is well known for his stories and verses. He is ranked highly among the realist literary writers of the 1930s. He was also one of the founders of the Albanian Communist Party in the city of Shkodër in 1941. He fought as a partisan for the liberation of Albania and on May 5, 1941, he was killed, at the age of 21.

†Dolores Ibaruri was the first secretary of the Communist Party of Spain and was known by the name of "Pasionare." In 1936 when the communists were defeated in the Spanish Revolution, she sought political asylum in the Soviet Union. Later, in 1960 at the Conference of 81 Communist Parties, she spoke out against the views of Enver Hoxha.

I remember that my brother found me reading the book and went to tell my father. My father listened to him and then told him to let me continue reading. He approved of my intellectual and political interests. The spirit of revolution was in my genes, and I began to look for more support for my ideas.

It was during this time that the ideals of communism began to be known among the people. I started to be active with other women and went door to door to talk with them. I encouraged women to attend school and to fight for themselves and their rights. When 1939 came (the year of the Italian occupation) I was a prepared person: a real rebel. There were many communist groups at this time, and I decided to join the Shkodër

Drita Kosturi.

group, of which Qemal Stafa was a member, with Nexhmije Xhuglini* and Selfixhe Ciu.

In 1939 I finished secondary school. Unlike the other girls of my age, I was given a great deal of freedom by my family and was very active politically. Because of my freedom and activities and the role and position of my father, I quickly came to the attention of the fascists. In this same year the old veterans, including my father, took part in a demonstration in front of the grave of Naim Frasheri. A group of my friends and I participated as well. I myself raised the flag in protest against the occupiers. Afterward, an Italian official sent for me and told me that I was being sent to study in Italy at no cost to me or my family. In fact, it was a form of exile.

While I was in Rome, the Italian police made a practice of rounding up all of the political dissidents, intellectuals, and students during Mussolini's speeches. As a result, I met many revolutionary people: antifascists, nationalists, communists, and others. These people influenced me and later I found that I had left Albania as a nationalist and had returned a communist. It was an exhilarating time.

In Italy I also met Qemal Stafa again and we were engaged to be married. What we shared was that we were young and idealistic—two students, two communists. I was not very attractive, and I remember once he was asked why he was engaged to such a plain woman. He responded, "I have never thought of her face. It is her spirit that I love."

On April 7, 1940, the first anniversary of the Italian occupation of Albania,

*Later the wife of Enver Hoxha.

I participated in an antifascist demonstration. Afterward, I returned to Albania and was immediately arrested by the Italians and sent back to Italy. There, I was tried and sentenced to prison for antifascist activity. Therefore, in September 1940 I entered the Regina Celli Prison, where the following words were inscribed over the door at the entrance to the prison: Forget All Hope: Coming in Here. I suffered six months of imprisonment. I am not sure why, but I was then released by order of Mussolini himself.

Fourteen days after my return to Albania, I went to fight in the mountains. I learned that the Communist Party had been founded and that I was automatically a member, since I had been a member of the communist group in Shkodër. On May 5, 1942, I was one of those present when the house that served as a hiding place for the partisans near the Muslim Medrese in Dibër Street was surrounded by the Italians. Qemal Stafa, who had been betrayed to the Italians, fought bravely against them, but the partisans were outnumbered, and on the bank of the nearby river he was shot dead. I was then sent to prison again by the Italians for being present there, and I served eight months of my sentence. I then escaped with the help of a prison guard in January 1943 and became a fugitive in the mountains in the Gjirokastër region. Afterward, I went to Vlorë and met the Albanian doctor Ibrahim Dervishi and an English doctor, Jack Dumoulin,* who were working for the Albanian Red Cross in partisan medical service of the Gjirokastër-Vlorë region. I fought for the Liberation and worked with them until the Liberation. My brother Skender was also killed whilst fighting.

In 1944 I went home and found the house emptied of goods and my father old and weak. It would be the last time I would see him. During this time, however, I found that I was being watched by the Communist Party and was left out of political life because I had expressed my opinions about the betrayal of Qemal Stafa. I had accused high-level communist leaders of complicity in his death. I continued working for the Red Cross, but in 1945 the first intellectuals were expelled from the Communist Party and I was one of them. They simply told me, with no explanation. In addition, two people were sent to our home and demanded that my father surrender his gun and other firearms. I had taken proper measures to hide them before the men came, but my father was insulted and said to them, "The gun and the wife are not to be handed over to you!" It was the beginning of severe persecution of well-known, intellectual families. I don't know how to express or describe the communist regime's ugly and savage behavior toward such families.

A period of special trials had begun for me and my family. After this incident, a person from the defense ministry came to my father and demanded that he give a statement that his son had been killed by a certain person. My father refused, saying, "I won't because I know that he was ordered to kill my son. They are the killers. He did what he was told to do." Then occurred a moment I will never forget.

---

*In a letter to me (the author) Dr. Dumoulin added, "I was a medical officer in the Royal Army Medical Corps attached to Special Operations Executive. From June 1943 British officers with wireless operators were infiltrated into then Italian-held (after September of that year German-held) Albania. I parachuted into Albania in December 1943, where I joined the partisans (Enver Hoxha's group). I met Drita soon after my arrival and for the best part of a year she acted as my contact with the partisan authorities, as the person who administered a small hospital, who did much work in them. She was very intelligent and hard-working and, particularly in the winter, suffered great deprivations."

My father turned to me and said, "We have fought for the sake of the fatherland. We might have consciously made mistakes." I didn't ask what he meant, but went to my papers to see if I could figure it out myself. I was so young and didn't think that I had done anything wrong, but I came to the conclusion that what I had done wrong was to have become a communist.

At this time I began my relationship with Myzafer Pipa, a young lawyer who was trying to protect the nationalist intellectuals who were anticommunist during the war and were subsequently against the dictatorship. Myzafer and I met in a library and were later engaged. He was well qualified for his work, brave and honest.

However, in September 1946 after the Revolt of Postriba, which took place in Shkodër where his office was, Myzafer was arrested "in the name of the people." I was arrested one week later on September 13. From that date followed three years of interrogation and torture.

The Horror of Interrogation

At the time of my arrest I was found with a letter from Dr. Jack Dumoulin* in my pocket. The return address included his Royal Air Force title, so the pretext for my arrest was that I was a collaborator with the English: a spy.

I was 26 years of age when I was arrested and I remember that I was wearing a light cotton dress. There were six prisons in Shkodër at that time; even the church was a prison. I was taken to the former home of the Suma family—one of the wealthiest families in Shkodër—to be interrogated. There, I was sitting in a chair with my legs crossed. An officer asked me why I was sitting in this manner "as if you had single-handedly liberated Albania." I didn't react. I was asked to leave the room and go into the hall. There I saw the others. The interrogator held up a mirror for them "to see the faces of the traitors." I was beginning to understand the nature of the psychological torture.

During this time the tortures began—psychological as well as physical. By nature, I was strong and they didn't make much impression on me. However, I had read about the Polish women patriots and I remembered one heroine who had to go to the czar and make him fall in love with her to get some keys. She had thought of ways to commit suicide in the event that the plot failed. I then thought about how I would be able to kill myself. I found a razor blade and thought of using it to cut my veins if I could not face the tortures successfully. I knew I was to undergo terrible tortures and was afraid of saying things under the pressure of pain and suffering. I understood that they would try to force me to accept their accusation that I was an English spy or that they would demand that I bear false witness against others. I knew I was strong, but I also understood the cruelty of the torture to which I would be subjected.

My first real shock was that I was taken to a crowded cell filled with men. Men of all classes and backgrounds: laborers, students, hoxhas, priests, and intellectuals—

Dr. Dumoulin suggests that this was a piece of paper with his address on it. "It would have said 'Capt. J. G. Dumoulin, RAMC.' It was the RAMC part that mystified her interrogators, who could only assume that it was a secret code; Drita had no idea of its actual meaning."

all types of men. I was the only woman in the cell. (Later I learned that there were other women in the same prison, but that it was part of the mental torture that there was just one woman assigned to each cell.) I asked the guard where I was to sleep. He just shouted to the men to make room for me. We each had 40 centimeters (less than 16 inches) in which to sleep. We had to sleep on our sides. Nothing existed to make life endurable: no water and no place to sleep. You can imagine how difficult it was for me in the thin dress I was arrested in.

Despite all the wickedness I saw at this time and the pain—physical and moral—that I experienced, I can neither say nor believe that our people are cruel and sadistic. I say this because you cannot imagine how kind the men and boys in that cell were to me. They knew that I suffered and that I had no family in Shkodër to look after me. The men found me a pair of pajamas and a blanket and shared with me the food that their families brought to them. They were so human and kind toward me. They were respectful and concerned and treated me as their sister. No, better than their sister! I will never forget their kindness.

Gulielm Suma, the son of the family in whose house we were imprisoned, slept next to me on one side and I had the wall on the other. He used to joke that he never imagined that he would sleep with the daughter of Ali Fehmi Bej. When they took Gulielm to be interrogated, a peasant took his place. He was not as careful with me, throwing his arms and legs over me as he slept. I couldn't sleep and began to become impatient for the interrogation to begin to escape the cell.

There was one time that I heard Myzafer's voice as I was on my way to the bathroom. He had learned that I had been arrested and shouted "Why have you taken Drita in?" Afterward I used to shout "It's me, Drita," but I never got a response. I found out later that he was taken to another prison.

Then the day of interrogation came for me. I was sent to the room where I was first arrested. My interrogator was waiting for me. As I entered the room, my eyes fell upon the stove in the room on which iron bars were placed to get hot. I had heard from other prisoners that the interrogators used them to pierce the flesh of the prisoners in the course of the interrogation. The minute I saw them I fainted. They took me out and revived me with cold water. When they brought me back into the room, the iron bars were gone. They had understood why I had fainted. However, the interrogator said, "Don't worry. You will experience this torture too if you fail to speak."

The first questions I was asked were about Myzafer. My answers were curt. "He is a lawyer." "He is my fiancé." Nothing else. I was then asked why I had become a communist. I responded "Because I had two pairs of shoes and wanted to give you one pair." At this moment, I was reminded of a French Progressive by the name of Clemenceau who said "When you are 20 you are a communist and at 30 you are a powerful, a strenuous anticommunist." By this he meant that 10 years of experience teaches the real nature of communism. My life has proven this saying.

Soon I was put into isolation. I was left in a room with no bread or water and told to stand all day and night. When I collapsed from exhaustion, they poured cold water on me and forced me to stand again for days on end. I don't know precisely how long this went on as I could only count up to eight or nine days. When I was finally at death's door, they took me to the hospital where I remained for two weeks.

When they brought me back, they began the interrogation again, this time with a different interrogator. He was a totally ignorant man who asked foolish questions. I was beaten, kicked, and tortured with handcuffs always on my wrists fastened so tightly that my hands bled.

I was then imprisoned with two men, this time in a room of a building that had been a church. One of the men in the cell with me was Gjon Serreqi and the other was a young man. I thought the young man was deliberately put in the cell to provoke me, so I thanked my interrogator for the company of the young man. The next day he was replaced by an ignorant old hoxha. The hoxha was so naive and uneducated that when Gjon's family brought a bra for me that was embroidered with roses the hoxha thought it was so beautiful that he wanted one too, but just one cup. He had never seen a bra before as he had never seen his wife nude above the ankles! This hoxha also wanted to read to me from the Koran. However, when he came close to me to read we discovered that we were both ticklish and everyone wondered what was going on between the old hoxha and young Drita! He also forbade us to eat pork in accordance with the Muslim tradition. However, Gjon and I convinced him that we were given nothing but pork to eat and that under these circumstances it was all right to break with the tradition in order to live.

Later I was sent to isolation again in a room in the cellar of the church where the dead priests had been buried. Again, I had no water, no bread. My hands were tied and I counted up to 15 days that I stood in these conditions, listening to the mice scratching around the cell. I had nothing to do all day but observe all that the mice did. I watched them store their food—bits of bread and nuts—while I had nothing. I was found unconscious and sent to the hospital. I stayed in the hospital for a long time. It was here that I learned that Myzafer had died during his interrogation. His interrogators had placed red-hot iron bars across his body that seared their way through to his bone.

It was also in the hospital that I met Pal Doda, an elderly priest who had attempted suicide by jumping out of a window to avoid further interrogation. However, despite his 80 years and the wounds he received in the fall, he had the misfortune to survive to be tortured again. I washed him and cared for him like a baby. He had great confidence in me and shared many of my opinions. He said "Drita is an angel sent from God to care for me, not a spy."*

When I came back from the hospital, I was sent to the *dhoma e territ* (the dark room). In this cell there was no light, only the light that came through the keyhole; there was no light day or night. There were 10 or 15 people in the cell and the prison was especially crowded at this time with priests. On my way to the bathroom I saw many priests cruelly tortured. I observed the profound faith of the priests who were being so treated. For example, one priest was tied to the ceiling and dropped to the floor. He hit the floor crying, "Long live Christ, my King!"

After some time another group of enemies was discovered by the regime and it was necessary to rush our interrogations. They prepared a false witness against me and the intellectuals who were in prison with me. This witness claimed that I had said to him "I know a great deal, but will not tell them." Since I had not known the man before, it was clearly fabricated. Just before the trial the interrogators experimented on me with electric shock. It was one very powerful shock and didn't last

After the democratic reform, Father Doda's body was reburied and the medal that he received posthumously for his bravery was given to Drita Kosturi by President Berisha in recognition of her kindness to him.

long, but I fell off my chair with the jolt. When I went back to my room, I put my head on my pillow and the hair on that side of my head came off. My eye was swollen and turned black. I had lost that eye. My teeth were all broken off. I was then taken back to the cellar and forced to stand night and day again, with no bread or water and with my hands and feet bound. This time I didn't last long because I had a vaginal hemorrhage. The entire floor of the cell was covered with my blood. I was again taken to the hospital and I wondered, "When is my end coming?"

The Trial

The day of my trial came. It lasted only a quarter of an hour. The sheet of paper with the information on which I was convicted was blank. They only had the names of my family and no others. The accusation on which I was tried was, "During the National Liberation War, in appearance serving the people, she has served the Intelligence Service and the spies, she has had links with the American and English Missions in Albania."

I was found guilty and sentenced to death. When the trial was over, I was tied hand and foot and placed in a cell in isolation to await my execution. I had only a small amount of dry cornbread and a bit of water. Because executions were always done early in the mornings, I woke every day at three so that they would not come and find me sleeping on the morning of my execution. Ever since this ordeal I have woken at three every morning.

In the cell next to me was Kol Prela, a Catholic intellectual, who was also sentenced to death and waiting, like me, for the moment of execution. We had only a small hole at the bottom of the wall to communicate through early each morning. We heard only each other's voices for three months. After three months the prosecutor and others came to inform me of a new decision. They entered and said "Stand up!" I replied, "I can't. You have bound my hands and feet." After they cut loose my feet, they informed me that my sentence had been reduced to life imprisonment. I was also told to send a telegram to the People's Assembly to thank them for the new sentence. I told them that I would do so after I had informed my family, but of course I never did. Kol heard the voices and the announcement and asked me to take a message to his mother. He was later shot.

I still don't know why I wasn't executed. Maybe it was because they did not have enough evidence or because I was well known and popular. Only one woman had been executed up to that time, Zurika Mano, who was part of a famous group of intellectuals who were accused of sabotage in Maliq in the Korçë district. I would have been the second woman to be executed.

Imprisonment and Exile

So I entered prison. The first night I was there the other women demanded that my cot be placed near the door because I smelled so awful. You see, in the three years of interrogation I had never bathed, not even in the hospital. Another prisoner, Ana Daja,* helped me to wash. As she started, all of my skin formed blisters as if I was burned all over my body. This reaction was caused not only by the fact that I had not bathed in three years but also by the lack of vitamins in my diet.

I had no family in Shkodër except the mother-in-law of my brother. She met me in prison and it was she who told my family of my arrival there. They had thought I was dead. The first family member to meet me after three years was my sister-in-law, Josephina, who insisted on seeing me. Later my sister, brother, and others came.

Although I was informed some months after I had arrived that my sentence had been reduced to 20 years imprisonment, I was unfortunately among a number of prisoners who had to feel the consequences of political events outside the prison. Whenever these events occurred, we were put into isolation. In prison we were allowed to come out of our cells twice a day, each time for just one hour.

One night in 1953 a number of prisoners were told to come out into the yard and get ready to go to prison in Burrel. I went out and saw my brother's friend, Hilmi Seiti, who was now a general and the chief of the Sigurimi in Shkodër. He said to me, "Have a good time in prison." I answered, "We can be broken, but not bent." While the others left, I was told that I would not be going. Hilmi called me to his room and showed me that my name was on the list of those to be sent to Burrel. He said, "You didn't go because it is I who decided that you should not go, but stay in the prison in Shkodër." Therefore, I was kept there secretly. All of my documents, however, show that I went to Burrel.

In 1953 I was sent to work in a large sewing enterprise in Tiranë. Many prisoners were sent at that time to sew things for the army. There I met the sister of Pjeter Arbnori,† who had been imprisoned for trying to cross the border and had been sent there from the prison in Burrel. We were given an incentive to work hard because our prison terms could be reduced by the amount of production we did that exceeded the daily norms. I was told in 1955 that my sentence was reduced to 15 years, and through hard work in the factory (producing two to two and a half times the daily norms) I was able to earn an additional two-year reduction in my sentence.

In 1956, while I was still in Tiranë, three of us, including myself, Frida Sadedin,§ and Musine Kokolare, were rounded up and sent to the prison in Vlorë and later to Shkodër. Then once again we were sent to Tiranë to the sewing factory, not to work but to be held in the underground prison beneath the factory.

Ksanthi and I met Ana Daja by chance when we were interviewing in Shkodër. She told us, "We used to tease Drita 'We know why you are in prison, but why are we here with you?' I was the daughter of an artisan—a copper worker. I was brought up in a religious family and never liked communism. There was much anticommunist activity in the early years and I distributed leaflets. As a result, time and again I was suspended from school. Later, I was expelled from school and in June 1947 I was arrested. I had many terrible moments in prison. Once an investigator struck me in the face, almost in the eye. Another time I was plunged into a huge pot of feces and was forced to clean such a pot with no soap to clean my hands afterward. For two weeks in October I had to stand at one end of a hall and a man stood at the other. Our bodies were doused with water and the windows were opened. The man had tuberculosis and died, but I survived." When we asked what had been her source of strength, Ana looked at us with her clear and piercing eyes and said with a strong voice "God."
†*The head of the Albanian Parliament in the first democratic government.*
§*We found Frida living in the center of Shkodër in Kulla Markagjoni, a 400-year-old house*

Drita Kosturi's friend Frida Sadedin.

with fortified tower and walls that belonged in earlier times to Frida's great-grandfather. Frida told us, "I have not done so much for Albania, but my mother and father were patriots. My mother was Marta Bib Doda, a niece of Preng Pasha, and she embroidered the first Albanian flag in 1903 when no one knew exactly what the emblem of Skanderbeg had been, a single or double-headed eagle. The local padre went to Rome to the archives, found the design, and brought it back to her. Later, in 1918, my mother headed the first Albanian women's organization in Kopliku.

"My father, Ahmed Anton Sadedin, was a Young Turk and was sent by the Turkish government to Albania as a punishment. He fell in love with my mother. Although this great love did not end well, my father contributed much to this country. He constructed the first hospital in Shkodër and was the founder of the Albanian Red Cross. As the only child in the family, my parents wanted me to have a good occidental education so they sent me to study in Italy and in Austria.

"My mother was arrested in 1947 for not having declared that she was from a family of which a member had fled the country, and my father was arrested in 1946 as a supporter of the West. In 1949 I was arrested as an agent. I was in prison almost 11 years and for 20 years afterward I was in exile."

When we asked Frida where she found her strength she replied, "First is God. I am extremely religious and I kept the faith alive in myself. The prison guards were superstitious and didn't stop me from praying and told others not to interrupt me. I am also strong-willed and optimistic for the future. When I am desperate I am aggressive, maybe beyond the limit. This is not as a result of prison, I have always been this way. I regret the life in prison and exile. It is an emptiness in my life, a dead time. I couldn't even read. There were people who suffered as much or worse. What is common for all of us, that is if we all suffer, it is not as bad. It is only half the suffering."

In 1959 I was released from prison, some months after I should have been released. My release was delayed because they were deciding what to do with me. It was decided that I would be released directly into exile and that I was not to be allowed to meet my family, even for an hour. I was sent directly to Shtyllas, a village in Fier, where I worked in the fields and had to check in with the police three times a day for five years.

After five years I no longer had to check in with the police and I was called a "free worker," but I couldn't even go to the town of Fier without getting permission from the police. I was still not free. My sister used to come and see me frequently and her visits gave me joy. I remember one time she came to visit me without her husband's approval and the bus on which we were riding had an accident. Although my sister was uninjured, I broke my arm. Still, I thought of nothing but getting her back to Tiranë.

In 1976 I retired from working in the fields and received a pension of 350 new lekë a month (equivalent to about $3.50) in recognition of my service during the war and my work in the field. After this time I used to come and go to Tiranë with permission. For example, I was able to come when my brother died. Later, in 1988, I had a stroke that almost paralyzed my left side. From that year and that event on, I didn't go back to Shtyllas. The situation was a bit more liberal so I didn't return. I asked that my documents be moved to Tiranë and petitioned to be a citizen of Tiranë. I have lived here since.

The Source of Her Strength

My strength comes from several sources. First, my father has been the guiding compass in my life. He was a democrat and a patriot. He encouraged me while I was in Rome to get to know the outside world and take the positive side of that world.

Also, when I was in prison in Rome there was a statue of the wife of Garibaldi, Anita, nearby. I knew her story well and I tried to find the force in myself to be like her, but could not.

Finally, I admired the wife of Hassan Prishtina, an Albanian patriot who was in the government of Fan Noli. Although she was not an Albanian, I found inspiration in her. She was never found without a pistol in her belt. Once, when her husband was in exile in Austria, she followed him. When she found him she said, "You cannot do anything to help Albania sitting in a coffee bar, but come to your country."

The Role of Faith

If you define religion and faith as the Catholics do, then I can't say that I have faith. We respected the feasts, but did not celebrate them in our family. I do, however, believe in a greater force. This greater force has been a consolation, as if someone were protecting me and when I do wrong, something inside me instinctively says, "Forgive me, God."

Drita: The Essence

Drita's is an irrepressible spirit, a rebel that is unbent and still fighting for her beliefs. At one point she even said, "I feel sorry, very sorry, that I do not enjoy good health and do not see better. I would surely have been involved in political work now." Early in the interview she remarked, "I have suffered so much I can no longer laugh or smile. I find people who do to be frivolous and silly." She then went on to recall several incidences during her imprisonment in Rome that made her laugh and us with her. She also sprinkled funny stories about the old hoxha and his naivety throughout her narrative of the time of her interrogation. Drita's eyes filled with tears when she recalled the tortures of others and the death of Kol Prela. She moved us to tears, not with her own sufferings but in recounting the sufferings of others. Her sacrifice has been extreme, yet she maintains her optimism, sense of humor, and dignity.

Drita's story is one of a lifelong struggle, of rebellion against tyranny, and of the strength of the individual against the forces of repression. Her ideals and beliefs brought her into confrontation with the forces of fascism and dictatorship. Her life was destroyed, but her commitment to her ideals is undiminished.

Part III

THE GRINDING OUT OF COMMUNISM

Chapter 9

The Middle Generation of Women in Albania

The women of the middle generation, those between the ages of 30 and 59, are those who came to maturity and have lived the greatest portion of their lives under communism. Most of their lives have been characterized by endless hard work, the struggle for survival, deprivation, and tedium, and those experiences mark their faces still. For all its difficulties and monotony, however, life with all its passions went on. People celebrated marriages and births, had affairs, grieved for those who died, and dreamed of the future. Children played and laughed.

It is hard to understand how one person could subdue so forceful and determined a people. The poverty of the country Enver Hoxha left at his death has an artificial and unnecessary quality that is inconsistent with the country's rich natural and human resources. To understand what happened and how events shaped the lives of the people, it is important to look back at the ruthless establishment of the regime, the policies and intentions of the Hoxha government, and the means used to accomplish the regime's Marxist-Leninist ideals.

It is equally important to understand that the people were attracted to the new leader and the communist ideals and that many people benefited, especially in the early years. For this reason there was both a push—the forced aspect of domination, and a pull—the attraction to the new form of government.

What Existed Before the Communist Regime

As noted previously, the Ottoman rule of Albania left the country as poor and backward as it had been 500 years earlier. There were no road or rail systems, no sanitation, no education, and no industrialization. The needs of the vast majority of the people had been neglected with the desire of the Turkish rulers to profit from their control of the country. Only a few educated and wealthy families benefited during this period,

Further, a series of weak governments failed in their three primary goals: to establish their governmental authority; to create an economic base for providing basic services to the Albanian people; and to protect the borders of the country against the expansionist goals of Albania's neighbors. As noted earlier, not until the 14-year rule of King Zog did a true unification of the country begin. At that time, with the help of the Italians, the establishment of a government and the construction of physical structures finally began to meet the needs of the population.

At the beginning of the War of Liberation, Albania was still a backward country, with virtually no industry or modern infrastructure and an uneducated population that was largely reliant on agriculture for subsistence. Medical care and hygiene were primitive in most parts of the country, and life expectancy was low by European standards.* The unification of the country was not yet firm, and the people's definition of themselves and what constituted being Albanian was not yet clear.†

Into this period of turmoil and uncertainty came the Italian Occupation. Although the economic ties with Italy had brought greater wealth and development than had been known before, the threat to the country's nascent independence was considered by many Albanians to be the paramount issue of the time. Therefore, during the occupation of Albania by the Italian fascists, a number of resistance movements were formed. The first of these to be formally organized was the Balli Kombëtar (the National Front), founded by Midhat Frasheri in May of 1939, just one month after the occupation. In addition to seeking the expulsion of the Italian occupiers, this organization sought agrarian and social reforms and the reintegration of Albanian lands that had been given to Yugoslavia and Greece earlier in the century. The Balli Kombëtar was led by land-owning and educated patriots who expected support from the Allies in the form of supplies and actual military intervention. Also, as early as 1928, communist groups began appearing in Korçë, Shkodër, and other areas, attracting "primarily the poor craftsmen, workers and peasants who were discontented with Albania's medieval economy."**

Although the Communist Party was not established nationally until November 1941, its local and regional members—along with communist

---

*Edwin Jacques cites an astounding statistic: "Under the Enver Hoxha regime, life expectancy rose from 38 to over 71." Jacques, The Albanians, p. 540.
†Stark Draper, "The Conceptualization of an Albanian Nation," Racial and Social Studies, 20, no. 1.
**Jacques, The Albanians, pp. 415–16.

sympathizers and other antifascists and idealists—began the fight for freedom in the cities and in the mountains using guerrilla tactics. Their ideals included belief in the equality of people and the emancipation of women, democracy and freedom, and self-determination. Few of these people knew anything about communist ideology, the writings of Marx or Lenin, or the Soviet experience with communism.

The Coming to Power of the Communist Party

With the assistance of Albanian advisers from the Yugoslav Communist Party, the Albanian Communist Party was established with about 200 members. Enver Hoxha was elected as provisional party secretary and an effort was made to unify disparate elements under the banner of nationalism and the call to expel the occupiers. Even after the establishment of the Communist Party, the communist ideology was downplayed in favor of an inclusive, patriotic, and unifying image. So the National Liberation Movement was formed as an organization that sought to bring together all of the antifascist fighters in a coordinated manner. Further assistance was given to this group by the Yugoslav communists in the form of military supplies and training, in addition to propaganda materials. This—combined with the refinement of the guerrilla warfare strategy—made the communists the best equipped and most effective liberation force in the country. As a result, in 1941 Great Britain, which at this time (prior to the involvement of the United States in the Second World War) was the only Allied country capable of helping in the Albanian struggle against the Italians, decided to back the communists as the liberation organization with the most potential for success. Therefore, Britain provided intelligence and medical officers, as well as military advisers and supplies, in support of this cause, first against the Italians and then, after the fall of Mussolini, against the Germans.*

Great Britain also sought to mediate between the factions represented within the resistance movement. However, whatever cooperation that had existed previously between the Balli Kombëtar and the Communist Party ended at the end of 1943. The German government had announced that at the end of the war it would withdraw from Albania and give Kosova back to Albania. With the defeat of the Italians and the occupation by the Germans, the policy of the Balli Kombëtar changed to open support of the Germans—whom they considered to be only temporary occupiers—and

*This assistance was limited in nature and represents the only contribution made by the Allies to the defense of Albania against the Axis powers.

equally open confrontation with the communists. This reorientation lost the Balli Kombëtar much popular support. At that time (September 1943), just after the defeat of Italy by the Allied forces and during the Second National Liberation Conference, the Communist Party "declared a war of extermination on all members of the BK (Balli Kombëtar), branding them 'enemies of the people.'"* This signaled the beginning of the Albanian civil war, which continued simultaneously with the fight for liberation through November 1944, when the Germans were defeated. The occupation by the Germans was brutal and destructive, but the National Liberation Movement was able to defeat their troops and crush the anticommunist forces at the same time, with the limited help of military supplies and other assistance from the Allies.

With the defeat of the Germans on November 29, 1944, at Shkodër, many of the anticommunist leaders fled the country and the communist government came into power.†

The Toll of Victory

The destruction of Albania was vast and the people were desperate due to hunger, the destruction of homes, and the prevalence of disease. With this suffering came new, unimaginable challenges and hardships.

Under these conditions the people were convinced by the new government that tough measures were required to reconstruct the nation and help it achieve the idealistic vision painted by the communists. Enver Hoxha was presented as the man to design and carry out this radical plan. Throughout the period of the War of Liberation, it was his vision and determination that led to the ultimate success of the communists in defeating Albania's foreign enemies, as well as the dissenters against communism. It is clear from Drita Kosturi and Dhora Leka's stories that Enver Hoxha was engaged at an early date in the extermination of individuals who represented possible obstacles to his climb to power and of groups or classes of people who might be threats to him and his political beliefs. It is also clear that Hoxha was not averse to using treachery and other devious means to gain the political advantage and power that he sought.

The use of the term "enemies of the people" to describe the members of the Balli Kombëtar in 1943 has a chilling sense of foreboding about it,

---

*Jacques, The Albanians, p. 422.
†Jacques notes that on the evening of the victory, "Enver Hoxha and his colleagues attended a religious service of thanksgiving to God for the final liberation." Jacques, The Albanians, p. 424. This is especially interesting in light of the religious persecution during the Hoxha regime.

as the first priority of the new postwar government was to eradicate all dissenters. Intellectuals, middle-class business people, and wealthy people, along with known anticommunists were among the first targets, as their wealth and property could be confiscated by the state for the purpose of easing the desperate economic conditions. These people were taxed heavily under a war profiteering tax, and many were arrested and sent to prison or shot for suspected treason. The Albanian people were told that such measures were necessary to protect the country from enemies and to redistribute wealth from the rich to the poor so that all of the citizens would be equal. Other early targets were the Catholic clergy, who were accused of being foreign agents, and the property of the churches was duly appropriated. For those who were the objects of eradication this was a reign of terror, and for those who were benefiting there was the rationalization that the means were justified by the ultimate attainment of their ideals.

The Benefits of Victory

As in any victory, there was euphoria. The liberation of their country essentially by their own hands was an accomplishment of which the Albanian people were proud. Naturally, they were filled with nationalistic spirit and pride in the sacrifices they had made to accomplish the victory. The ideals of the war and those presented to the people by the new government were lofty and stirred hearts and minds. There was a mood of optimism in the midst of the destruction of the land.

The spirits of the people were buoyed by the propaganda of the government, and physical needs began to be met by relief from the UN Relief Agency and by wheat supplies from Yugoslavia. Initially, the sacrifices of the postwar period seemed a small price to pay for the independence of the country and the freedom and equality of the people.

The new government wasted no time in devising ways to improve the lives of the people, even as it sought ways of exerting increasing control over the thoughts and actions of that same population. Many areas of life were targeted and addressed in a manner consistent with the government's goals throughout communist rule—with or without the help of the countries with whom Albania was aligned. Among the primary issues addressed were land ownership, increased agricultural production, the industrialization of the country, the provision of municipal and social services, and transportation.

Land Ownership. Land reform had been a desired goal since the country's independence from Turkey, and now the communist government sought to begin this. Although the stated goal was the redistribution of the land from the wealthy landowners to the agricultural workers, the actual result was the transfer of private ownership of the land to the state. A large part of this transfer was effected almost immediately, with some land remaining in the hands of the people. However, over time the amount of private property allowed was reduced in increments that eventually left families with insufficient land to support their needs, leaving them totally reliant on the state. This same model was applied to the ownership of livestock; it was eventually prohibited for families to keep even chickens.

Agricultural Production. Even before the war, Albania had not been able to produce adequate agricultural products to feed the population. At the end of the war this situation was even more critical due to the destruction that had occurred throughout the country. Therefore, one of the primary goals of the new government from the beginning was to increase agricultural production at least to the point of self-sufficiency. Among the methods employed was the creation of agricultural cooperatives that employed the villagers in routine agricultural work.* In addition, the villagers—along with students, professionals, and other "voluntary" laborers—were engaged in the clearing and terracing of lands to increase cultivation and to construct irrigation systems. Production goals were set and the people held to these goals, despite the hardships caused by increased work hours and the general lack of machinery to accomplish the heavier tasks, such as clearing new lands. Unfortunately, the rapid population growth in the communist period led to the needs of the people outstripping the increased agricultural production throughout the period. During the periods of alignment with Yugoslavia, the Soviet Union, and China, these partners provided much needed wheat to compensate for the shortfall. In the years of isolation following the break with China, the government "met" the needs of the citizens largely by proclaiming them met. During this latter period, food was strictly rationed and inadequate, while fruits and some vegetables were exported for currency.

Industrial Production. A central aim of the Hoxha government was the development of an industrial base in Albania. For this reason, 50–65 percent of the budget in each of the five-year plans devised by the regime was dedicated to industry, and aid was sought from each of the successive foreign partners to assist in this goal.† The successes of this program can be measured in the number of factories for processing food, producing textiles and steel, mining chromium, and other purposes scattered throughout

---

*Most of the labor was manual throughout the communist period, despite some agricultural machinery provided by the Soviet Union and China during the periods of Albania's alliance with these countries.
†Jacques, The Albanians, ch. 28.

the country. Towns and cities were literally created as sites were chosen in which to place these factories, and one of the key accomplishments of the regime can be said to be the urbanization of Albania that came along with the industrialization. Unfortunately, the industrialization was frequently accomplished using obsolete technology exported to Albania from the countries with which it was aligned. In addition, the maintenance of the factories was problematical after the ties with the individual countries were severed, as replacement parts were no longer readily available. As a result, these plants were ineffective and environmentally unsafe.

It is also important to note that much of the emphasis of the communist government was on industrial production that related to exports. Hydroelectric power, for example, was exported and Albania was the third largest producer of chromium in the world. This export activity allowed the government to raise much needed budgetary funds, but it was still unable to meet the demand for consumer goods.*

Education and Literacy. One of Hoxha's primary goals was universal literacy and education of all the people. Literacy programs were established in all areas and education through the eighth grade became obligatory. Emphasis was placed on a secular, atheistic approach. Although there was a strong propagandistic element in which access to certain books was controlled and many ideas were not tolerated, there was an emphasis on excellence and achievement. Education was also thought to have three components: classroom learning, labor, and military training. Therefore, the classroom was only one place in which the education of the children took place. "Actions" were organized for high school classes to build railroads and harvest crops, and there was a month of military training required each year.

Also, during this period institutions of higher education that had not previously existed were established. These included the university in Tiranë and schools of higher learning in other cities, the Academy of Science, and other scientific institutions.

Health Care. In the postwar period health services were free of charge. A number of hospitals, clinics, maternity homes, and sanitariums were established. In the early postwar years many medical professionals were educated in Russia and other Eastern European countries. Later, after the creation of the medical school and of the University of Tiranë, doctors and other medical personnel were trained in Albania. As a result,

---

Today the industrial base of the country is almost nonexistent as the factories are mostly abandoned as too inefficient or dangerous to operate. This has, in turn, led to significant unemployment, especially in the new cities that were created with the establishment of the factories.

the number of doctors grew exponentially and it became possible to provide basic health services to a larger number of people. With a greater number of doctors and the use of antibiotics and vaccines, epidemic diseases—such as malaria, tuberculosis, and sexually transmitted diseases—which were widespread before the war, were effectively eliminated. The overall health of the population was also positively affected by the isolation of the country, which kept out some of the more virulent diseases, including polio and AIDS.

Nationalism. In his appeal to nationalism Hoxha sought to give the Albanians a keener sense of being one people in the following ways:

1. Standardization of the language.* The creation of a unique literary language was greatly encouraged to replace the two former existing dialects. This process of standardization had begun in the nineteenth century, but was now considered to be an immediate necessity to ease the work of the administrative institutions, the schools, and the media. To this end, Albanian as it is used in the Tosk dialect, with the inclusion of some Gheg elements, was adopted as the official, or literary, language. In addition, an effort was made to eliminate foreign (especially Turkish) words.

2. Condemnation and, in 1967, abolition of religion. The government sought to eliminate potential divisiveness among the people by outlawing religion and encouraging intermarriage among families of different religious backgrounds.†

3. Egalitarianism. Strong measures were taken in an attempt to bring the standard of living in the villages up to that of the cities. In addition, the emancipation of women was sought through various means designed to break the power of the existing social code and to provide educational and employment opportunities previously not considered.

4. National values. The Hoxha regime did much to strengthen nationalism by emphasizing the contributions of the Albanian people from ancient times to the present day in the history and cultural development of the region. These values were reinforced not only through the educational system but also through an intensive propaganda campaign designed to boost national pride. The slogans

---

*Based on a conversation with Anastas Dodi, a prominent professor of the Albanian language.
†Jacques proposes that "Albanianism" represented a "substitute religion" in which the communist leadership represented the deities, the war heroes became the martyrs, sports and culture became the religious observances, and strict adherence to the laws was the orthodoxy or fundamentalism of the faith. Jacques, The Albanians, pp. 546–59.

sought to convince the people that they were capable of producing everything they needed by relying on their own experience. The slogans also told the people that they could do without the experience of other countries because the Albanian people have developed in their own special way. Although this propaganda had a positive and unifying effect on the population in the early years, it reached a fevered pitch in the period following the breakup with the Chinese, when Albania was totally isolated from the rest of the world. In fact, it became xenophobic and more clearly unreasonable with each passing year.

Some of the benefits brought by the communist rule began to be felt by the majority of the population in the early postwar years, and the years that followed brought increasing prosperity. This was true as long as there was foreign aid from some source (Yugoslavia, Russia, or China) to support the economy of the country. During this period—prosperity reached its zenith in the early to mid–1970s—many, if not most, people were proud to be associated with communism and with the Party of Labor of Albania. To be a supporter was not only necessary but patriotic. To be a member of the party was prestigious and brought practical advantages. Also, until the early 1970s there was a certain liberalism in Hoxha's dictatorship. Foreign books were allowed into the country and there was a degree of cultural permissiveness, for example in dress and music. Tiranë in the early 1970s is shown by Ismail Kadare in striking contrast to immediate postcommunist Albania: Tiranë is described as having pleasant cafes and a graciousness that was not apparent in the early part of 1994.*

The turning point came in the final years of the alignment with China (after 1972 when President Nixon visited China). At that time Hoxha became concerned about the foreign influences, especially in light of what he saw as the weakening of China's adherence to Marxist-Leninist principles. In response to these concerns, his policies became stricter and the life of the people became harder. It has also been suggested that at this time the long-term effects of Hoxha's illness—diabetes—and his resulting weakness caused him to become increasingly paranoid. The combination of these factors and the eventual break with China led to a radical "go it alone" policy, in which the Albanian people were exhorted to sacrifice to the maximum to meet the country's industrial and agricultural needs. Also during this period, which extended up to the time of Hoxha's death in 1985, "enemies" were identified with increasing regularity and punished in extreme

*Ismail Kadare, The Concert, New York: William Morrow, 1994.

ways. The class struggle intensified and the poverty of life increased to the breaking point.

Impact on the People

The Albanian people had good reason to be both pleased and frightened by the turn of events. There was a sense of life improving. People were chosen from the lowest socioeconomic levels for favors, including education and recognition for production and good work. Some of these changes came very quickly and must have given the Albanians, especially the rural poor, a sense of accomplishment and optimism. This feeling was further buoyed by the propaganda of the regime that continuously told the people that their sufferings and sacrifices were not in vain. The repression, the poverty, and the total isolation of Albania from the rest of the world were all justified in the name of the creation of a new society. This new society would be "free of the wounds of capitalism, without capitalist exploitation of the oppressed classes, and without moral degeneration or prostitution."*

At the same time, life became predestined. As long as a person's biography remained unblemished, he or she could expect certain things in life: education, employment, and social services. The limits of that life were circumscribed, but there was little uncertainty about its basic form and progress. A typical week might involve regular work and military training or voluntary actions as well as the endless waiting in lines for food. There was frequently no day of rest and little leisure time. There also was the constant effort to ensure that a good biography was maintained and that it was not tainted by contact with a person with a bad biography or by actions that could be judged unpatriotic.

If a person's biography had a black spot on it, he or she also knew what to expect in life: limited education as studies beyond the eighth grade would be impossible to attain; low-level, most likely physical, work; and constant observation by the Sigurimi for "crimes." That person would live in a state of constant vigilance or fear of punishment for suspected crimes. This was especially true in periods when the class struggle became sharper, that is, in times when Hoxha found new enemies to condemn in an effort to intimidate the people. Some of these people with bad biographies were born in exile and remained there until the coming of democracy in 1991, suffering the punishment for their families' crimes their entire lives.

---

*This is a summary and paraphrase of the propaganda slogans of that time.

Chapter 10

The Lives of Typical Women

"I have had a quiet life, but it has been monotonous," Xhina.

"Life has always been difficult and I have always been tired," Liri.

"The scandal of my life is that I had to live in such conditions. We were obedient animals, but nothing more than animals," Barije.

"I worked in a plant because the regime gave me no other option. I was not given the right to pursue higher education or to go into the line of work I desired. When I was young, there was military training. Imagine me as a girl three months away from my family. Once in a village I felt ill and wanted my mother to come. My mother was not allowed to come and I wasn't allowed to go home until I had finished my military training," Rexhina.

"The women of Albania are heroines. It was our life—we had to survive," Meri.

The preceding statements are typical of the women of this generation summarizing their existence. Despite the improvements in their lives and the government's goal to emancipate females, the women of this generation experienced lives of unrelieved hardship. They found strength in a variety of sources: within themselves, in their families, and in their work. However, this generation was largely deprived of the freedom to learn of their faith or to worship. Therefore, for the majority of the women, faith (especially if defined as "religion") played little or no role in their lives.

Issues That Affected Women

There are a number of issues that serve as background information in order to understand this generation of women and the leitmotivs in the responses they gave to our questions. Some of these issues stem from the actions or ideals of the government and others are sociological issues.

Unlike their mothers, for example, the women of this generation were raised with the expectation of being educated.* Education for girls as well as boys was highly valued and the opportunity for young people to pursue university or specialized training was an important goal. Parents, for the most part, encouraged their daughters to continue their education as far as possible and supported them in heroic ways. As in other aspects of life, the field of study in which a girl (or a boy) was allowed to enroll was decided by the state, based on the current and expected need for skilled workers. However, it was also the goal of the government to give equal opportunities to girls to pursue studies in the sciences, mathematics, and engineering, as evidence of the emancipation of the Albanian women.

This equality in the treatment of women was also evidenced in the requirement that the girls participate, along with the boys, in the military training and youth group "actions" (such as construction or harvesting) previously mentioned.

However, while girls of this generation were afforded greater opportunities to study and to spend time away from their families with other young people, their upbringing remained conservative and restricted. This was not only based on societal customs but was also supported by the government as a positive value. Girls were carefully monitored by their families and the community at large to ensure that they were honest and good—that is, they did not talk to boys or show interest in any one boy. Any evidence of their sexuality was discouraged to the point that they were forbidden, both by their families and the government, to wear slacks or makeup, and girls in their early teens frequently bound their breasts to hide their "shame." This shame was most obvious when they had their menstrual cycles. Since tampons and sanitary napkins were unavailable, the girls used rags which they had to wash and hang on a line outside to dry.

In addition, the family continued to be the strongest influence on the girls. They learned about life and what was expected of them both from their fathers and their mothers as well as from their grandmothers, who were frequently their primary caregivers when they were young children. Mothers taught their girls to be hardworking and to care for the house. The family's training of the girls was to prepare them to marry, to be an asset in the family home of their husband.

Although the communist government encouraged interfaith marriages and marriages for love, arranged marriages within regions and faith groups continued to be the rule rather than the exception, especially in the

---

*"Before liberation, 92 percent of the Albanian women were illiterate; by the 1980s all could read and write." Jacques, The Albanians, p. 557.

rural areas. However, the conditions of the arrangements showed signs of liberalization in this period. For example, more women were introduced to their prospective husbands and given an opportunity to get to know them before the wedding. Also, in some regions, the arrangement began to take the form of a recommendation as opposed to a requirement.

However, the engagement and marriage of daughters in this generation were major problems because of the large number of factors that had to be considered: religion; politics (particularly a person or family's biography); the honor and reputation of the family; and sometimes the wealth of the family. Finding a good marriage—one that met all the requirements of this list—was difficult, and families continued to be unwilling to leave the choice to chance factors or love.

Other issues revolving around marriage include the relationships that the women have had with their mothers-in-law as well as with their husbands. The position of a wife depended on the birth order of the husband and the number of other married brothers in the household. For example, the wife of the oldest son usually had a more privileged position than did the wives of the younger sons. Occasionally, we even heard stories of the husband's commitment to his mother superseding his commitment to his wife.

The Hoxha regime encouraged the people to have children, going so far as to provide cash gifts to families upon the birth of a child. In addition, contraceptives were outlawed and unavailable. Abortions that were obtained illegally and at high risk to the health of the mother were the only form of birth control available, and many women, especially those in urban areas, had two or more such abortions. Many women were fatalistic about conceiving and having children. Also, there continued to be value placed on having boys rather than girls and many women stated that they had continued to have children until they had a boy.* Midwives were provided free of charge by the state and, as a result, childbirth became safer. All of these factors led to an explosion in the population during the communist period.

Despite the emphasis on families, it was also the stated goal of the communist government that women should be treated as equal with men. As a result, women had a relatively high representation in the Communist Party, in various levels of the government, in the universities, and in the workforce. Women working in agriculture and industry had the illusion of

---

*"When a girl was born the very beams of the house began crying." This Albanian proverb pertains to two aspects of the birth of a girl. First, the parents would both be sad because the daughter would cost them more in terms of a dowry and would not be as productive in contributing to the household as a boy would. Secondly, the mother would frequently grieve for the difficult life that lay ahead for her child.

economic independence in that they earned a wage that was actually paid to them. For many, however, the wage was so low that they were free only to the extent of being able to buy a loaf of bread with their daily wage. It was clearly not enough to support an independent life.

Women did have a certain amount of independence in that they were safe from crime or attack. It was safe to walk in the streets alone at night and people did not fear for themselves or their possessions. As one person described it, "The police knew if you took even one cracker from your neighbor and [they] would punish you. How much more do you think you would be punished if you harmed another person?"

All of these issues affected the women of this generation to some degree. However, although the communist government sought to equalize the conditions in the villages with those in the cities, the most striking differences in life events and outlook are between the village and city women. Therefore, the rest of this chapter focuses first on typical women of this generation from the cities in different regions of Albania and then on typical women of this generation from the villages in different regions. These are women who suffered no serious political persecution and represent the majority of women of this group. (Chapter 11 recounts the stories of women who did suffer such consequences and were among those politically persecuted by this regime.)

The Lives of Typical City Women

PESHKOPI

We traveled to the northeastern city of Peshkopi from Homesh via minibus. After a long and dusty wait by the side of the road trying to hail infrequent cars and buses, a minibus driver who knew our host stopped and found room for us by telling three other passengers to squeeze into the back. The conversation on the minibus was lively and primarily concerned with politics, but only started after we satisfied the curiosity of the other passengers regarding who I was, where I was from, and why I was there. On arrival, the minibus left us in the middle of the city right next to the bazaar, which was crammed with white tented stalls from which came competing strains of loud music—Albanian-Turkish style. Other vendors were gathered on the road where the bus had left us and they hawked their wares at us loudly and aggressively. There was a smell in the air of cooking food, mixed with the fumes from the factory that belched black smoke in the valley behind the bazaar. Our host from Homesh, who had accompanied us on the trip, left us near the bazaar in order to ask for directions. I wasn't quite sure what he was asking for since we knew only the name of the woman we were to meet. However, when he came back he led us confidently away from the bazaar and toward a residential district.*

We stopped after some distance for additional directions, and the man we asked turned out to be a relative of the woman for whom we were searching. As he was giving us precise instructions to her house, Sanije herself came along and he introduced us. She had received the news just that morning that we were coming and was returning from the bazaar with food to prepare for us. With only a few hours' notice, Sanije managed to bring together 22 women† at a small restaurant and to arrange for the gathering to be paid for by a local merchant. The format was more open than most of the interviews, and this led to a greater variety of issues being raised. However, the majority of the women addressed the social and economic aspects of their lives. The following are typical of the responses:

Tefta, a retired teacher in her fifties who is married with three children, said, "I remember many things from my childhood. We had a lot of dreams, but we didn't believe that dreams could come true due to the economy and fanaticism."§

A 49-year-old economist named Nadire told a similar story, "I was one of nine children and was raised in a village. Although we were poor, my father was a teacher and wanted me to be educated. He prepared all the documents and forms for me to attend the university, but my brother tore them into pieces because he had no education and was jealous. My father struggled with my brother and won. So I left the house to go to school with only 50 lekë [old lekë, each worth about a tenth of a cent today] and I encountered many economic difficulties."

Our hostess, Sanije, a stylish woman in her early forties, added a different perspective on her generation's preparation for life: "I graduated from university in 1967. At that time, my friends and I expected to get married, but found ourselves completely unprepared for our lives as wives and mothers. This was because our mothers didn't want to discuss these issues. There was no sex education."

A flippant response to our questions came from Irma, a hairdresser

---

*It was here that I learned the wonderful expression, "From Albania you can find Istanbul," meaning that you can find your way anywhere by asking. This is fortunate since there were few road or street signs, very few telephones, and no telephone directories.

†They were all Muslims, as are the majority of people in Peshkopi.

§The words "fanatic" and "fanaticism" are frequently used by the women to describe extremely conservative social attitudes and opinions that dictated and limited the role of women.

and wedding consultant in her mid-thirties: "If you really want to understand the life of the Albanian woman, spend a night in Peshkopi in the winter." She then continued, "In my profession I see many people. People say that the people from the south are as mild as their weather and that the people from the north are wild like their winter. This is true, but it is not nature, but rather mentality. It is said that we Albanians are going toward Europe, but the northern women aren't. They are still extremely timid. Those who are disobedient are few because of the continuing role of fanaticism. Instead of having taken a step forward, we are moving a step backwards. It is considered to be the 'law of nature' here that woman must be under man."

When asked about their source of strength in meeting the challenges of their lives, yesterday and today, the group members shot brief responses at me, "Tradition." "Love of children and of life." "We cope with difficulties and make the necessary sacrifices." "We are full of confidence about our future." "We say, 'May God be the first to lead us.'"

SHKODËR

In the city of Shkodër we found religious differences to be most acute of anywhere in the country. This is primarily due to the early and ongoing persecution by the government of the Catholic priests and believers. The early rationale for this persecution was the accusation that the priests were foreign agents because they were accountable to the Vatican in Rome. However, many of the Catholics of Shkodër were also among the intellectual elite and the merchant class and thus represented another threat to the government. Finally, the majority of the Catholic community was strongly linked to the Balli Kombëtar and other anticommunist groups. As a result, there are few Catholic families who did not suffer consequences at the hands of the communist regime.

Irena's story

Irena is 36 years of age and a chemistry teacher in the secondary school. Hers is typical story for Shkodër, especially in the Catholic community.

I was born and raised in a cultured intellectual family. My father was originally from Shkodër and graduated with a degree in agriculture from a university in Italy. My mother was from a cultured and wealthy family. However, although she received a scholarship to study in Italy, her family would not let her go because they were fanatical. My father traveled from town to town for his work and met

Sanije and her mother in Peshkopi.

my mother. They married for love. After the Liberation, my father was sent to Kamzë to teach at the agricultural institute there. In 1950, however, the regime asked the professors to go out and work in the fields so from 1950 to 1960 my family moved from Tiranë, to Fier, to Lushnjë, to Durrës and finally to Shkodër where I was born.

Although my father was talented and successful in his profession, he was seen with a "bad eye" by the government. He was always seen as a bourgeois person because he had studied abroad. Despite this, Enver Hoxha himself praised my father once because he did so much for the progress of agriculture. However, just three months later he was called a "saboteur" and sent to a village just to work in the fields there.

The following three-year period was a very difficult time for our family. We were five children and I was the youngest. My other brothers and sisters were obliged to go to work and not continue with their studies. The life was hard with five children and my grandfather living with us. I remember that the most difficult time was when my mother went and sold her blood so that she would have more money to feed us. When we learned what she had done, we kissed her arm. She did this especially at the New Year so that she could set a good feast table. It seemed a terrible thing to us children that she would sell her blood for our bread and we cried when we saw her arm all black and blue.

Despite the hardships suffered by my family, I remember my life with my family as the golden period of my life. I had a wonderful father and mother. In fact, I don't ever remember my father raising his voice to my mother. The way he treated her is something I always want to remember. In addition, we children were brought up having the freedom necessary for children. We were not under strict control, but they never took their eyes off us. I remember all the family moments—sitting around the breakfast table, for example, and wanting our father with us because we loved him. We were extremely poor, but even though there was only cheese and tea for breakfast, the table was always set properly and we always sat together for meals. There was harmony in our family and we felt happy when we were together.

I was fortunate, given my biography, to have an opportunity to attend university. However, after my graduation from the university, I was sent to teach in Pukë for four years because, as my father's daughter, I was considered to be a "microbourgeois" person. Later I was allowed to come back and teach in a village near Shkodër. However, since I had been in Pukë for four years and was older, I had to decide to get married immediately before I was considered to be too old. Three men had already declined to marry me because I had been in Pukë so long and away from my family. They were worried that anything might have happened since I had been out of the control of my family for so long and I might not be an honest girl. Afterward, two men were being considered to be my husband. One was 44, when I was 27 at the time, and I started to cry: "How terrible is my situation to be offered such an old man!" The other man who was offered was a young man whom I liked, but who had such a bad biography. He had all the good qualities I was looking for. He was handsome and had a good family, even if he didn't have a house. I decided that it was better to take the young man who was offered than to have to marry an old one. After that, my husband and I saw and met each other, we walked and talked together for a couple of months so at first it was a sort of friendship that we had. We were engaged after two months and three years later in 1990 we were married. It has worked out well and we now have a four-year-old son and a one-year-old daughter.

At the beginning of our married life for a year and a half, we lived in a house that was like a cell. A total of 14 people lived in two rooms. It was impossible for me to live there. Although they were a patriotic and cultured family, my husband's family was suffering the consequences of having one uncle who was a Balli Kombëtar supporter and another uncle who had fled to America.

The source of my strength has always been the example of my mother and father. I have tried to see the positive things and replicate them in myself. I would most like to emulate my mother's spirit of sacrifice. She has never complained of being tired. It seems that my generation could never be like that of our mothers. The degree of their sacrifice was unimaginable.

When asked what role, if any, faith had played in her life, Irena answered,

I have not mentioned the role of faith in my life out of modesty. My family believed in God. While my grandfather was alive (before 1971) we never had a meal without saying grace. We always celebrated the feasts. After my grandfather's death we stopped praying. It was the influence of the outside world. However, I believe and have always believed. All that is spoken about religion makes sense to me. We were told and taught that religion was not to be considered, but something inside of me told me that God existed and I went on believing. My sisters and I had religion inside of ourselves.

So really, you see, my strength comes from my family and my faith together. Let me tell you an example of what the power of faith means to me. Before I was engaged to my husband, Pjeter, something happened that had an effect on me. One of our neighbors, an old man, died suddenly. He had been a good man. He told us many stories and we loved him. The family was not prepared for his death and I helped: it just came out of me this desire to help. I did everything I could when he died. While preparing the room and seeing the dead man lying there, I prayed to God, "I am doing something good for people without benefit or reward, please help me to become engaged to a good man." I saw the results just three months later. Pjeter's father had died at the same time as this old man. In fact, before I knew of Pjeter, I saw the grave of his father and this man having the same date of death. Three months later I met Pjeter and we became engaged. Later, my mother said that the spirit of the old man whom I had served had spoken to the spirit of Pjeter's father to make this possible. For this and other things I thank God every night.

Lili: A Story of Today

Lili is a 53-year-old retired teacher of Albanian literature and language in a high school. The significance of Lili's story is that she has had to surmount challenges in all periods of her life and yet she retains her optimism and zest for living. Her story too is typical of the women in the Catholic community of Shkodër.

My father was an intellectual and Enver Hoxha was against all intellectuals. He had graduated from the Fultz school and worked as a translator. I was three years old when my father died. He was arrested and sentenced without trial in 1946. At that time we were told that he was being transferred from one prison to another, but actually he had been shot. Later, the minister of internal affairs declared that my father had not been guilty of any crime and issued a document stating this. I was consoled to some extent having this document and it helped me to obtain approval to continue my studies.

After I completed my schooling, I was sent to a village to work. I was so happy there. It was a village of communists, but I had good relations with the villagers. All the villagers loved me so much and I hadn't told anyone of my father's death. However, it so happened that at a certain meeting everybody had to tell what his or her family biography was. It was such a difficult moment for me to tell them that my father had been shot dead by the regime. I had the document that proved that he was not guilty, but ... I don't like to remember all this. I want to forget this moment.

Democracy came, but I have had bad luck during this period. My husband had two brothers in America, one working at Voice of America. Of course, my husband never admitted this earlier, but after 45 years we were finally given the right to visit them. My husband went to the United States in 1992 and came back with money that we used to buy and fix up the house I am now living in. The first few years of democracy were wonderful.

In 1994 my youngest son and I went to visit my elder son in Italy where he was studying and sorting out his documents for citizenship (based on his grandmother's Italian citizenship). One night while I was away my husband and his sister were alone in the house when thieves broke in and killed my husband right in front of his sister. She couldn't save him and it was useless to call the police as the thieves were the postman and two policemen. Although this terrible thing happened under democracy, nothing shakes my faith in democracy and the Democratic Party.

I have always found strength in two things: faith that some day things would be better and faith in God. For example, He sent Marilyn* to our house. She has become my sister—a member of the family. She arrived five months after my tragedy and has helped me deal with this difficult time in my life. I have always believed that one day at least my children would have a chance to live a better life; that the dictatorship would die. This belief also served to make me strong.

TIRANË

In Tiranë, in central Albania, the subject turned to politics more often than it did in other regions in the country. A greater number of the women interviewed seemed to want to appear persecuted or to apologize for or excuse their roles in the communist regime. These tendencies made it difficult to learn about their lives, as women, whatever their political orientation. Our discussion with Barije, 55, was typical:

I came from a working-class family that had a relatively more comfortable life since my father was a butcher and we at least had meat to eat. When I joined my husband's family, I found myself in a family that had very little and I was always

*A Peace Corps volunteer who, with her husband, was staying with Lili during their two-year teaching assignment.

hungry. That being said, I have had a good life because I had a good husband and family. We obeyed orders, there were no quarrels, but there was constant poverty. I was unemployed at the time my children were born. Time and again I took in work (making straw hats, sewing) to make some extra money to supplement my husband's salary as a carpenter. Although I found employment in a pharmaceutical enterprise when my younger daughter was three years of age, it was challenging working with two small children at home. Despite the hard life, I enjoyed being considered a good worker and was happy to hear praise. Also, although my job was demanding, the real challenges in my life were those at home. We had no running water in the house, so I had to fetch water for all the family's needs from somewhere in the neighborhood. We had very few clothes so I was always washing clothes (outdoors in the rain and cold in the winter). Although there were problems, I found pleasure and satisfaction in working hard and well.

At the same time that we interviewed Barije, we interviewed her neighbor. Both of them described their lives in fatalistic terms with such expressions as, "People have to live life as it is given." and "There is an expression in Albania, 'Women have seven souls not only one.'" However, when asked about their sources of strength, they replied, "Sacrifice is in the blood, in oneself"; "This was our world and we always believed that things would get better"; "A strong desire to live creates a great hope for a better life and we drew strength from the joy we experienced in our children, the good words of our supervisor, or happy events, such as weddings"; and "Like other women of our generation, we were brought up with certain virtues—love of work, love for life, and honesty. These have been good guides for life. We were taught by our parents and others not to take more from society than we deserved.

Barije elaborated this theme by talking of her mother-in-law.

I remember especially what I learned from my mother-in-law who was so kind to me and set an excellent example for me. My mother-in-law saw how I suffered from hunger living with her family. She tried to feed me extra food and never complained of her own sufferings. We also learned some things from books, but we had nothing to compare our lives with other than the communist slogans and promises of better times, which had a positive effect on our ideas.

Barjie, a Muslim, stated clearly that her strength and the source of her optimism in life had come primarily from her family. When asked what role faith had played in her life, she responded simply, "God is first and we are secondary."

Barije's neighbor, who is Orthodox, stated that she believes that the Christians and Muslims are all worshipping the same God. Therefore, when her daughter was expecting her first child, she went to pray not only at the Orthodox church but also at the shrines of the Muslim saints.

BERAT

The Road to Berat

Our first trip to interview women outside of Tiranë was to the central Albanian city of Berat. Ksanthi knew a teacher there who agreed to gather a group of women for us to interview and offered her hospitality. To keep costs down and because we had no car at that time, Ksanthi and I decided to travel by public transportation.

The adventure started at 8:00 A.M. on a Wednesday morning in June as Ksanthi and I walked to the bus center in an open area on the other side of town. When we arrived, the dirt field was full of dilapidated buses, none of which looked at all promising to get us out of the city, much less to our destination. One of the most decrepit turned out to be the next bus to Berat, of course. We spent some minutes trying to decide if we were brave enough to take it or whether we should wait for 45 minutes for the bus that looked marginally better. While we debated, a man sitting in the prime location (the seat right behind the driver) got up and offered us the seat. We accepted it quickly as it offered the possibility of fresh air and, ignoring the fact that the front of the bus was only inches off of the ground, we hopped aboard.

The trip itself turned out to be quite pleasant as the exhaust fumes, which must have overwhelmed the people in the back, were mitigated by the air from the driver's window. The otherwise alarming noise of the bottom of the bus scraping on the ground every time we went up even a slight incline added to the sense of adventure.

As we were pulling our things together to get off of the bus in the center of Berat, Fitore, Ksanthi's friend, stuck her head in the bus doorway and gave us a warm greeting. We followed her to her apartment, which has a spectacular view of the old city and the castle. There we found the interview group ready and waiting.

The stories of the women of Berat were typical of their generation. Fitore, a 40-year-old teacher of English, sparkled when she talked. Her eyes and face smiled as she described her life and answered our questions:

> My parents taught me to be honest, frank, and sincere, to have respect for others and to be hospitable. Since they were from the northern part of Albania, hospitality was part of their personality. They taught me by their own examples, but there were also many books in the house and I was encouraged to read them and discuss what I learned with my father and later with my older brother. My father played a very important role in my education. I remember my mother primarily as working, washing, and keeping house. She didn't have much education, but she was well-respected and managed her family well.

I think that for everyone their personal source of strength is inborn. Everything comes from the heart. If you can dedicate yourself to helping others, this is the source of strength and helps you overcome obstacles. You must always strive to be your best.

Another woman in the group, Violetta, is 49 years old. She is a quieter person, but clearly a woman with a strong spirit. Although she was born to a poor family of six in Vlorë, she had an opportunity to be educated and now works in a library.

What I remember most is the conservative nature of my father and the effect he had on my life decisions. I wanted to be a teacher and was given an opportunity to extend my education through high school. As recompense for that opportunity, the party told me to go to Skrapar to teach. I was enthusiastic about leaving home. I was 16 or 17 at this time and I wanted to be with my friends. Although it was the "call of the party" and I was expected to answer the call, my father was against it. With the support of my mother, I ended up going and enjoyed both teaching and being away from my family. However, in Skrapar I met and fell in love with my husband who was from Pogradec. Both of my parents were against the marriage, but they finally relented and I was married in 1962.

Another problem I have had in life is that my husband is extremely jealous and this has always hurt me. However, I have always been optimistic and have thought of a brighter future. I have tried to be a friend to my children and to have a good relationship with them based on good communications. I have also sacrificed for their sakes and, in return, they have inspired and encouraged me.

My primary source of strength is summed up in remembering the Albanian saying "Neither the bad nor the good has an end." Also, my faith has made me feel younger. Although I was born and raised as Orthodox, I am now Baha'i.

One woman who asked not to be identified, but whom I will call Vjollca, spoke frankly about her relationship with her parents and her mother-in-law.

My parents were extremely conservative—they were fanatical! In fact, they would not allow me to finish high school because they were worried that I would be subjected to sexual abuse if I went away for further schooling since I was so attractive. Although I found a way to study for a profession, I worked only a short time because my parents arranged a marriage for me.

I was engaged and married quickly, knowing nothing of my husband or his family. It was worse than I expected it to be and I have had to face all kinds of hardships alone. The primary source of my problems has been my mother-in-law who is bad-tempered. She has always complained, gossiped, and told my husband untruthful things about me, fueling my husband's jealousy. Although my husband has treated me badly, I couldn't consider divorce because of the social consequences I would have to suffer. I don't feel that I am unusual because most of the Albanian women are under the dictatorship of their husbands.

I have led a poor life, economically and spiritually, but thinking of my children and their welfare gave me the strength to carry on. Love for my children has been my total source of strength and I have sacrificed everything for them. I look forward to brighter days ahead, knowing that everything good that happens to my children will be good for me.

KORÇË

The women of the southern city of Korçë exemplify in many ways what is most typical of the city women of this generation. They are, for the most part, well-educated; they espoused the atheist-secular culture; and they accepted the life that they were offered, with the belief that it would improve, just as the propaganda promised. However, they appeared to have fared much better than their counterparts in other areas of the country— both in the cities and in the villages. The reasons for this are diverse, including the fact that this city began the communist period with many advantages.

1. The city and the surrounding area were the source of a large pro-portion of the Albanian émigrés to the United States and other Western countries, most notably Greece, in the 25 to 30 years prior to the war. This resulted in many families in this area accumulat-ing a previously unheard-of wealth and having an ongoing source of clothing and sometimes money throughout the communist period.

2. As noted earlier, Korçë is known as "the cradle of Albanian nation-alism" and might also be known as "the epicenter of Albanian com-munism." A large proportion of the communist partisans who fought so valiantly against the occupiers and simultaneously—at Hoxha's instigation—so aggressively against the anticommunist enemies came from this city and many of the nearby villages.

3. Although Enver Hoxha was born and raised in another southern city, Gjirokastër, he spent time in Korçë studying and teaching there. He is reported to have developed a great love of the city and its people.

The first of these advantages cushioned many Korçë families from the impact of the years of great national poverty. The other two resulted in Korçë and the district receiving preferential treatment by the communist government when it came to public works, including the electrification of the villages and the building of secondary roads.* In addition, although

*It should be noted that the main roads and the access to the Greek border were deliberately underdeveloped to thwart both a potential invasion by the Greeks and the constant efforts of Albanians to escape to Greece.

there are families in Korçë who suffered persecution under the regime, many stories that were told suggest that the incidence and degree of punishment of such crimes was less than it was in other parts of the country.

Nowhere else in our travels did we meet more people who described their families as idealistic communists or were themselves previously active supporters of the communist regime. Even more often, it was clear from the stories the women told that many of them had been privileged by the regime in ways that only communist supporters and others with good biographies had been. If they weren't outright communists, they were at least not openly or actively anticommunist. This earned them a certain amount of consideration and better treatment by the government.

Ironically, the people of this region have become some of the most ardent supporters of democracy and many prominent political figures in the first years of the new democratic government came from this area. This may be explained by the relative freedom that the people had, the connections they maintained—however limited—with their families outside of Albania, and the overall high level of education and sophistication in the area.

Klara's Story

This interview with Klara took place in a seedy hotel in the lakeside resort town of Pogradec on Lake Ohrid. Although we spent about two hours looking for Klara, who was reported to be spending the weekend there, the wait was worthwhile because we had an opportunity to hear at length from this lively and passionate woman.

I was born on July 30, 1941, in Korçë to a family from Panarit village. My parents were idealists of the communist variety. My father was a tailor and had his own shop. He employed four people, but ran the business on the model of a commune so the people worked as a team. My mother, Ollga, was an activist of women in Korçë. In 1943 she founded the antifascist women's group."*

In 1947 I started in kindergarten at the first such facility to be opened after the war. It had received aid from the UN Relief Agency and had many beautiful toys and books and good food to eat. This was a wonderful time in my life. One

*At another time we interviewed Klara's sister, Drita. She told us this about their family: "My parents were simple people with almost no education at all. We were among the poorest families in Korçë, although my father was the head of a factory. Also, although my parents were communists we had no advantages. I admired my mother because she was honest, energetic, tolerant, and loving. She was also emancipated for her generation and gave us much freedom. She told us that when she died she didn't want speeches. Instead, because she had been one of the first to take part in the antifascist demonstrations, she wanted us just to sing a partisan song. I always felt very close to my mother and have been glad for her support all my life."

particular memory I have of this time is the celebration for May 1. We marched along the boulevard in Korçë waving three flags—Albanian, Yugoslav, and Russian—and shouting "Enver, Tito, Stalin!"

My parents were liberals. They gave me much freedom and I visited all parts of Albania with the Pioneers.* I enjoyed being with my friends and I had a feeling of solidarity with them. Also, at that time—that is before 1959—there was a clear-cut difference in the classes in our society. I would go with three dresses and return with just one because I was always giving my clothes to other more needy children. At other times I would divide what was on my plate with a poor friend. It became a saying in our family "Whatever belongs to Klara belongs to others as well." I was not only a literary and sociable sort of person, but I was also philanthropic and courageous. I inherited this from my family.

In 1959 I went to the University in Bucharest until 1961, when relations were broken with Romania. Then in 1962 I began my studies again in Tiranë in pharmacology. However, soon after I started, I fell under the eye of those who thought that I did not dress properly. My parents were called by the Central Committee of Tiranë about my attire. My parents and I were offended by this and I came back to Korçë.

There I fell in love with the man I married. He was a liberal from a noble, declassed family. He was a football player and a teacher in an elementary school. I married him consciously, knowing the risks: that I might suffer political consequences with him. We married without ceremony because no one, including my parents, agreed to the marriage. I went to his house and by that action we were married. This was unusual for the time. The day after this "marriage" my mother came to me to offer her love and support. She told me "I want you to come every day to our house with your husband." The consequence was that my mother was terminated from her position as the director of an enterprise and my other relatives did not see me in my husband's house, although they continued to help us indirectly. My in-laws never questioned why my family didn't come: they were noble and knew why.

All the people around me tried to help me, but my husband and I understood that we had to work hard and take care of ourselves. It was good fortune for us when the class struggle was less intense and we were given the right to complete our studies. I studied Albanian language and my husband studied physical education. Many times I know that my name was on the list of persons to be exiled, but the people of my family helped to keep us out of exile. My family was highly respected in Korçë and loved as idealists.

But you might ask me "How did you build up your life in these circumstances?" Everything was cut when I married. This was typical in such marriages. What is interesting and worth mentioning is the attitude of Albanian women like me who didn't mind the consequences of the class struggle. We did what our hearts told us to do. I know I would have succeeded in other ways had I not married such a man. I worked hard and loved books and had a passion for the work I did in the library. I had a library in my home, but I found a larger one at my husband's house. My father-in-law was a polyglot and this inspired me to learn languages, particularly the Romanian and Slavic languages. Later, since I knew these languages, I was asked to work in the Albanology section and to do translations from Romanian

*The communist youth group.

and French into Albanian. I was also a part-time translator for the only publishing house in Albania at that time. I am respected particularly for the translations I have done from Romanian into Albanian.

The most important factor for me in building up my life is that I started studying Albanology in 1963. It gave me an opportunity to know all of the history of Albania. I have read all that has been written and that has allowed me to have independent thoughts and has made me love my country even more. This, in turn, has allowed me to become a journalist. Since the beginning of the democratic period, I have written about 300 articles on historical, political, and cultural issues.

The feeling of motherland is the common denominator of these. This love of the motherland was given to us and our children by our parents.

Klara from Korça.

While all of the children were being taught verses about Enver Hoxha, my father-in-law taught our children to recite verses written by Naim Frasheri and about the history of Skanderbeg."

I also remember listening in secret to the radio transmissions from foreign countries. Before 1990 my first political impression that the regime in power could be overthrown came when the Trepçe Strike* took place in Yugoslavia. I said then, but only to myself, that maybe such a thing could happen here.

How did my parents feel about the reality of communism versus the ideal in which they believed? There are two moments in my family that I will share to illustrate my response. At one point, one of my three sisters wanted to join the party and my mother discouraged her saying, "No. They just pass the time gossiping in their meetings." Later, a few years before his death, my father used to have intimate conversations with me, since I was his favorite daughter. He used to say "These people (the party people) consider the undone things done. 'They' pretend to be brave after the war." This is why he was very reserved and had high respect for the family of my husband."†

The Trepçe Strike was a miner's strike against the government that took place in Yugoslavia in 1983.

†*Drita told us, "My parents were among the first communists. They were idealists, however,*

My moral education was as an atheist.* I was not brought up with communist ideals. My grandmother raised me and my sisters and she didn't bother herself much with such things. People in my generation studied with books from the time of Zog, and the people who taught us were educated abroad. They had not been inculcated with the communist ideas. We studied Latin and Greek literature and read precommunist modern writers, including Hemingway and Ruskin. After 1960 the situation became worse in this way because the teachers that graduated in this period were politicized. While I was in Romania I never thought of politics. I never had communist ideals and, besides, the communists didn't like independent thinkers like me.

What gave Klara the strength to maintain her optimism and joy for living in the face of the challenges of her life? She answered this question with one word, *mirësia* (kindness).

This feeling is inside me, an inner impulse. Kindness has been a drive. I want to see people happy and that's why I have been surrounded by people with lots of troubles, so I can help them. I don't know revenge; I forgive easily.

Although I have accumulated many offenses in life since my marriage, I am energetic. I have come to know the lives of the persecuted people: those who studied and graduated abroad and ended up whitewashing houses. I felt so sorry for these people who were born rich and died in poverty. I remember my father-in-law who wanted two cups of coffee a day and he could only have one.

By nature I am rebellious. I can't explain why. I have read a lot and come to learn much about the international feminist movement, well-known Albanian women, and the women's movement in Albania since its beginning. This has led me to establish an association like the Qirjazi sisters' association† for culture and

---

and knew nothing of Marx. They taught their four daughters to be simple, modest, and to love life. They didn't think of making us communists and, as a result, I am not aligned with any party. I am independent."

Drita explained the impact this fact had on her life. "We were atheists for generations, my grandparents, my parents, and me. That is why I dedicated my life to science and have been a chemistry teacher for 25 years."

†*Parashqevi Qirjazi (1880–1970) graduated from college in Istanbul in 1904. She then came to Albania and dedicated her life to teaching. In 1909 she published* ABC for Elementary Schools, *thereby making history as the first Albanian woman to write a school textbook. She also committed herself to realizing her objectives of expanding educational opportunities, especially those for women, throughout the country. Later, in 1909, along with her sister Sevasti Qirjazi (1871–1949), she founded a women's association in Korçë called "Ylli i Mengjesit" (The Morning Star). In 1917 she also began publishing a magazine of the same name in the United States and took part in the Paris Peace Conference in 1919 as a representative of Albanian emigrants to the United States. Parashqevi returned to Albania in 1921 and remained active in educational and cultural activities until her death. Sevasti is remembered for her publication of textbooks and for her political activities, which included working with Ismail Qemali in the period following the independence of Albania from the Ottoman Empire, heading up the Albanian National Party with its headquarters in Worcester, Mass., and defending the rights of Albania in international organizations. She defended especially the right of women to be educated and to participate in the political life of their country.*

patriotism. I founded it two years ago, with the intention of getting women together to think about the necessity of having their own rights. When democracy came into power in our country, it couldn't have come without the women's contribution. So, I thought to gather the Korçë women together in a patriotic and nonpolitical association with the clear intention of supporting democracy, but not aligned with any political parties. Our association is a social one, aiming at the further emancipation of women. I believe that women should be involved in fighting for their own rights. I feel strong and energetic and I try hard to do something for the women.

Although Klara had already said that she was an atheist, I asked her about the role of faith in her life because she had also spoken of the influence her father-in-law—a Bektashi Muslim, had on her. "Faith had no role in my life or in the family of my husband. This may be because Bektashi has none of the rites of Islam. The fact that my in-laws were Bektashi helped me because there were some well-known Bektashi writers and historians and I got to know their writings. I respect all religions, but have none of my own."

Nikoleta's Story

Nikoleta, an attractive and youthful 45-year-old woman, told us a story that illustrates the historical divisions within the society. It was interesting to hear a personal account of the conflict between the communists—who in this area were predominantly Orthodox—and the Balli Kombëtar supporters—who in this area were predominantly Muslim. It also contrasted significantly with the composition of the factions and the stories of those women from Shkodër.

My family is from a village near Korçë called Polenë. The village is at the foot of a mountain and was the ideal place for resistance during the war. All the village was a base for the partisans during the War of Liberation. I remember the stories I was told of the bravery of my grandmother who was killed during the war. She accompanied some partisans to show them an escape route, but was shot on her way to that place. When she felt a sharp pain, she couldn't make it to safety herself. After that, my father and his brothers took up arms as partisans.

Polenë was the only communist village in the area and was surrounded by Balli Kombëtar villages. Because people in the surrounding area collaborated with the occupiers and our villagers fought against them, we suffered much from these other people. In fact, we felt that we suffered more from Balli Kombëtar than from the occupiers. For example, while my family was in the mountains trying to escape, the Balli Kombëtar people came into our houses and stole all the dowries, including the blankets that had the names woven into them. Even today when we visit in their houses we see the things their families stole from our families and can recognize them by the family names woven into them and by the different style and patterns of the weave.*

My parents were married in 1949 and I am the eldest of three children. After the war we moved to Korçë where my father was an army officer and my mother was a nurse in a kindergarten. My father's job was to follow dissenters and protect the border.

I was married through an arranged union, even though I knew the man I was engaged to, contrary to my parents, who married for love. Some other people wanted to marry me, they serenaded me,† but who knew what kind of people they were? It was safer to have an arrangement.

I had some troubling times when my son was in the second year of medical school. It was the time when democracy came. Our office was closed and I lost my job. We had only my husband's small salary and I had to figure a way to help my son go on. I shed many tears and did all sorts of things to make money: embroidery, everything. It was my son who found the solution. He started working on the third shift at the hospital and went on with his studies. He was given the job of anesthesia assistant for two or three years. It did him a world of good. That's why he now knows how to make his own decisions. This experience had a positive impact on our children and they learned a good lesson. My son is now working in Greece to make money to pursue his career in medicine.

I say that others have more time for such things as makeup and clothes, but my life is too hard for that. If someone asks me what I remember best I can remember only much work. What has given me strength is that I never liked my children to be in a lower position than others and I have worked hard to ensure that they would not be in such a position. Also, by nature I am smiling and optimistic. I'm just like that.

What role has faith played in my life? Well, in Polenë it is a characteristic that the people are very religious. I remember when I was little our parents took us to church. As a result, I believe when I am in trouble. Then I pray. I like to be present for religious celebrations, but I don't like the attitude of those who are very religious.

Other Women of Korçë

We met Rebeka, 31, and Alma, 33, in a large group of women. They were both dynamic and enthusiastic. Their stories are typical of those of the younger members of this generation in Korçë.

Rebeka told us,

I admire my mother. She was always dead tired when she returned from her work in a mine. Her dream was to help me to continue in school. My father was also fanatical about this. I'm glad that I realized this dream. It was my dream

*The traditional patterns, colors, and styles of weaving are distinct from village to village and from Orthodox to Muslim regions.
†Serenading is a courting custom of the Korçë region where a young man sings love songs under the window of the woman he loves and would like to marry. There are a great number of such beautiful love songs that have been written in Korçë.

specifically to study medicine. I was given the chance and chose then to specialize in pharmacology. I am pleased with my profession and have just opened my own pharmacy, a small one.

I think that what has given me strength in my life is that I have never felt pleased with what I have achieved. The desire to have a business of my own pushes me forward now.

Faith has played no role in my life. I belong to that generation that grew up when the churches were closed, but I think religion is a good thing.

Alma explained,

I was born in the village of Polenë, near Korçë. My mother was a cook and my father worked in agriculture. I remember my mother as artistic, romantic, and very beautiful. She loved to read, and read even while she was weaving on the loom. I couldn't continue to advanced studies because I was the second child. I wanted to, but I wasn't given the chance, even though I had high grades: it was a policy of the government.

Polenë was such a small village and all the people there were Orthodox. Since it was surrounded by Muslim villages, we had no choice but to marry within our own village. However, I married for love. I was 21 at the time and my parents agreed. It has worked out well. Now we have two children and have been living in Greece for the past year. I think we will stay there for some time, but we will return. Motherland is motherland.

There have not been many challenges in my life. I believe that we Albanians aren't offered much from life, so we don't ask much. Therefore, we are satisfied with what we have because we don't expect to have anything. However, I have drawn strength from my faith. Belief in God has nourished me since I was a child. I am very religious.

Among all the women of Korçë whom we interviewed, we found that the majority of the women of this generation identified their primary source of strength as coming from their families and from necessity, as Eli, 53, and Klea, 37, have done:

Eli: "I have found my strength in my love for my children and in the great pleasure and great joy I felt when my husband came home."

Klea: "I just had to be strong and accepting. I was not the only one. Where does hope come from, but from necessity."

The Lives of Typical Village Women

Xhevat Jella, the father of our young hostess in Homesh, gave us a clear picture of the lives of the women in this northeastern village during the communist period. This description, in its essence, applies to the lives of all village women in Albania and provides a context for understanding their circumstances.

From 1945 to 1990 the area around Homesh was an agricultural cooperative, which was organized in brigades. There were 40 to 50 persons in each brigade and 30 to 35 of these were women. In fact, all of the hard work in the fields was done by women because many of the men and young boys left the village and went to work in towns or in mines, forestry, or enterprises.

The work year had a definite cycle. After each new year, there was a special action called "opening the land." During this time, from 8:00 A.M. until 4:00 P.M. the workers would work clearing land that had not been cultivated before. This was extremely hard work involving breaking land through ice and snow and the action lasted for two months: January and February.

Beginning on March 15 there was spring planting to be done. All the women were forced to go into the field from 5:00 A.M. until 8:00 P.M. each day with only a lunch break in the field.

There were no nurseries for the children so many women simply locked their children in their houses. When they came home at the end of the work day, the women had to prepare dinner, but frequently the children fell asleep without eating because it was so late. Sometimes people had to wait until 10:00 P.M. to buy bread and this was too late for little children. In the morning, children often went to school with no breakfast because their mothers weren't there to feed them. There was not much time at lunchtime either. If the women were allowed the time to go home, they might have two hours, but in that time they had to cook, do the washing, and eat. Since most women had more than three children, they had to run to do the wash of the small children and get it dry. In spite of all this hard work, the women did all of this with great patience. In addition, they frequently had guests in the evenings; two to three visits per week were common. Women had to serve the mostly male visitors until 12:00 midnight. It was hard work and they had no time for other pursuits, including radio, television, or books—even if they were available—which they generally weren't.

Harvest time was another difficult time for the women as most of the harvesting was done by the women in the mountainous areas and the day started at 3:00 A.M. There were no holidays or days off. In order to visit parents or others outside the village, the women had to ask permission and no permission was granted during harvest time.

The most difficult period for the villagers was from 1970 to 1980 because the private sector was almost abolished. Previously, they had small plots of land (three-tenths of a hectare) they could work on for themselves, to grow food for their families. After that, they had almost no land—one-tenth of a hectare for an entire family—and that didn't meet their needs. People were entirely dependent on the cooperative and the little amount of money they earned. The private markets were closed so they could not sell produce. The state was obligated to supply them with everything—including rice, flour, macaroni, and fruit—and there were great shortages of food and goods. There was, for example, no place to buy beans. Occasionally, the cooperative would distribute to each family the equivalent of 10 to 11 kilograms per year. Although this was a productive cooperative, the state took too much and the village government took the remainder. There was simply not enough to go around.

The difficulties increased even more from 1980 to 1990, when the livestock were collectivized. First the sheep were collectivized, then the cows. People were not allowed to have any animals, not even hens.* The milk that was available was full of water because part of the original milk had been stolen and those who stole it had to make up the part they stole. The economic situation of the cooperative families was bad; the cooperative gave its members very little. The quantity of corn, wheat, and white dry beans that they received didn't meet their needs for the whole year. That's why many families made a habit of stealing these products, mostly during the night.

The typical village woman, in my opinion, was strong: her personality was not destroyed. Still, she tried to enjoy life. She could have committed suicide, but she did not do that. Instead, she found the force to enjoy life, especially through her children.

The source of strength is the same for all our people. It is based on our history. We were brought up to maintain our national character and language. It was a matter of survival for our country.

Education also helped the women during this period. Women were educated through the eighth grade. It was obligatory. Schools were politicized, but people were educated. This helped in the development and emancipation of women.

Since 1990 women have worked mostly in the home as housewives and raising their children. In the spring the woman helps in the fields, and summer is a trying period. The work in the field is lessened, but she now has much more work at home: milking the cows or baking bread. There is still no mechanization of agriculture.

Our hostess in Peshkopi also gave us a picture of the village women of this time.

In my opinion, the source of the village women's strength is the Albanian tradition and especially that of hospitality. I have so many good memories from the time I headed the women's organization and had a chance to visit many villages and meet many women.

I remember especially that on January 4, 1984, I went with a group of people from Peshkopi. There were seven or eight men and I was the only woman. We went to Lurë, one of the pearls of nature where the seven lakes of Lurë are. It was so difficult to pass the roads in the dark on foot and in the snow. We met many women coming home from the fields one by one, each loaded down. When we said good evening, they not only smiled, but said "welcome to my home." One of the men said "Is your husband at home?" Her answer was "If not, I will find him." The lesson I learned from this is that Albanian hospitality reaches its ultimate in this area.

In Lurë, I had a phone call to return to Peshkopi because a party leader in Tiranë wanted me to go to Tiranë regarding some women's issues. It was terrible

Since this represented a great hardship for the people, many families found ways to keep animals in secret. An amusing story from this period is that of the man who kept pigs in his cellar. When he was told that he was viewed so favorably by the party that a high-ranking party official from the area would come to his house for dinner to honor him, he worried that this person would discover his pigs. So, before the dinner he decided to give his pigs a party and gave them enough raki (a strong alcohol drink made from grapes) to put them to sleep. Unfortunately, the party official enjoyed himself so much that he stayed until the pigs began to wake up. Fearing that the party official would hear them, the man excused himself and went down to the cellar and fed the pigs more raki to keep them quiet a bit longer.

because I was supposed to stay in Lurë for a week. The snow was up to my waist. I had only cloth shoes and a light coat. Friends asked two men to accompany me. As we traveled, we stopped at all the houses we passed and we were welcomed in by the women. My clothes were soaked and at each stop the stove was ready to be lit for a visitor. They dried my clothes and I went on. I will never forget the kindness of those women. I had to walk for eight hours through the snow and I didn't feel tired because I found such a nice atmosphere among the women. The collective work made them feel closer to one another and helped them to be with each other, sharing their lives and stories. That kind of life brought them together and made life bearable for them.

Now I have been finding something different in the villages. It used to be that everyone was not only interested in themselves, but they wanted to do something for you. Now they are more interested in themselves.

THE WOMEN OF HOMESH

In some ways time stood still for the women of Homesh. While they talked of the advantages of working on the cooperative (being with other people, especially other women, during the day, and having a regular salary), at home they continued to live lives that were similar to those of the women of the older generation. Frequently, for example, the women were raised by their mothers to be good wives so that they would not dishonor their families when they were married. Then they were married by arrangement to men whom had never seen prior to the wedding. Livere, 41, related her upbringing: "My mother taught me to do housework and cooking and she beat me when I didn't do it well. My mother taught me how to keep house. She told me 'when you go to your husband's house, don't sleep late.'"

Zamone, 51 years of age, told us about her marriage with both humor and resignation in her voice: "I married at the age of 17 under an arrangement. I was veiled until marriage and it didn't matter whether I liked my husband or not, I had to take him." Despite the circumstances of her marriage, Zamone has had a good relationship with her husband. "Although he wouldn't wash up or take care of the children, he cut wood and helped in other ways, like looking after the cow."

Both women talked of the difficult times in their lives, under the communist regime and now, and the poor economic situation of their families. Zamone continued: "I remember that my house burned down. It was in the time of Enver Hoxha. I was caring for my children and both my mother- and father-in-law while I worked. I worked only for bread: I earned 3 lekë [old lekë, now worth about a tenth of a cent apiece] for the job and cornbread cost 3 lekë. I was exhausted by the work in the field and by raising the children."

"I have always been extremely poor. Yet, I have been satisfied with my work," Livere said ironically. "I took three lekë per day in pay. However, more recently (since the coming of the democratic period), our house was pulled down by the owner of the land where the house was built many years ago.* So we had to build a new one, very close to the former one. It ruined our financial situation and we now have only 500 square meters for cultivation to support our family."

What gave Zamone and Livere the strength to surmount their difficulties?

Zamone told us,

> If you love your children, you have to work. If you don't work, you won't have anything. That made me strong. Everything is hard, but you just have to do it. My mother prepared me for life with these words, "Be honest, be loyal to your husband, and be respectful and hardworking.'...
>
> Life offers me all sorts of things, good and bad, and God has given me strength to face everything. I believed but didn't let anyone know. I have always had faith, in part because my grandfather was a hoxha. God has my life in his hand and I have always believed that He would help me. Present life is not worth living, but I am optimistic. Perhaps for my children things will get better.

One other woman in Homesh who was typical of this generation was Rrufie, aged 50. Her husband was an army officer who had been wounded during maneuvers. Although she told us that "the economy of our family was not so bad because army people were better off than others during the Hoxha regime." Rrufie continued, "the work was hard, especially during the time that we were working on the bunkers." When asked what gave her the strength to survive in this particularly difficult time, she said, "I don't know how to explain strength. We ate bad bread and that was all. Being strong was just a necessity. There was no way out: if you didn't work, you had nothing."

When asked what role faith had played in her life, she answered, "I believed, but I couldn't worship so I just believed with my heart. When my children were sick and the doctors couldn't help, my prayers were answered."

Our hostess's mother, Dhilhixhe, is a 40-year-old teacher of Albanian at the local school, which is in Shupenzë, an hour by foot away from the village. Although she is an educated woman and is employed full time in professional (nonagricultural) work, her life has not been much different

---

One of the goals of the democratic government is to restore all state land to the prior owners, that is, the pre–1944 owners. This has resulted in many claims being made to the government and those that have been settled have created new difficulties for the people and institutions occupying this land.

from the lives of the other women of the village, except that there are no other educated people in the village with whom she finds friendship. Dhilhixhe's life is circumscribed by a certain exhausting routine. She walks to school and back each day, prepares the lessons and teaches, works in the family field, cares for the cow and other animals, does the housework, cooks, and cares for her mother-in-law, husband, and three children.

I am from a village near Homesh, Boçevë. My father was a Bektashi Muslim priest, and my mother worked in a cooperative kitchen. My mother always wanted me to do things better and never praised me. She was serious and demanding and never expressed her love—not that she didn't love us. The greatest problem for my mother was to make sure that I was well-behaved and clean. I became very demanding of myself and am still that way today.

I married at the age of 20. It was both an arranged marriage and a marriage for love. I married my teacher. I was fortunate in my marriage that I found a partner and friend. I have excellent relations with my mother-in-law, although she has always been sick. She hasn't asked me to do too much housework, and she helped me with the children, especially when I was attending university. She knew that I had a great love of studying.

I have found strength in myself because I have enjoyed good health, but I have also had both love and hope for my children. I have high expectations for their education.

PERONDI

Through Ksanthi, we were able to stay with the family of Flutra, a young English teacher, in this village of 10,000 near Kuçovë, in central Albania. The bus took us to Kuçovë (formerly known as Stalin City), where Flutra met us. The fact that she met us as we stepped off the bus is a testimony both to the patience of the Albanians and the fact that meetings can actually be arranged even without a telephone. Ksanthi had simply told Flutra that we would be going to Berat and doing an interview and that we would arrive in Kuçovë in the afternoon on Wednesday. Amazingly, she had only been waiting there for 30 minutes. We walked through several city streets and then up a hill, past the outlying parts of Kuçovë, the middle school, and several new apartment buildings. The village started at the point where the last satellite dish was in evidence. We passed some women sitting on their doorsteps spinning yarn, and stopped to greet Flutra's sister who lives close to the border with the city (where, we later learned, the last of the piped water is available). We continued for about 15 more minutes uphill, remarking on the fact that the road was paved (in fact better than the street in front of our house in Tiranë). Flutra explained that since the cooperative in the village had been named "Enver Hoxha," they had been given a good road. Also, although there were some fences and walls along the road, the houses themselves were hidden and there was no sense of being in a village. On each side of the road there was green, because each house had grapevines and fruit trees that shaded and covered it, giving the appearance of uninhabited nature. We finally turned into a small walkway and then came quickly to the gate of the house on the right. We entered a small courtyard dominated by a large fig tree. Off to the left was the stable area with two cows, a donkey, and a dog. To the right there was another work and animal area with another dog. Straight ahead was the house. The chickens with their chicks and the duck with her ducklings had the run of the yard, and the cat made himself at home inside and out.

We received a warm welcome from Flutra's mother, Safide (affectionately called Safo) and were served a cold drink consisting of milk and water.* Flutra told us that every woman in the village wanted to be interviewed. We were also fortunate to have the chance simply to observe life in the village. In the process we surmounted certain challenges in the interviewing process: donkeys and cows making such loud noises that we were sure that the person's voice on the tape recorder would be drowned out.

Upon our arrival we decided to begin interviewing immediately. The village women arrived in small groups and individually over the next 30 or 40 minutes, and we interviewed continuously until 10:00 P.M. Since this was the first village I had visited, it seemed very odd to finally get the chance to talk with women dressed as I had seen some village women dressed in the market in Tiranë. There were especially three "old" ladies in their sixties who had their hair bound by cloth wrapped tightly around their heads with small "tails" sticking out to the side.

After our interviewing ended, Safo served us an enormous dinner. There were two kinds of meat—chicken and lamb—boiled eggs, cheese with oil and garlic, *kos* (yoghurt), *byrek* (a pastry stuffed with cheese and lots of butter), a salad of tomatoes and cucumbers, bread, and raki. Our hostess reminded us that everything was fresh and produced by them, except for the bread, which came from the state bakery. It was truly delicious, but one complicating factor was that the food was served with a tiny fork (almost like a pickle fork) and a huge spoon, and I had not a clue as to how to use my utensils! It turned out that the big spoon was to eat some of the dishes directly out of the same bowl that everyone else was eating from. The raki was especially potent and delicious. I managed to drink about four or five

---

*As an adviser to the dairy industry had told me that 100 percent of the cows in Albania had tuberculosis or brucellosis, I avoided as many diary products as possible. Since I also avoided water due to the contamination of the drinking water by the sewage, I declined to drink this combination.

sips (to keep up with all of the toasts that Flutra's father gave) and then my cheeks started turning numb.*

The next morning we woke up about 7:00 A.M., feeling a little guilty, knowing that the family had been up for hours already and that Flutra had already gone with the donkey and fetched the water for the day.† We tidied ourselves up as much as possible and then went into the kitchen for breakfast. Safo gave us a huge bowl of kos, some bread and jam, and our leftover food from the night before. We ate as much as we could and had one interview immediately after breakfast. The 65-year-old woman in the group told us that she had been in the field at 4:00 A.M. and had returned and dressed up for the interview. She was then going back out to the field. We also set out for the field after this interview, taking all of our recording equipment with us.

As we walked through the center of the village, we saw what the residents believe to be the oldest Orthodox church in the Balkans. The village also has a school, a mill with ancient equipment that has been restored to the family of the prior owner, a hair salon for men and women, and a medical center. Each person was given 1,500 square meters of land when the cooperatives were privatized, and the land is served by a dilapidated irrigation system. The land of Flutra's family was planted with feed for the animals, squash, corn, beans, watermelon, and hay. As it was hay harvesting time, the combine was being used to harvest on the various plots and the village women were carrying huge loads of hay to their homes, mostly in huge bales on their heads.

Although I was struck by the difficulty of the life in Perondi, it appears to be somewhat easier than that in Homesh, simply because the village is in the plain rather than in the mountains. The fields are more accessible and the climate is more temperate. However, its history and the demands made on the women are similar.

The Women of Perondi

We actually learned more about our hostess's mother, Safo, from observing her while we were there and from the stories told by others,

---

*It was here that we learned the following story about raki. "The first raki grape seed was planted and watered with the blood of a sparrow, the second raki grape seed was planted and watered with the blood of a pig, and the third raki grape seed was planted and watered with the blood of a wolf. That is why the first glass of raki makes you happy and makes you sing like a bird, the second glass makes you sloppy like a pig, and the third glass makes you aggressive and predatory."

†There is no running water in Perondi except once a month. Then water comes out of a pipe into a ditch near Flutra's family's home. Electricity only came to the village in 1971.

than we learned in the interview. She has been a great friend and an inspiration to the women around her. She is a warm, kind, self-effacing, and self-deprecating person, with a ready smile and eagerness to laugh. She herself told us,

> I am 53 years old and originally from Kuçovë. My father died as a martyr in Yugoslavia when I was young and because my mother remarried too soon afterward, I was not allowed to see her. Therefore, I was raised by my grandparents in Kuçovë. When I was 15, my uncle thought it wise to marry me to someone close to Kuçovë and he arranged a marriage with a man who was 10 years older than I was. I moved in with his large family. There were 50 people living together in one family. They were a hospitable and hardworking family. My father-in-law was a hoxha and loved me very much. He did, however, ask me to conform to the ways of the village. He asked me not to wear makeup and told me to wear my hair tied up on my head in the manner of the village women.
>
> My dream was to have two children, a boy and a girl. I had a girl and then two boys who died at the age of one year. I then had three more girls and finally a boy. The fourth daughter I named Flutra (Butterfly) with the wish that the girls would fly away. Finally, I had a boy. The greatest happiness I have felt has been visiting the families of my married daughters and hearing good words from their mothers-in-law.
>
> Love and desire or hope for a better life has given me strength to surmount the difficulties in my life.

While some of the women spoke of the economic and social difficulties of their lives in the communist period, several spoke of the challenges of today.

Hyrie, a 37-year-old teacher of English, who is single and living in Kuçovë now, told us,

> My mother married at the age of 14 during the National Liberation War. She has been an example for me all my life. She is hardworking, thoughtful, and considerate. She also values honesty highly. My mother struggled all her life with poverty, but she is optimistic by nature. Our mothers have lived for others and not for themselves and have lived with the ideal of building a good and just society.
>
> We now have four generations living together in our family, but this is not a major problem. However, people keep asking why I don't get married. I am opposed to arranged marriages and until I meet the right person I would prefer to remain single.
>
> I am basically an optimistic person, but have suffered bouts of depression as a result of events in my life. For example, after I graduated with high grades I was sent to teach in remote villages rather than in better posts. Even in democracy the Albanians are not free of prejudices. [Her last name is Hoxha, but no relation to Enver.]
>
> My mother's example has always been my greatest source of strength. If I am even half the person she is, I will have sufficient force to meet the challenges of my life.

Another teacher, Mimosa, aged 33, also told us of her problems in the Albania of today: "Present life is difficult. I have been married for six years and live in a small flat with nine people. There are three small rooms in the flat where my mother-in-law, my brother-in-law and his family, my sister-in-law, and myself, my husband and my four-year-old son live. My husband is out of work and I work for all. There are quarrels sometimes and the situation is nervous."

Qamile, 45, added, "We have been poorer before the coming of democracy, but more joyful. We had to work late, but didn't fear going home alone in the dark. The villagers don't even go to weddings now for fear of robberies. Crime has increased and we are all full of anxiety for the children when they go to school. The government needs to do something. It is of no value to be rich if you have no peace. It is especially important for a child because the greatest wealth is a child."

Highlighting the twin problems of unemployment and emigration that currently plague Albania, Kujtime, 35, concluded, "This transition period has been very difficult. Both I and my husband have been without work. Finally, my husband had to emigrate and sometimes I find that people are mean and take advantage of my situation."

We also found Perondi women—including Qamile and Zymbyle who are Muslims and Mimosa who is Orthodox—expressing their faith as their primary source of strength.

"Life is full of difficulties and obstacles, but men are created to live life successfully" Qamile said. She then added, "My primary sources of strength have come from my children, my family, a desire for a better life and to realize my objectives, but I also believe in God. God gave me hands and capability. A lazy man prays to God 'Give me what I want.' God says 'But you haven't done anything. I have given you hands and legs, etc. Those who are wealthy have earned it.'"

"I believe very much. My grandmother was a very religious woman; all of my mother's family was religious," said Zymbyle simply.

"Belief in God, in myself and in the future have given me strength to overcome the difficulties in my life," said Mimosa. "I learned this from my parents. I was told the good and the bad and was taught both by example and with inspirational stories. Also, I am optimistic by nature."

THE WOMEN OF VITHKUQ AND BELLOVODË

Although Vithkuq, in the south, is relatively more prosperous than the other villages in which we interviewed, the lives of the women of this generation were still characterized by hardships and social expectations. Here we met Majlinda and Eli.

Majlinda, 32, began by saying, "My life has been only hard work." Then she continued,

I was one of five children and was born into a poor family. We were raised in poverty and with hard work. What I especially remember of my earliest childhood is picking medicinal herbs to sell to bring in more money for my family. I finished the eighth grade and had no money to go on studying so I went to work at the age of 14.

I married for love when I was 17 years of age and it has worked out excellently, although my family was against the marriage because my husband was Walachian.* My father even said, "I will kill you if you marry him," but after a week he accepted it. On the other hand, my husband's family longed to have me in their home.

I always worked hard on the cooperative, as did my husband. Now we have our own land, but I spend most of my time now at the loom making rugs and blankets.

I have had a life filled with hard work, but I draw strength from my hope for a better future. I want to be strong like the others and to make life better.

At the end of the interview Majlinda thanked us for talking to her because it gave her an excuse to rest for a while.

Eli, 42, was also born, raised, and married in Vithkuq. She told us a story that is untypical in many ways. She is an independent woman who has been able to break with tradition and flaunt authority through her own hard work, based on the role model provided by her father.

I was one of four children and very fortunate that my father was a hard worker. Although we were brought up only on our father's salary, we lacked for nothing. I was my father's favorite child and I have my best memories of him. I remember that I was a very religious child and my father did not prevent me from worshipping and I appreciated that.

I began working in the fields when I was 14, but at the age of 20 I got a job as an accountant for the cooperative because I had graduated from two secondary schools, one in economics and one in agriculture. At the age of 29 I was married under an arrangement, but I got to know my husband first. I was married late for two reasons. First, I had a good job and didn't feel that I needed someone to support me. Second, I had a black spot in my biography. My mother's brother, an intellectual, was imprisoned for agitation and propaganda. It was later proved that he was not guilty and he was released.

After I was married, I only lived in my in-laws' house for one month because there were so many people. So we came to my family's house because they had no one there, and we lived with them for ten years.

In general, my married life has been good. I was out of work for four years in

A person from Walachia, the southern region of Romania.

the beginning of the transition period, but now I work as an inspector for the insurance company. I believe that my life will be better in the future and I will work hard to make it better.

In fact, I have drawn strength from hard work and think only of my children. I want them to lead a better life. I have also appreciated the support of my parents. They have always been a great support to me even in my married life.

What role has faith played in my life? I have already said that I have always believed. A funny story comes to my mind, however, to illustrate my feelings. When the churches were closed and no one made red eggs in observance of the Orthodox Easter, I threw a red egg under the door of the office of the party secretary. When he found it in his office, he shouted at us, trying to find out who had dared to do such a thing.

On the way back to Korçë from Vithkuq, we stopped in the small village of Bellovodë. Unlike Vithkuq, this village has a sense of being at a crossroads, on the way to or from somewhere. It is a busy place, but there is a sense of poverty here that does not exist in Vithkuq. However, that poverty does not extend to the spirit, as we learned in our interview with Viktori. At the age of 48, Viktori is a stunningly beautiful woman in a classical sense: handsome, fine-featured, and almost regal in bearing. We sat talking on the front porch of her house with her three daughters and her mother-in-law, whilst also waving away the men who wanted to listen and interject their ideas.

Mine was a family of migrant shepherds. We lived in the mountains in tents and huts. I was engaged from the time I was four years old. My husband's grandmother told my husband's mother that she would not rest until her grandson was engaged to me. I didn't know my husband and I only saw him officially at our wedding, although I had seen him secretly before. We were married in 1970 when I was 21 and our lives have progressed well.

In all the challenges I have faced, I have thought only of my daughters. I have sacrificed all for their dowries.

When I asked what role faith had played in her life, she responded,

We were religious and always kept our icons with us. I have always believed that we were with God from the time we were born.

Summary

Although the typical women of this generation, whether of the city or the village, lived lives that were better than those of their own mothers, they still experienced great hardships. And, like their mothers, they faced their difficulties with courage and amazing strength. It is important,

Viktori (second from right) with her daughters and mother-in-law.

however, to understand that life with all its joys and passions went on. It is true that it was circumscribed by the economic and physical conditions of life and by both societal and government limitations. However, these boundaries seem to have given special meaning to the connections that existed between family members and neighbors and to the events of life: marriages, births, and deaths.

The women of Albania, of this and all generations, also understand better today the difficulties they faced in comparison with what they now know about the Western world. Most of them have seen American and Western European television shows, some have traveled outside the country, and many have met women from abroad and learned about their lives and their expectations. For this reason and because there is now freedom of speech, the Albanian women are expressing the challenges they have experienced in their lives more freely today. This has the potential to bring healing to those who have suffered and whose lives are now improving. It also has the potential of dividing society, because there are those whose lives are untouched or, in fact, poorer as a result of the political and economic changes. There appears to have been a solidarity that had less to do with the propaganda of the times and more to do with the unifying nature of common suffering. So many women said that they did not feel their sufferings so much because everyone in the society suffered the same. As the economic and social potential of a significant proportion of the women increases over that of another large proportion of other women, what will be gained and what will be lost? What implications does this have for future generations?

Chapter 11

Atypical Women of the Middle Generation: Lives of Persecution

Regardless of where they lived, women of all generations (including this one) had the potential to be subjected to political persecution. This persecution resulted from being born into certain families or was due to the actions of others in their families, often their fathers, husbands, or brothers. This chapter is devoted to their stories.

SHAZIE'S STORY

Shazie is 34 years of age. Although she is originally from the village of Boçevë, we met her in Homesh. She told us,

My father was a brigade leader in the cooperative. However, he spent 25 years as a political prisoner because his brother crossed the border into Yugoslavia. My father was sent to prison because he had gone to the border with his brother and didn't denounce him. First, he was imprisoned in Peshkopi and later in Spaç (one of the worst of the prisons). He was not released until democracy came.

I had to start working when I was 9 and was married under an arrangement in 1978 at 16 years of age. I had to be married quickly because of my biography problems. My husband had some biography problems of his own that only came to light after we were married.

The biggest troubles I have had to face have been caused by poverty. I have six children ranging from 17 down to one and a half years of age and there has never been enough to feed them. Now that my husband is engaged in trade and I work in the field things are better. There is just enough.

Love for my children has kept me strong. I had to choose to either die or live. I also believe that things will get better. My personal dream is to have a better life economically for me and for my children.

AISHE'S STORY

We also met Aishe, aged 50, in Homesh.

My father died of cancer and my mother and brothers worked in the fields. I had six brothers and I was the only girl. Although we struggled, my family had a good political biography and there were no problems for me before I got married.

I married at the age of 17 in 1963 when the class struggle was not so sharp. However, my husband said something against the government and was imprisoned for 18 months. For 18 years my brother didn't come to see me and I was separated from my family, though my mother came to see me secretly. My children were denied education.

We have suffered much and that suffering is deeply engraved. The only thing we didn't experience was literally being ground in the grindstone. You see, I am 50, but I look older because of the hard life I have lived. Great sufferings, bad people around, and all day working in the field—that was my life.

I found my force through hard work. I just worked hard. A hard life makes a person stronger, but not bad. Now I have a cow and a sheep and I live better. My sons go abroad and bring good money. Now let God be careful of us not to have any more trouble.

FILOMENA'S STORY

Filomena is now, at the age of 50, the headmistress of a school in Shkodër. She told us,

To tell the truth, my childhood was very bitter. In 1951, when I was 5 years old, my father, who was a private shopkeeper, was arrested for agitation and propaganda. The truth was that the Sigurimi wanted him to work for them, but he didn't accept. He was put in prison for 6 years. We were 4 children. The youngest was only 3 months old at the time and the oldest was 12 years. My mother was not employed until my father was imprisoned, but after that she had to do the most difficult work because no one wanted a prisoner's wife working for them. For example, she carried heavy loads and washed clothes in a hospital. My oldest sister, who was very good in school, had to quit school before 14 years of age and start working in building construction. It was a very difficult job for an Albanian woman. [The same was true for] my older brother—he was very talented in school—but his dreams were crushed before they could advance.

I was the third child. When I was five, I had to take things to my father in jail and these visits were always accompanied by the sarcasm of the police, but I was a powerful child with a sense of courage. I had the bitter experience of seeing my father 9 months after he was sent to prison and just before he was tried. When I met him on that occasion, he was completely changed. We children began to cry because we couldn't recognize him, he had changed so much. Also, he seemed like an old man. All his teeth were broken, his skin was white, and he was like a creature without life.

Despite the conflicts with the communists and the persecution of my father, I did not feel the effects at school. I was bright and got good results, so the teachers were good to me. However, after I finished secondary school, I had another bitter experience that affected me for life. I finished high school with good grades. My oldest sister was married and my brother had joined the army. My mother was sick and my father was an invalid because after prison he had worked in construction doing the most difficult tasks. During work he had an accident that caused a cerebral hemorrhage and he lost his memory. Even after a year in the hospital he was a total invalid and unable to walk. I was given the right at this time to go on for advanced studies in engineering. My older sister agreed to do the housework and care for our parents so that I could go to school in Tiranë. I was very happy then: my dream was being realized. However, my happiness lasted only one week. The people in charge of the university told me that I was not to have this right. It was unimaginable to me. They explained that it was because I had a bad biography. I left and came home, giving my parents one more cause for suffering.

Later, in December of that year, I was accepted to attend the two-year institute in Shkodër because of the difficult economic conditions of my family. I finished there and was assigned to teach in the mountains of Pukë, in the village of Flet, the remotest village in that area. I lost the best years of my life there and I cannot forgive the people who sent me. However, the villagers were extremely poor and I worked wholeheartedly because I felt sorry to see those poor children. After two years the local government there gave me the right to complete my studies by correspondence. So I finally graduated in Albanian language and literature.

Even so, after five years in Pukë, I returned to Shkodër and worked for 12 more years in villages around Shkodër at a time when less qualified teachers were being assigned to the teaching positions in Shkodër itself.

I have always remembered with nostalgia the advice of my mother and her encouragement of me. That has given me strength. Also, my faith has given me strength, made me optimistic, and given me the persistence to achieve my goal. I pray to God at difficult moments to help me overcome obstacles.

The Women in the Library: Korçë

Although I have made the point that the extent of political persecution appeared to be less in Korçë than in other areas we visited, it is clear from the stories told to us by Zhani, Tefta, and Natasha that persecution did exist in this city as well. However, it continues to be striking that, despite the consequences suffered by these women and their families, the extent of their suffering and punishments was relatively mild, at least in comparison with that of people with similar crimes in other parts of the country.

ZHANI'S STORY

Zhani is a determined and forthright woman of 58 years, with excellent training in her profession as an ophthalmologist.

I was born in 1938, the only child of two intellectuals. My father was an agronomist and had studied in France. My mother was a teacher. Both parents were very interested in my education. I began my studies during the War of Liberation when my mother was teaching in the liberated areas. She took me with her and started teaching me from the time I was five years of age. After I went to high school in Korçë, I studied medicine in Poland. I studied there for two years, but had to return in 1956 because of the uprisings there at that time. I completed my medical training in Tiranë. Later I specialized as an oculist.

There are difficult times in my life that I remember: being an only child and traveling far from home to study in Poland, and then later studying for my specialization. Fortunately, when I was studying to specialize, my mother cared for my children to help me. Now that I am taking care of my grandchildren, I know how much she sacrificed for me during this time.

However, the most difficult moment in my life (I always cry when I think of this moment) was when my uncle, Nesti Nase, minister of foreign affairs, was declared to be an "enemy of the people" and sentenced to imprisonment.* I knew that my family would suffer the consequences. My mother was a well-known and well-loved teacher, but when she died people were afraid to come to speak at her funeral. When no one else spoke, my 16-year-old daughter got up and spoke some lovely, warm words. Later, before he died, my father said, "If no one speaks at my funeral, please ask one of your daughters to do the same thing for me." I remember the kindness of people who called themselves communists who came and expressed their concern at this time. It is so meaningful to me.

I have found my source of strength in my desire to survive and in the kindness of those who helped us in the difficult periods. I remember these individuals and the strength they gave us to go on.

TEFTA'S STORY

Tefta, 53, told us a story of how Enver Hoxha treated even his so-called friends,

I was born in Korçë in 1943 also to an intellectual family. My father, Foto Bala, was a real figure in Korçë. He was a graduate of Montpelier University in southern France and became a professor of philosophy. He was also a deputy in the government.

In 1946 our troubles began. My father was one of those deputies tried in a special court.† First he was sentenced to be shot, then to life in prison, and then to 20 years of prison, all of which he suffered. Can you believe this? My father had been a friend of Hoxha's from Gjirokastër, they had gone to school together in both

---

*Nesti Nase was a high official in the Albanian diplomatic corps and served as ambassador to the Soviet Union, ambassador to the People's Republic of China, and minister of foreign affairs. He was expelled from his position with the accusation of having revisionist views.
†On December 2, 1945, elections for the Constitutional Assembly took place. A group of nationalists (persons who had supported the National Liberation War) were elected deputies to this assembly. These deputies were against the communist reforms that would lead Albania along the socialist road. In 1946 the "group of deputies," as they were called, were declared traitors to the country. They were tried in a special court and the majority of them were sentenced to death. This group was accused of collaborating with U.S. and English agents.

Korçë and Montpelier, and they had shared a room and sometimes even the one suit they owned. They were friends, but it didn't matter. Most of the intellectuals were either shot or imprisoned by Enver Hoxha. There were 28 friends, intellectuals, and deputies who were tried in a special court and of these 25 were shot and 3 were sent to prison!

My mother was allowed to continue working as a teacher until 1955, when we went to Tiranë to live with other family members. There she was told to work in an enterprise. We were allowed to live in Tiranë until 1962, when we were sent into exile in Gradisht for five years. We only stayed there for three and a half years, until my father was released from jail. Since we were not allowed to go to Tiranë, we returned to Korçë. At that time we were all without work. My mother worked occasionally sorting potatoes, but my father couldn't work. Later, I worked for three or four years as a geologist after I complained to a minister, but after that the class struggle became more bitter and I was given a job as a worker.

In our family we have all found strength in knowing that others have suffered much more than we have. We saw their difficulties and my parents taught us to be thankful.

Faith was not strong in my family, but no one interfered with me. I have always believed in God. Although my family is Orthodox, I married a Muslim because I fell in love with him. When I was married, my father asked me how I had come to accept to marry a Muslim. He told me then that it made him happy that one of his daughters had married a Catholic and the other was marrying a Muslim because now his family had all of Albania represented in it.

NATASHA'S STORY

Natasha, 48, told us of her sufferings of the past and those of the present day.

I was born in 1948 in Korçë to a poor family from a village and I am still leading a life of poverty. My father and brother tried to cross the border to go to America and were caught and sentenced to prison. Both died in prison—my father after 6 months and my brother after 18 years. In 1966, soon after they were caught, my family was exiled to Moglicë for 4½ years, but then we returned to Korçë. When we returned, we were given a single room in which to live—all 7 remaining children and my mother. My mother worked on a tobacco farm to support us and I worked on a farm for 8 years as well.

I married for love and this is the great joy in my life. However, I am now unemployed and my husband has been in Greece, without documents, for two months. This has been a desperate and frightening time for me. I want him to come home. We are homeless and jobless and this has been the most difficult time in my life. After my husband left, we were told that we had to leave our house. The policemen came and abused me physically when I refused to leave. I was sent to prison because I didn't obey their orders. I was closed in a very dark cell in the cellar for a day. I have complained to them for this treatment, but no one gives me an answer.

God has given me strength. I have taken strength only from God.

MERI'S STORY

Meri is a 54-year-old writer and former teacher of English. She is from the lakeside city of Pogradec.

I was one of the gayest girls in boarding school in Tiranë. I was always in top form. After graduation I went to Korçë to teach English and was married four years after graduation. I couldn't imagine an arranged marriage so I married for love. My ex-husband belonged to one of the highest families in Albania. His grandfather had been a minister in Zog's government. For that he was shot and my husband's father was hanged by the communists. My husband and I were exiled to a village with a mine about 20 kilometers from Durrës, where he worked as a miner. I was prohibited from being a teacher so I cleaned office floors and cooked for the miners. Sometimes I worked as an accountant, but often I sorted coal on the third shift. For seven years we lived in a very small house—a windowless hut, actually—that had been built for ducks.

An especially difficult time came while I was pregnant with my daughter. My husband had an accident in which he broke his back. I stayed in the hospital with him for 36 days. That winter each day I had to carry 30 liters of water through the deep mud wearing my husband's large boots. My feet sank into the mud and I had to use all my force to take one step after another.

The birth of my child was also difficult and then it was hard to raise a child in such conditions. One day, when my baby was just five months old, lightning stuck the hut. In fact, it struck a lamp and the lamp shattered. The baby was naked and I had to hide her under a board to keep her dry. Later I was very ill and had to have an operation.* It was the second time in my life that I was very close to death, the first time being when I gave birth to my child. During the time that I was hospitalized, our house was flooded and we lost all our belongings. When I was released from the hospital, I was expected to go back to the same work, sorting coal, with no leave or other recognition of my medical condition. This was also the time that my daughter would have started school.

It was a terrible time and I had to make a frightening decision. I had to abandon my husband in order to survive and to bring up my daughter. After the divorce, my husband was sent to prison for 9 years. Here was a man who had nothing to do with politics—in fact even the word "politics" terrified him since his grandfather and father had both been killed—yet he was imprisoned on a political pretext. Six months after I returned to Pogradec I found work in a village and spent 15 years teaching gypsy children. During all this time I faced many problems with social and political opinion. The Sigurimi used to call and ask me if I would marry my husband again, did I still love him. They wanted to know if it was a sacrificial divorce.

When I was young, I always said to myself, "I want to be a wonderful wife, a good mother, and, if possible, a writer." I have not been a bad wife. My husband and I are on good terms, although he has remarried and we do not meet each other. I have been a very good mother. I think of my daughter as a gift from my husband.

*She showed us her scars. For what she described as an esophageal transplant, she had terrible scars and holes created by poorly stitched and dressed wounds across her abdomen and extending up her torso.

Meri in Pogradec.

She is not only my daughter but also my best friend. I have also now written two books. One called *Lasgushi në Pogradec* (*Lasgush in Pogradec*)* has been published. The other, which describes the period from October 1991 to the spring of 1992 is called "As në Qiell as në Tokë" (Neither in the Sky nor in the Earth) and not yet published. I want to live to complete my plans.

First, I had my daughter. My love for my daughter gave me strength. I wanted her to have a better life than mine. Also, I have been very near to death two times. When you are near death, you find that you can live. Also, I have read many books in my life. I dreamed that somewhere there existed a life that was different from ours. This is my native land and I love my country. My life is connected with this little town and with this country. I am very proud to be an Albanian woman.

The following chapters contain individual interviews with women of this generation, illustrating in more detail the lives they have led and the challenges they have faced. They also show even more clearly the impact of education and upbringing in a secular society. It is possible that women readers of this same generation in the United States and other Western countries will identify more with the stories told here than with any others in the book. There are similarities in the ways the lives of these women progressed—as career and economic opportunities opened up—while many other aspects of society remained the same, limiting their progress. These women also experienced the challenges of women in other countries: coping with the death of a spouse, divorce, and career advancement in the face of prejudice and other obstacles.

---

*Lasgush Pogradeci is the pseudonym of the well-known lyric poet Llazar Gusho. He was born in 1900 and died in 1987. Lyrics of love and of the motherland are the essence of his literary work and there is an optimistic note and a strong influence of folk poetry. His main works are Vallja e Yjeve (The Dance of Stars), 1933, and Ylli i Zemres (The Star of the Heart), 1937. Pogradeci is considered to be one of the most talented Albanian poets.

Chapter 12

Floresha Dado:
The Sacrifices of a Mother
and a Passionate Scientist

Floresha is a hard-driving and charming 49-year-old professor of the theory of literature at the University of Tiranë. Hers is the story of a woman from a simple background who scaled the intellectual heights and raised children in the face of hardship, with much personal sacrifice. Despite the challenges of her life—and maybe because of them—she exemplifies what she herself refers to as the "nobleness of the Albanian women," which comes from that spirit of sacrifice.

Family Background

I was born in Durrës to parents who were simple villagers from the southern part of Albania. My father was intelligent, but had no education. My mother also had no education, but she was clever. I have such lovely memories of my parents. Since my childhood I have understood what the spirit of sacrifice is because I could see it in both of my parents.

My father was a municipal official in the city of Durrës handling complaints. He was honored by the people of Durrës because he took seriously their complaints and tried hard to help them resolve their problems. However, there were four children in our family and only his income, so our family's finances were difficult. Despite that, my father knew I loved books and understood my passion to read.

It is fresh in my memory the times he took me by the hand and walked me to the bookshop. He let me pick out a book, then told the bookseller "give it to my daughter. I will pay you when I get paid." My father wanted his children to be educated, but he also told his daughters, "I want you to be able to face society your-selves—being masters of your own houses—and to overcome all difficulties by means of your education." He wanted us to be independent, not dependent on our husbands or others.

What I remember of my mother is that she was an ordinary woman who paid much attention to us children. She tried not to let us feel the problem of our poverty. For example, in order for us to have a new dress for the first day of school, she sewed all night and made us dresses out of her old ones. She didn't sleep all night.

It is a pleasure for me to remember these moments and to recall and acknowledge that what I have inherited from my parents is their sacrifice and their desire to give us every possibility to grow and to do well.

I also remember that I had a strong desire for literature in secondary school. I thought I wanted to write, but I found when I entered the school for Albanian language and literature that I did not have the talent. It became my dream to study literature and be a scientist in this field, to find a husband who would understand my passion for literature, and to have a house where the four walls would be lined with books.

Marriage

Fortunately, I found the man I had dreamed of and was happily married to him. My husband, Peçi Dado, was from a poor family, but at 16 years of age he started working as a journalist and had an opportunity to study scriptwriting in Moscow for a year. He then went to the university here and studied Albanian language and literature. He was one of the first scriptwriters in Albania and was the author of many important and successful Albanian films. Later, he was at the head of the scriptwriting department at the new Kinostudio (film studio) and dedicated his life to his art. He understood my passion for literature and I was happy with him.

The first years of our marriage were full of difficulties as we had no house and lived with my in-laws, who had different ideas about many things. It was a small house: two rooms and a kitchen. Our son was born in 1973 and our daughter was born in 1975 while we were still living with my in-laws. I also started work at this time at the Academy of Science in the Institute of Language and Literature. My dream was starting to come true, but there was so much work to do: postuniversity exams and the completion of my dissertation (a monograph on Çajupi). My mother-in-law didn't understand me well and did not help me.

The best memories I have of this period are connected with my life with my husband. We had very different temperaments, but yet there was understanding between us. He was very sensitive—he felt so much. I was energetic and ambitious. I remember one occasion when I wrote an article and I asked him to comment on it. I had thought that I understood the issues in the science of literature, but when he made his remarks, I realized that I was married to a man who was not only a writer but also a perceptive critic. His remarks made me realize that I still had much to learn.

There was a time I remember well when I had so much work to do and neither my mother-in-law nor my father-in-law helped me. I was always alone unless my husband helped me. There was an occasion when he was to go to Vlorë with the production crew, but had decided not to go because of the situation in the family shortly after the birth of our second child. He wanted to be there, at home, to help me. By chance, I met a friend of his who told me that he was sorry that my husband was not going with them. He told me that Peçi wanted to go, but would not because he understood my need for his help. I went home and told my husband to go, that I would find the time and energy to cope with the children. It was my desire to help him as he helped me and I wanted him to follow his passion, too. He was surprised when I told him to go to Vlorë, but this helping of each other is one of the things that maintained our good relationship.

Floresha Dado.

Seven years after our marriage Peçi had a heart attack and at that time my life took a turn for the worse. I had to do all the heavy work: to chop the wood for the wood stove, carry the heaviest bags, do the shopping, take the children to kindergarten—all. I also didn't sleep enough because I worried about losing him. However, I played a role: I didn't let him see that I was worried or that it was difficult for me because I didn't want to upset him. Three years after that first heart attack he had another. He died on May 24, 1981, when he was in Lezhë working on a script for a film *Qortimet Vjeshtes* (*Challenges of Autumn*) on the life of his great hero, Qemal Stafa.

In my opinion, the family is sacred. It was what brought joy into my life. I had a good husband and beautiful and nice children. Peçi's death was a great shock and I felt it as a great injustice done to me. In response, I said "God doesn't exist! If he did, he wouldn't have done this injustice to me."

Alone

And so I entered the most difficult period of my life. My son was eight and my daughter was six. For the first three years after his death, I used to go to the graveyard every Sunday and put fresh flowers on Peçi's grave. I lost weight and was weak. One day coming home from the graveyard, I was so weak that I thought I was dying. Finding myself in this position, I pulled myself together. "What am I doing to myself? What about my children?" I asked myself. Then, I remembered my husband's words when he was at death's door: "Take care of the children." Remembering his words, I decided not to think of myself and my grief but of them. I decided at this moment not to go to the graveyard so much, but to dedicate my life to my children—to work and care for them—and to become much more involved in my scientific studies.

My dedication to my children and my career in science made me feel that my life was not as difficult as it really was. The goal I had was to raise good and educated children. My daughter began to study the violin and I encouraged her. Both of my children studied foreign languages.

Poverty was a significant issue, not just in my family but in all families in Albania. When the situation was at its worst, I had no food to give my children because there simply was no food in the stores. With my neighbor, I would get up at 3:00 A.M., even in the dead of winter when it was freezing, to stand in line for a liter of milk or 100 grams of butter or maybe something else. I came home at 6:00 A.M. in a desperate mood. My desperation was for two reasons. First, I had to do so much by myself. If my husband had lived, he would have done so much to help me. Second, I wondered why my country was so poor that we did not have food. Why did I have to stand in line for so little food?

A detail I remember from this period was that sausage was only very rarely available. It just wasn't in the shops. When I did find it and brought it home, I never ate it, but gave it to my children. They always asked, "Why don't you like it?" They didn't understand that I was leaving it for them.

At this same time, I was asked to go be a teacher of the theory of literature. It was hard to prepare the lectures, partly because I was the first to teach this subject. Also, there were no foreign texts available in this area because what was treated by the foreign writers was considered to be decadent (that is, not in accordance with our ideology). I decided to find a way to make my life full and not empty. The way I did this was through work. It helped me forget all that had happened to me when I worked. I knew that when a wife loses her husband there are many solutions to her grief and loss. My solution was that I chose to work hard.

My day, which began at 3:00 A.M., continued with work. After I helped my children get ready for school, I was at the library at 8:00 A.M. There, I worked until 1:00 P.M., when I interrupted my studies (when I had no lectures) to go home and give the children their lunch. At 3:00 P.M. I was back in the library and worked until 6:00 P.M. When my son was older, I remember that he used to come to the library and get me. We then walked home together. I prepared dinner and ate it with the children. Then I worked with them on their homework. When they went to bed at 9:00 P.M. the day really began for me: the cooking, cleaning, and ironing. It seemed that I was always in a hurry and often I ended up burning or cutting myself as I rushed.

When I finished doing all this, I often felt desperate again. Sometimes I turned on the television so as not to feel so lonely. It was the only time I had to myself. I was "happy" because my children were sleeping and they would not see my desperation and my tears. I never wanted to show them how I felt.

There have been some beautiful moments throughout the anguish of this period. My daughter, Orjeta, distinguished herself as a lovely girl and as a talented violinist. I remember times when we had no electricity and no heating and I lit candles to give light to my children to continue studying. One such night, when my daughter was 16 years old, I was feeling particularly depressed. It was freezing cold, but my daughter picked up her violin and began to play a piece by Bach. It was very beautiful, but in some ways it made me more depressed thinking about my very talented daughter studying and playing the violin in the candlelight. Since then she has won prizes as a talented student and she is now studying in America.

My son, Edvin, who is clever, silent, and serious, worked hard to be successful in school. He won a competition and is studying in the medical school. I cried with joy the day he told me that he had won. The next day my children said to me, "We felt so sorry looking at you crying. We feared that something horrible had happened because we have never seen you cry before." My son has a good heart and I believe he will make a good doctor.

It seemed to me that I had overcome the difficult times when I saw my children succeeding in life. These are the things that have changed my life for the better. I have been offered some satisfaction from my children's accomplishments.

In addition, I have also had my own accomplishments that have repaid me for the hard work I have done. I was given the title of docent in science and later the highest title in my field: professor doctor in the science of Albanology.

I would like to mention something here. When my daughter first went to America, she was shocked by the comfortable life of the American family with whom she was staying. It was at this time that she became aware of how difficult our lives had been and how many hardships I had in raising her and her brother. I remember the letters I received during the first period of time that she was there. They are a treasure for me. She wrote, "Mom, please do me a favor. You have done so much for us. Now you should do something for yourself. Look at yourself. All you need is a little makeup. Do you know who Floresha is? You should think much more of yourself."

The Source of Her Strength

My desire to be a woman full of dignity has given me much strength in my life and has given me success. People tell me that I don't look my age. Perhaps they just pay me a compliment, but I know that what keeps me young is my passion for work and my love of and care for my children.

Always in my life I have had an intense desire to have a role in life and in society, just as my father had wished for me. I have always liked it when others have not considered me just as a woman but as a person worthy of their evaluation and recognition: knowing that I deserved it. In Hoxha's time, women were favored simply because they were women, but I did not want that. I put myself face to face with my male counterparts and I worked hard, much harder than some of them. Comparing myself with others who have achieved the same things—the men I mean—I am proud of my accomplishments because I did not have the favorable conditions that they had in the family. I was both man and woman.

You asked me what I will do with the rest of my life. This is my answer. In this new period of time in which we are living, I feel that I have a new responsibility for my profession, for my subject of the theory of literature. It calls to be brought into compliance with modern thought. Reconstruction needs to be done and I am eager to do something. Therefore, I will still work hard as there is still much to be done. I must respond to the new demands of society with continued dignity.

Now I will tell you a secret: to tell the truth and speak most sincerely, I feel very tired. I can't even express how tired I am. All the hard work and passion I have expended to excel in my field and to raise my children have left their traces in my life and left me exhausted. My one real regret in my life is that I never kept a diary. It was a great mistake in my life, but there was no time and too much pain. My secret dream now is to write.

The Role of Faith

Although my family was nominally Muslim, I was raised at a time when my whole education was atheistic. I belong to that generation. Therefore, I have been an atheist, but sincerely speaking I accept the existence of a supernatural force. It is a mystery to me, however.

My husband was Orthodox and now my daughter is Protestant and my son is Orthodox. In one of her letters to me, my daughter expressed her faith and her view of God working in my life, "God tested your force and this test is given by Him to those in whom He has confidence that they will overcome difficulties."

My people also have a saying, "God throws you down with one hand and picks you up with the other." I think my life exemplifies this.

Summary

By many standards, including the stories of other women in this book, Floresha's life has been an uneventful and undramatic one. It is characterized more by exhaustion and monotony, alleviated by the joys of parenthood and her career successes. Her pain and sadness upon the death of her husband are, however, universal, as is her desire to succeed personally and in the raising of her children.

Particularly impressive is the way in which Floresha's children spoke of her. They admire and appreciate her. They are beginning to know of and understand her sacrifice for their sakes. How many parents crave such a response from their children? What have they done to deserve it? What does it mean to sacrifice for children in a developed country?

Chapter 13

Diana Çuli:
A Life of Art and Service

At 45 years of age, Diana Çuli is a prominent writer and the head of the Independent Women's Forum of Albania. As a writer, Diana worked for 6 years in the 1970s as a journalist for the leading literary journal *Drita* and for 12 years was the publisher of *Les Lettres Albanaises*, a literary magazine written in French and directed by the well-known Albanian writer, Ismail Kadare. She is also the author of seven books and two screenplays for films created from her books.

As an activist, Diana founded the Independent Forum in 1991 and has served as its president since then. The Independent Forum was the first women's organization created in Albania after the advent of democracy. She has also served as a member of the board of Interbalkanic Women's Association, president of the Albanian NGO (Nongovernmental Organization) Forum, and board member of the Albanian Helsinki Citizens' Assembly. She has also been a guest speaker on human rights and politics at colleges in the United States and was a participant at the women's conference in Beijing in 1995.

Diana is a thoroughly modern woman: a successful, self-confident professional who has a zeal for improving the lot of the Albanian women. Although Diana is adamant in her political independence, she was one of the first people to speak out forcefully against the communist regime and was part of the movement that served as the catalyst for reform. Diana has been honored by foreign organizations and recognized in the press and in women's groups for her desire to serve her country.

The Influence of the Past

I was lucky to be born into my family because it was neither rich nor poor, but it was very patriotic. My parents had a strong feeling for Albania: a love of the

Diana Çuli.

mother country, the culture, and the literature. They were people of strong principles. My father and uncles had fought as partisans and my father told my sister and me long stories of the past. My father also loved to show me values that were positive and beautiful in life.

A very important person in my life was my grandmother. She was a typical Mediterranean woman from the Himarë area. She had five children whom she raised alone as her husband was in America, and she raised them to be cultured and educated, even though she herself only had three or four years of schooling. I was brought up listening to her stories. My grandmother was like a folklore encyclopedia and I memorized many of the verses.

My grandmother thought always of my grandfather and always wore black. She was tall and beautiful, but she never bought something pretty, only a new black dress.

As most girls are in our country, I was more attached to my mother than my father, but this is the tradition in Albania. Men are your danger, so mothers and daughters are close. Usually, the fathers have chosen the husbands and the brothers have served as bodyguards. Men and boys tell you what to do and mothers and grandmothers protect their daughters from the men. I also got my love of literature from my mother. She was always reading, even when she was cooking. She told me stories and started teaching me to read at the age of five. I was taught Russian, Italian, and English while I was still a small girl. I remember that my father's presents on my birthdays were mostly books.

My parents taught my sister and me to be modest, to help others, and to be serious. Maybe they helped us too much, but they also pressed us to study. We had to perform and get good grades. They were hard on us, but the principle was good. The difficult thing for me was that I had to be serious and not express my true feelings in front of others. I had to suppress my real nature and I still can't show my feelings today as a result.

The time that I was in middle school was a difficult time for me because I was no longer a child and not yet a young adult. I could not decide things for myself. My parents expected me to be an "honest" girl and not be involved with boys, not even to look at them. This was true for all the young girls in Albania at that time. The social rules were very strict. For example, when our bodies changed, my sister and I—as well as our friends—had to strap our breasts. Actually, we chose to do so because any evidence of our sexuality was considered to be shameful. Our teacher was good and it was she who explained to us about menstrual periods. Our mother was indifferent on this subject. She had wanted sons because she knew how hard the life would be for girls. Now I feel happy when I see girls living a different life from that of my generation. The relations between mother and daughter have changed for the better.

When I was 15 and first began working on the "voluntary" actions in construction and other things, I believed that I was doing something good for my country. I dreamed that in the future things would be beautiful.* When the country broke with the Soviet Union, relations with the West were somewhat improved for a time, but the new relations with China brought repression. I had my first suspicions about the kind of life we were living when the Chinese Cultural Revolution took place and its influence was soon reflected here in all areas of life. Many books and much music from the West were outlawed and "new" policies were applied as part of the "pure" communism of Enver Hoxha. Hoxha's theory that only Albania was purely Marxist and that the other communist countries were revisionist brought with it a very militaristic and spartan atmosphere. This made me less enthusiastic about the regime and the future. I remember, for example, the "circulation of the intellectuals" from town to villages. This was the temporary or permanent relocation of well-educated persons from more developed and important towns to less developed ones. This was practiced time and again to train intellectuals and "keep them safe" from bourgeois influences.

Later when ties with China were broken, fear and control were increased. It was also after this that our economic situation became worse and life in many aspects became more difficult. You worried that even your friend might spy on you, so you couldn't share your opinions with anyone. As young people, we were severely

---

*The "Revolutionary Triangle" dictated that education had three components: learning, physical labor, and military training, and these were the elements that made up the school curriculum. This curriculum was designed for the revolutionary education of the younger generation.

limited by the traditional family structure and social opinion on the one hand and political control on the other.

In the 1970s at the university where I studied at the school of literature and Albanian language, our lives were ideologically more difficult. We were afraid even of our friends. We lost our ideals and they were replaced only with the paranoia of the system. Despite this, we were fortunate that we had excellent teachers and access to the library—even to books that were prohibited.

A Talent Revealed

I had developed an interest in writing when I was 12 years old and published a short story in a children's magazine. I always said that I would be a writer when I grew up and people laughed at me. My father enrolled me for piano lessons at the age of 6 at the Pioneer Palace, but later, at age 11, I registered myself in the literary circle that taught us how to write, read, and understand.

Although I wrote for myself in grade school, I didn't try to get my work published. I didn't feel that I knew enough about what I was doing, even though my friends tried very hard to get their works published. Even at the university, I focused on reporting and literary criticism and went on to a career in journalism.

It was difficult to get nominated for journalism in Tiranë, but because I had written articles in several journals I was proposed to the Union of Writers' literary journal *Drita*.

It was wonderful to work at *Drita*. The best-known writers were working there and doing good work. There was an excellent library where it was possible to read prohibited books. The atmosphere was very good, with freedom of discussion and open-mindedness. I decided at that time to publish. I was 25 years of age and published a book of short stories. However, it was not easy for me to work in a field that was primarily masculine territory. For this reason, I had to publish five books before my name was even mentioned. I felt that I had to work two or three times harder than the men to be recognized.

At age 25 I was married. I had known my husband all my life because we were from the same neighborhood. He is an electrical engineer and 3 years older than I. We met through friends and so began a deep love. Three years later we were married. We had the same point of view on life, the same mentality. We have had some difficulties in our marriage, even though my husband has been quite supportive of my activities. As you might imagine, some of these difficulties had to do with the conflict of the artistic temperament with the scientific temperament.

During the time that I started to publish, my husband and I were also starting our family. We had a daughter and then a son. It was also a very difficult economic period for the country. I had to wake up at 2:00 or 3:00 A.M. to line up for milk, potatoes, and other foodstuffs, and then I had to line up for other items in the afternoon. It was also a difficult time for my husband because a writer's life is such a public one.

Many of the challenges in my life relate to my writing. As a young woman I wanted to publish my poetry, but didn't dare to: I didn't want to expose my feelings. For example, I never wrote about political issues because they were required to be treated in a positive way. Instead, I wrote about family and personal problems. In retrospect, I am not pleased with the things I wrote at this time. I am unhappy that I couldn't express what I wanted. It only pleased me that something I had done gave other people pleasure in reading it. Although it was not what I wanted to do, I was happy to give people the enjoyment of reading my work.

Now I am free to write whatever is in my head, but, instead, I have spent much time reflecting and searching in myself. People expect so much from a writer they know.

The richness in my life now is in my public life. Sometimes I think as a writer and sometimes I think as a social activist: these are contradictory. On the whole, however, I cannot imagine just staying home and writing books. I want to do something concrete right now.

Over time one of the difficulties in my life has been coordinating my marriage and my public life as a writer and as an activist. Public opinion also holds you to a high standard. You have to be perfect: a perfect wife, mother, and worker. When I traveled, people said that perhaps I wasn't a good wife and mother. When I wrote, people said perhaps I wasn't a good wife and mother. I have always felt the burden of public opinion very strongly. I have not been allowed even a small deviation and sometimes I think I would like to be anonymous because then I would be freer.

The Source of Her Strength

Albanian women are strong in general. I am not special. Other women have suffered much more and had greater problems in their lives than I.

To the extent that I have had to overcome difficulties and challenges in my life, my strength has come from my family. The women never lamented or complained of anything. They never asked for help from the men. I particularly remember my grandmother's story of when my grandfather left her for the last time to return to America in 1938. She told me, "As the ship my husband was leaving on pulled away from the shore, I looked down at the four children at my feet and the baby in my arms. My desperation was such that I wished the ship to go down and drown my husband." My grandmother went on living with her paralyzed mother-in-law and also caring for her own five children. Despite the difficulty of her life, she remained big-hearted and was always helping others. She did not become hard, but she did nurse the bitterness of the injustice of men against women. This bitterness was always there.

My mother was also an example to me. She was a woman of total sacrifice. The mother looks at the daughter as a projection of herself. There is, therefore, no conflict between the life of sacrifice and attachment.

The Role of Faith

Faith has played no role in my life. Although my family was Orthodox originally, I was raised as an atheist and I think people adapt to the environment in which they are raised. Although I have read religious books as human philosophy to understand what religion was, I am still not a believer.*

Summary

Diana's sensitivity to the problems of the women in her generation comes from her writer's eye for perception, and now she is doing something with that knowledge. Throughout her life she has seen and felt much that has spoken to her of the difficulty of the lives of the women. Now it is her determination and commitment that lead her to want to do something to improve the lives of the women.

*Diana's views on religion in Albania are included in chapter 22.

Chapter 14

Kozeta Mamaqi: The "Sins of the Father," the Life of the Child

Kozeta's story is one of reversal of fortune. It particularly illustrates what happened to those whose families supported the ideals of communism and then the regime of Enver Hoxha. After eliminating some of the brightest and most charismatic of the early supporters of communism, Hoxha gave others high positions in the government. As time went by, however, it was impossible for these people to prove sufficient loyalty because Hoxha perceived them to be a threat to him and his power. Therefore, with or without reason, he destroyed them—and with them their families.

I met Kozeta through a mutual friend early in this project. Kozeta is now a radio programmer with the state radio station (Radio Televizioni Shqiptar) and she was recommended to me as an articulate and kind woman with a story of hardship that was unrelated to her own activities.

On December 9, 1995, we went to interview her at her new apartment at the Seismic Center development in Tiranë. The land around the apartment buildings was muddy and litter strewn, and the roads approaching her building were unpaved and badly rutted. Not only was there much trash in the streets, but during one of our visits someone spent about 45 minutes breaking glass bottles against the wall of a building that had been started and abandoned. The apartment itself (two bedrooms and living room–kitchen) was spacious, but she reported that the plaster was already falling off the walls. She was also concerned because she had not yet taken title to the unit and did not want to lose her right to remain there. Her grown son lives in the apartment with her.

Childhood

My family is from Përmet, a well-known town in the southern part of Albania. My father's family was patriotic and he learned his love of the country from

Kozeta Mamaqi.

them. My grandfather, my father's father, died young at the age of 37. Although he did not attend university, he published five books of verses: his own and traditional verses he collected from others around the country. My grandfather was a patriot and proved his love of the country by traveling all around Albania as an actor and writer. He worked only for the love of the country. The money for the publication of his books came from well-known and wealthy people who made donations so that the books could be published. They recognized the value of preserving traditional Albanian folk stories and verses and I am proud of my grandfather's contribution to the country.

My father, Dashnor Mamaqi, graduated from secondary school at the time of the National Liberation War. He was also a patriot and took up arms as a partisan. His title was commissar of the battalion of Përmet.

My mother's family was closely allied with the Zog regime as my grandmother was one of four sisters, two of whom had married men who served in that government. My mother broke with her family's political orientation and fled to get away from an arranged marriage to a rich man they had chosen for her. You see, she had already met and fallen in love with my father. She and her sister joined the fight for Liberation because of their belief in the emancipation of women, and they were supported in their beliefs by their mother. After the war, my grandmother waged her own fight to help advance the cause of emancipation by going from village to village talking and working with women.

My father and mother fought together near the Yugoslav border and were engaged. After the war they married in Kukës where my father was sent to work.

In 1946 I was born, the first child in the family. While I was still an infant, my father was transferred to Tiranë. There he held the first of many important party functions: vice minister of education and culture, instructor at the Institution of the Central Committee of the Party of Labor of Albania (PLA), first party secretary of Durrës, first party secretary of Gjirokastër, candidate of the Central Committee—later a member of the Central Committee—and deputy of the Assembly. Also, between 1952 and 1959, he attended the High Party School in Moscow. My father was a member of the Central Committee until the end.

My father's position meant that we had a good standard of living and I remember being very close to him. I remember so many things from my childhood. He took me to many places with him after work—to football games, the dedication of monuments, plays—everywhere. My father spent a great deal of time with me, though he had little free time because he traveled a lot. He provided me with a love for literature and art and taught me Russian. I admired my father greatly. He created such a wonderful atmosphere in the family that we were happy whenever he was with us. My father was proud of me and my good school grades. He was naturally affectionate with everyone in the family and greatly respected my grandmother, who lived with us.

I remember my father as a correct person. One time at a ceremony outside of Gjirokastër some villagers invited me to eat some fruit from the plum trees. My father was very angry that I had eaten the fruit because he said that it belonged to the cooperative of the area, and he paid for the fruit I had eaten. Later, when all the families of the senior party officials had the opportunity to choose good furniture that had been confiscated from rich people, my mother took some armchairs for our home. Father asked where they had come from and made her return them.

It is a testimony to how highly regarded my father was that on his fiftieth birthday (February 1, 1973) many people came to pay their respects, including Enver Hoxha, who praised my father with many superlatives. He told us that we children should be very proud of our father.

My mother was at one time the vice director of the Artistic Lyceum. Before that she had worked in nurseries and personnel positions. During my childhood I remember her as loving and hospitable. Our home was always referred to as the "big house" because our friends were always welcomed there, even when we weren't home. My mother has always smiled, even when she has had very little to offer. She attended a two-year school to be a nurse and now helps the former political prisoners in Durrës. They call her "Nënë Tereza" (Mother Teresa).

Although I always loved and respected my mother, I was always much closer to my grandmother, my father's mother. She sacrificed for me much more than my own mother did. For example, since we had no alarm clock, my grandmother would wake me up early in the morning when I had exams so I could study. She also brought me food when I was studying. Although my grandmother had no education, she was very intelligent and extremely optimistic.

My childhood was quite happy and I loved to be with my friends. My parents never restricted my activities. In fact, I felt quite free. Although I wanted to become a doctor, my father persuaded me to become a journalist. So I did my university studies in Albanian language and literature and studied journalism for two years.

In secondary school, the most handsome boy fell in love with me. I told my parents and then they explained to me that he had a bad biography. He was from a rich family and was being watched carefully by the Sigurimi. The story ended there. However, when I was in the university, my father was first party secretary in Durrës. My mother and Mrs. Balluku* knew a certain young man and spoke to me on his behalf. At first I said, "No." Later when I came home from school, I found him waiting for me at the train station with my sister. I was angry because I had already stated my position and yet there he was. He cried and I had pity on

*The wife of Beqir Balluku, member of the Politburo of the Central Committee of the Party of Labor of Albania and defense minister.

him. I felt that in fact he loved me so I said "Yes." Later, I was crying about it and my father told me that the important thing was that I should be happy and that I didn't have to marry him if I didn't want to. My decision was the most important, not what others wanted for me.

When I graduated from school, I was assigned to work at the radio-television station in Tiranë while my fiancé, the head of Radio location (the military radio command center) for the navy, lived in Durrës. In August his family invited me to go on holiday with them and I didn't want to accept at first because this would not be considered correct. Finally, I decided to go and to consider myself married from that moment. After the vacation I moved into my mother-in-law's house. She did not want me to travel to and from Tiranë to work, so I quit my job. Then I had a hard time finding work in Durrës. For example, I could not work at the newspaper *Adriatik* because I was not a member of the party.

My husband and I were officially married in 1967. We had no wedding ceremony and I wore only a very cheap white suit. One reason that I did not have a real wedding was that I had lived with my husband after the vacation with his family. Another reason is that it was the style to have a simple wedding, especially since it occurred after the abolition of religion in the same year.

Later, I was offered a job at *Adriatik* if I would join the party and I took a job as a journalist. I worked very hard at my jobs: part time at the newspaper and, later, part time as a worker in the TV manufacturing plant in Durrës as well. For three years I worked as a party member candidate and three more years as a party member at *Adriatik*. Also, I had my first child during this time—one and a half years after I was married.

In general, my husband's family was a good family. My husband was a bit more dependent on his family than his peers were on theirs. He was also used to living a different kind of life—a life among men—since he had always been in the military. Although he graduated in the Soviet Union where society was more civilized, he did not approve of my participation in different activities. For example, he didn't express his appreciation of me or my work. In this period, however, I published a small book of short stories and sketches, *Studentja e Konservatorit* (*The Student of the Conservatory*).

In time, my husband was transferred to Tiranë to work in the ministry of defense and I began working for the magazine *Ylli*.* I was responsible for the problems of education and culture. I wanted to work at this magazine for both political and artistic reasons and the people who worked there all had good reputations. It was an excellent experience for me because I loved my work there and I began to feel successful. I also began work on my second book.

Crisis: "He Ate All His Friends"†

However, my happiness in my job lasted only one year before the difficulties began. I had just been told that I would be promoted to artistic editor, but everything took a bad turn because on my son's second birthday, on December 17, 1974, my

A politico-social and literary-artistic magazine.
†*The expression used by Kozeta here is reminiscent of a phrase used among the people whenever the class struggle became sharper as Enver Hoxha sought out new groups of enemies (often his closest associates): "The bitch who eats her puppies"* (Bushtra qe ha kelushet e saj).

father was expelled from the party. We were gathered for a celebration with my family when my sister came in and told us. My husband's family was there at the time and they never came to our home again after that.

In 1973 my father had been asked to work as second party secretary in Tiranë. It was the time when the PLA began the task of fighting against bourgeois (revisionist) ideas in art and culture and against the liberal attitudes toward these. He was considered to be the right person for this fight. The plan was to take action against those who manifested revisionist ideas in ideology and art, the so-called liberals. Paradoxically, when my father was sentenced, he was accused of being one of those he had fought against.

Hoxha's praise of my father at his fiftieth birthday celebration is a particularly bitter memory, since this was a time when Hoxha had "discovered" a new group of enemies headed by Beqir Balluku. Balluku had saved Hoxha's life during the war and later served in various senior government positions, including minister of defense, vice prime minister and member of the Politburo. My father and Balluku had been close friends and visited in each other's homes, so my father was called upon to explain the nature of his friendship. He was expected to confess that it had been bad that he had been so friendly with such a man. Later, however, Hoxha asked my father directly why he had not discovered that Balluku was a traitor earlier than everyone else since they were such good friends. My father replied "He was closer to you. It should have been you who discovered this. Why do you ask me?" At the moment Hoxha heard this reply, he accused my father of being a provocateur, a traitor, and an enemy.

The magazine I worked for didn't know what to do with me when my father was expelled from the party. Finally, they sent me for a month of physical labor, even though it would not normally have been the time for me to go. This was a regularly scheduled event for intellectuals and others. The timing was just changed in my case to give them the opportunity to think about my situation. I felt isolated, even among the people I was working with, and worked harder than ever because I didn't know what else to do.

I went through the four stages of punishment. In early 1975 I was finally expelled from the party because I was my father's favorite daughter and was accused of not being sincere with the party. They thought I was not sufficiently vigilant to understand the antiparty and antistate ideas of my father. I was also fired from my work and was unemployed, so I went around seeking help from one office to another, but nothing happened.

Also, in March 1975 I was officially divorced. My husband came to me with tears in his eyes, saying that his family had decided that he should divorce me to protect his family, including his uncle who was on the Central Committee. They had forced him to sign the document for our divorce.

I had nothing to live on so I sold empty bottles for bread. My son was ill so he went to my husband's family because I couldn't care for him. Then, I was sent to work at a brick and tile factory. However, out of pity for me (that is, not wanting to see me doing the backbreaking work there), the director told me that he had no work for me. I was unemployed for some time, but then I was sent to work at a vocational school for some months, typing and preparing textbooks for the pupils of this school. At this time, I was the only one of my family still living in Tiranë. My parents were originally sent to Burrel and then to Selenicë, whereas one of my sisters was sent to Tepelenë.

I remember being very angry: first at the government because I saw no wrong that my father had done and then at my husband because he had a responsibility to me and our sons. I blame him for protecting his family and not staying with our family. My husband continued to visit me secretly, but we always quarreled.

On October 15, 1975, I was sent to exile in Selenicë in the province of Vlorë. I didn't know why I was being sent there and couldn't believe my ears when I heard the news. There were eight people on guard around my house and I was afraid I would be arrested. The night before I left, I wrote in my diary: "I am writing for the last time in Tiranë. I leave for exile tomorrow. Oh Gods, whom have I wronged? Why is all this happening to me? No one can explain. The two little boys are sleeping on the sofa not covered by a blanket, but by the sofa cover. Vangjel* didn't even come to see the children. Sokol keeps asking for his father. I feel so sorry for the children."

The next day I left for five years of exile with three Sigurimi and one armed policeman accompanying us. My son said, "My father is bad." When I asked him why he said, "Because he didn't come with us."

The Period of Exile

Selenicë was a small village with a few houses and two apartment buildings near the mines. The men all worked in the mines and the women worked in the fields. Since by this time my father had been sent to prison and the rest of my family had been sent to Selenicë, I lived in my mother's house there. My father had been sent to prison to live, as he described it later, "in a coffin" for two years. During this time he was interrogated and his weight dropped from 89 to 40 kilos. Our family had no idea where he was. Finally, my father was sentenced to 15 years imprisonment. However, he suffered 9 years in total: 3 years of interrogation and then 6 years in prison, first in Ballsh, where we went to meet him on foot from Selenicë, and then in Lezhë, where he died in 1984. We never knew the cause of his death.

On October 28 of this same year the problem of the children was sent to court for the first time. My husband won custody and it was decided that I had to pay 700 old lekë [about 70 cents] for the older child and 500 old lekë (about 50 cents) for the younger child monthly to my husband. This was at a time when my total monthly salary was only 3,000 old lekë [about $3]. Then on November 10 a second court hearing, the appeal, was held regarding the custody of the children. It was again decided that the children would go to their father. When this court in Vlorë gave its decision, I fainted and fell down the stairs. It was a very difficult moment because none of the other women who were in the same position as I had their children taken away from them. I was a special case, I don't know why. I wasn't even allowed to keep one because of "political and moral reasons." They didn't expect me to educate them and bring them up correctly because my family was an "enemy family."

It was a terrible day for me. Then they came to execute the order. My eldest son was eight years of age at the time and my little one was three. The children

*Their father.

were with me in the house when the police came to take them. I didn't find the strength to go out of the house and accompany the children to the car: a taxi that the family of my husband had sent to take the children. My brother and sister took the two children out and described the scene to me later. All of Selenicë was gathered in the square shedding tears because it was a very dramatic situation. The children refused to go into the taxi and the police forced them in. They were crying "We want to stay with Mommy!" For more than a week I couldn't go out of the house and didn't even go to work. I couldn't do anything, I couldn't even sleep.

I was given the right to see the children three times a year, but only for one hour and in the presence of the people responsible for the district where my children lived. From time to time I called from the Post Office to the Post Office in Durrës to speak to my children, but they never came to the telephone. They weren't allowed to talk to me. Even as I tell this I experience again the bitter taste of that moment when my children didn't come to talk to me. I also sent greetings to them at the kindergarten on their birthdays, but they were always returned to me unopened. My meetings with the children depended much on the current state of the "class struggle." When it was most severe, I had difficulty in meeting them. In the periods when it was not so severe, I could meet the children more easily and I felt better.

When they took my children, I kept asking myself if life was still worth living. I could not see anything beautiful. Two or three times I came to the decision that life was not worth living, but the difficult work kept me going. Also, I loved beautiful things, and I looked for them everywhere. If I tell you now, you may wonder if I am quite alright, but it made me so happy to see the first spring flowers. I always looked for something to ease the pain in my spirit.

On May 27 of the following year I went back to Durrës for the first time. I don't know by whom or why the order was given, but I was told that I was to go back to Durrës to live with my husband and children. It seemed impossible, but I went anyway. When I got to Durrës, I found that no one knew about the order and learned that my youngest son had been hospitalized to have his tonsils removed. My husband's family would not let me see my older son and I was refused admission to the hospital to see my younger son. However, a kind man, a surgeon at the hospital, allowed me to go and stay with my son and I spent a night with him there.

The year 1977 was significant because in this year my grandmother (my father's mother) died. She was buried with only the immediate family present and her body was carried by a handcart. My brother and I dug the grave ourselves. We had no idea how big and deep to dig it. As we were digging, a shepherd saw us crying, not knowing what to do, and carrying the coffin. I remember his kindness well. He stopped and helped us. He also helped us lower the coffin into the grave with some rope.

One of the most vivid and saddest recollections I have of the period of my exile is of an incident that occurred one year when my sons were able to visit me during their summer holiday. A mother dog, Fiora by name, used to come to our family because we fed her. When my boys were visiting, they played with and fed one of the puppies. That puppy became everything to my son Sokol. One day the nephew of the chief person in the municipal government, a boy of 12, poured gasoline on the puppy and burned him, calling the puppy "the dog of the enemy." My son's pain and sorrow stayed with him and led him later to write a poem about the dog.

The Beginning of the End

Although my punishment was for only five years and I was no longer officially in exile after that, I was not granted permission to move. However, on the December 26, 1986, I moved to Shijak, a very small town 11 kilometers from Durrës. I had been asking during the entire time I was in Selenicë to be moved because I wanted to be closer to my children. I was originally petitioning to Mehmet Shehu and was in his office to look into the status of my petition on the day he "committed suicide."* I had wanted to be moved to this town because it was close to Durrës, but I was not given permission to go into Durrës because it was a first-category city. Here, in Shijak, I shared an apartment with another family and had only one room in the flat. However, my eldest son, who was working at the time, came and slept in my room every night until he joined the army. My younger son was still in the eighth grade and continued to live with his father and stepmother.

I stayed in Shijak and worked in a tailor's shop ironing 120 men's shirts a day. Later, in 1990, I was given a job teaching literature in a grade school in the village of Luz i Vogel, about two and a half hours away by bus. I left my home at 5:00 A.M. and returned at 5:00 P.M..

As soon as my younger son, Sokol, received his degree, he became the head of the Democratic Youth movement in Durrës. One day as I was returning on the bus from teaching, I heard shots and was told that some leaders in the Democratic Youth movement had been shot. My son was afraid that I would be given this news and I found him waiting for me. He said simply "I am alive." Then he gave me a note from my elder son. "Dearest Mother, please forgive me thousands of times. Ardi." My elder son had boarded a ship with his uncle (my brother) and many others to go to Italy. Sokol and I ran to the harbor, but we were too late. We met my ex-husband there because he too was worried about the boys. We knew that the ship was not in good condition for the trip and we were worried when we saw them on top, but the ship had already pulled out. It was one of the last boats out.

In March 1991 I stopped working as a teacher along with the other teachers, because in protest the people had cut down the trees from Durrës to Kavajë (the route to the village). It was impossible to get through and school was closed until the end of the school year. Later, I was told that I could go back to Tiranë. I went back thinking that I would work again at *Ylli*, but it had closed. So, I went to work at the radio-television station. I spent 2 years living at the Shkolla Partisë (the Party School) dormitory where 37 families shared one bathroom. It was entirely occupied by exiled and persecuted people.

Mehmet Shehu served as coordinator of the partisans' guerrilla activities during the War of Liberation and was the highest party official after Enver Hoxha. He and Hoxha together formed the Communist Party's policies and directed their implementation for almost 40 years from 1944 through 1981. His death on December 19, 1981, was officially reported as a suicide following the progression of a nervous disorder. However, it is widely believed that this suicide was actually another of Hoxha's purges and that Shehu was killed on Hoxha's command. Some of the many theories proposed as to why he was killed include that he posed an imagined or real threat to Hoxha's power, he disagreed with Hoxha regarding the isolationist policies, or his loyalty to the regime was now suspect because his daughter married a man with a questionable biography.

The Source of Her Strength

Although I was pessimistic about my personal future, I tried to find strength in myself just because of my love for my children. I did as much as I could for my children when they were with me. For example, I often read them stories about families and relationships. One particular story by Victor Hugo was about an orphan taken care of by his grandfather. The grandfather died and the boy couldn't understand what had happened. One day he was found frozen by the grave of his grandfather. My children shed tears over this story. It touched them very much. I wished for a day when they, having been brought up in a family with a good biography, would be able to say that they have a mother living in Selenicë and it is our right to be with her. It seemed to me that this day was far away. I never thought that it was so close. In retrospect, I still wonder if the Berlin Wall had not been pulled down and all the changes in Eastern Europe had not taken place, would anything have happened in Albania? All of these changes quickened the pace of change in our country beyond what we could have expected.

I felt that life had been unjust to me and I felt the heavy burden of the existence I was leading. I didn't know before that such things existed: that there was a group responsible for sending people away. It started especially after 1974. I had to accept everything as it was given—as it was told to us. I couldn't understand because my father was with them "in the same pot." Such things as the imprisonment and exile of others were discussed in the family as my father understood them. If I couldn't learn about these things in my family, I could find them nowhere.* I asked a friend and she told me that she knew about them, but had never said anything for fear of reprisal. Was I a hypocrite?

When my grandmother lived with us in exile she always said, "Don't pay much attention to the house. We will go back to Tiranë." Very few people in exile were optimistic: only two, my grandmother and an old intellectual. When the intellectual said optimistic things, we all said "she's crazy," and when my grandmother said optimistic things, we all said "she's an old lady." We dismissed their optimism. I now have respect for my grandmother's optimism and have learned other important things from her as well. She was a model of a stoic woman; and she deprived herself of everything personal and dedicated herself entirely to her son and all her family; and she was always with us and had more strength than any other woman. Her optimism was based on her faith that her son (my father) was guiltless: that he had served his country and the government well and blamelessly, only to be "eaten" by Hoxha.

I also learned from my mother. She fought with my father for the liberation of the country and for a society that would live up to her ideals, even though this turned out to be an unattainable utopia. My father and mother were an excellent couple. There was harmony in the family and it left good impressions on me. As I was growing up I was surrounded by good examples and models. My father was intelligent, tolerant, and loving. My mother was a good wife and mother.

Although I have lived through very difficult moments, I still consider myself to be a strong person. I am also sensitive and I shed tears easily; for example, in

---

*Kozeta's mother was present at the final interview and added the following: "We educated our children badly. We never judged. When I doubted, I blamed or questioned myself."

touching scenes in movies. People embody contrasting feelings and I have feelings of all kinds. I have always struggled and will always struggle for something I consider right, and I will always fight against those things I consider wrong.

I also had a strong desire to make one dream come true: to raise two good citizens, good people. I have realized this dream. In all my meetings with my sons I kept this in mind. They are two young men with no vices and I take much pride in them. They love to work, and work hard. They are honest and know the difference between good and bad. I am also happy that they respect each other's differences. My eldest boy is very religious and my younger boy is an atheist, but is interested in politics. They respect each other and try to accommodate each other. They are spiritually connected even though each has found his own way in life.

I was also lucky throughout my exile to have had good friends among other exiles and the villagers. One old man was extremely poor. He worked hard all day long and lived on a cup of yoghurt, water, and a piece of bread a day. He always wanted to do something good for me because he knew how much I suffered. Once he gave me a flower, although he had never given a flower to a woman before. Another old man saw me reading a book during the lunch break and asked me to read something to him. These people encouraged me to overcome my problems. They listened to me and that helped to ease my problems.

The Role of Faith

My family was Muslim by origin, but my grandmother was an atheist so my father was also. Therefore, I was raised as an atheist. I have always been superstitious, but now I believe. Maria, an Italian woman whose Albanian husband had died, lived in Shijak. She was a great inspiration to me and helped me to develop my faith. I believe that there is one God for all people.

I had no optimism that this day of freedom and democracy would come. I thought the dictatorship was the worst and that this day (the day it was overthrown) would not come. I prayed to God when I found no strength in myself.

Summary

Sadly, Kozeta's story is not that rare. Many people suffered for their family names or the actual or fabricated misdeeds of their family members. Whatever her father's role in the regime was and however one feels about that role, can such consequences and their impact on the life of the daughter be belittled or ignored?

Kozeta's face sometimes shows the tiredness and anguish of someone who has worked hard and suffered. Sometimes there is an edge in her voice that comes from the continued anxieties of life. However, when she speaks of her children, her face is soft and beautiful, her voice is loving. Also, when she speaks of her faith—as she did walking down the street with me one day—she smiles with her whole face and says "I believe. I believe completely."

Chapter 15

Liri Kopaçi:
Born and Bred to Succeed

Liri is a bright star, a success story. From a small village and a poor family, Liri has succeeded largely due to her own intelligence and drive. Despite her humble background, this 31-year-old woman now represents what is typical in the younger urban women of this generation: those who have made the most of what they were offered and pushed to achieve even more. She has flaunted many of the social strictures and ignored the voices that said that she was striving for the impossible. Liri is strong and determined.

For all that she is driven to succeed, Liri is also warm, kind, and full of fun. She respects her family and has repaid them for the sacrifices they have made for her.*

Childhood

I was born in 1965 in a tiny village that no one has heard of, the village of Qukës-Skenderbej, which is a half-hour drive from the city of Librazhd. I was the fourth child born to my family, but two died, a boy at the age of three and a girl at one month of age. Later, my parents had two more children, making us a family of four girls.

For all that my father came from a family that had a good reputation and his brothers held good positions, my family was very poor. My mother was from the nearby village of Fanj and came from a family that was economically better off than my father's because my grandfather—her father—had a great many sheep. My grandparents on both sides were old friends and arranged for their children to marry each other. When they were married, my parents had seen each other before, but had never spoken to each other until their marriage.

In fact, my parents still don't communicate much with each other, but have, instead, concentrated on my sisters and me. My mother has a very strong personality, while my father is softer, which is strange to me because his brothers have

This interview was conducted entirely in English.

197

Liri Kpoaçi

always been forceful decisionmakers. Anyway, my mother has never compromised or obeyed much.

I admire my mother's strong personality in comparison to my aunts, who are quieter. My mother is extremely hardworking and strong. That's what has helped her get through life. I would like to be like her, to be as hardworking as she is, but I don't think I will ever attain this. If it had been a different time and if she had received an education, she would have made an excellent professional woman. I also admire the fact that my mother could make something useful out of nothing. The expression we use in Albania is that she has "golden hands." Mother did all the knitting, weaving, sewing, and cooking, including the cheese and curd. She taught us to do hand work, but I never seem to have time anymore. Only occasionally do I do this when I want to make something to thank someone.

I also remember that my mother was unforgiving, especially with us children. She would punish us by giving us ten times more housework. She never praised us or bragged about us to the neighbors. In fact, she always complained and denigrated us. It is not that she wasn't kind, but rather that she just had so much work and needed for us to behave. Also, our parents did not take much care of us because they worked so hard. My mother worked in agriculture, on the cooperative in the area, and my father worked in Librazhd in a low level position in the army. Many times my mother would take us to the field with a cradle when she was working close to home. Other times we would stay with our grandparents or with some of the many relatives we had in the village.

Most of my good memories from childhood relate to the time I spent in the village. I remember so well the day we moved to Librazhd when I was five. My family often talks about my first day of school there. I didn't want to go; I just wanted to go back to the village. While everyone else was smiling, I was crying. Eventually, they gave up and so I missed a year of school.

At first my parents thought that I would never learn anything in school because I wrote my numbers upside down. Soon, however, I began to get good grades and after that my parents just expected me to continue to do well, in spite of the hard work I was expected to do at home: housework and caring for my little sister. My mother expected me to do well without studying much because she thought it was a waste of time and besides we had so much other work to do.

I was fortunate that I still had an opportunity to spend time in the village during the summers. I used to go there and, from the time I was seven or eight years old, I would work with the other children in agriculture. We woke every morning at 4:00 A.M. to collect tobacco leaves and then strung them up all day. I wasn't told to do this, but all the children did it to earn extra money for their families, so I did what my cousins and the other village children did.

School Days in Tiranë

At the age of 15 I moved to Tiranë because I was accepted into the high school for foreign languages. At the end of elementary school I had the choice of quitting, going on to the local high school or applying for a professional high school in Tiranë. My parents—really my father—decided on the latter. It was a privilege to attend this school, but at the time I wasn't enthusiastic. You see, I was playing volleyball for the city of Librazhd with a team of adults and I thought that my future was in sports. I enjoyed traveling and playing volleyball with 19- and 20-year-olds. I was never a timid child, but I think that playing on the team helped me grow up faster and learn about life more quickly than I would have otherwise. I got used to seeing places that other children of my age didn't get to see and I spent a lot of time away from my family. I had a great deal of freedom and my parents didn't discourage me in this activity. In fact, my mother encouraged it and I never experienced any negative social opinion of this activity while I was in Librazhd.

However, my father thought differently about my future than I did. I was one of two people chosen to attend out of eight or ten applicants and so I went to the foreign language school.

My first encounter with Tiranë was tough. I never showed that I was scared, but I felt discriminated against here. People would look down on me and forget me immediately. I felt from the first day that for them I didn't exist. I knew I was from a good family and I remembered the strength and reputation of my family. The only way I could handle the situation was to say to myself that their opinion didn't count and I ignored them. Fortunately, there was a teacher who had taught in Librazhd whom I got to know. She wasn't my teacher at first, but she cared for me and was a great support. The situation changed over the years, but it took a strong person. If you were not strong, you would crumble. I say it changed, but it changed mostly in theory. In social situations you could always tell the girls who lived in the dormitories. We lived with 12 girls in a small room and had no shower or hot water in the building. As a result, we couldn't take proper care of ourselves and we were poorly fed and dressed.

It was also while I was at this school that I first encountered a negative opinion about my sports activities and had to give up volleyball. The headmistress even came to see me in my room to convince me to do so. However, my friends and I still had fun. We were always daring ones and we would sneak out to have a coffee in a café or see a film.

When I graduated from high school, I went on to study English at the university in Tiranë. I remember that by the third or fourth year of university it was fashionable for girls to become engaged and marry, especially those girls from outside of the capital city. They wanted to marry someone with education and stay in Tiranë. We got to know the boys in our classes, but once they went on a date with one of them they were expected to get married. You were a "bad girl" if you didn't do that. The result was that you had to marry the first man you met. People were already very prejudiced against those of us who lived in the dorms. We had a bad reputation just for that. I saw so many bad marriages that came out of this and there was no way out for the women. If a relationship broke up, it was always blamed on the woman.

My reaction to this situation was to say, "No! I don't want a boyfriend." I was happy for this decision because I was free. My friends who had boyfriends or lovers had to get their permission to go anywhere. For me, my friends were enough compensation.

Back Home

However, after university I had to go back to Librazhd and was there for four years. I was better off materially than I had been before I went to high school in Tiranë, but was worse off morally and socially. What I mean by that is that Tiranë wasn't the best place for me, but it offered some sort of entertainment and culture, while Librazhd, a city with a population of only 6–7,000, had nothing. I coped better than my friends, one of whom referred to Librazhd as the big hole. At least I didn't get depressed. It's true that I had a lot of family there, but I had changed a lot. I became bored with the same conversation every night and hearing much criticism because my mother and father thought I was lazy. They said this, even though I got up every morning at 5:00 A.M. and took a bus for 45 minutes and then walked 30 minutes to get to the school where I taught by 7:30.

After teaching for some time, I began working at the local Youth Committee. My job was to deal with the administrative issues in the secondary schools, organize academic competitions, and follow up on problems. The one aspect of this job that I loved was working with the children. I met many talented young people with whom I still keep in touch. On the whole, however, I hated this job because I worked for an ignorant woman and because I had to conform to the party's policies. In addition, it was a time when the party was changing and was eager to increase the number of promising young professionals in its membership, and so the local party members put increasing pressure on me to join. Other members of my family were already members of the party and I didn't see why I too should join, so I refused. I knew that I could suffer the consequences of this refusal, but my uncle, who was influential, got them to accept it. However, I left this position and found another teaching job in a different village. The last village I taught in was two hours away by foot, uphill going and downhill coming back, and, naturally, I didn't get paid when I didn't go.

At the end of 1991 there was chaos in Albania as the political system collapsed. There was so much destruction and frustration in the country that it made me pessimistic. It was painful for me and I was scared about my life and myself. I was going down, down, down. I was in Librazhd and I was panicking. My parents were terrified and became more conservative. I began to believe that all that was left was for me to get married and stay in Librazhd.

However, I found a reason to go back to Tiranë, at least for a couple of days. I didn't have my diploma yet and I was required to show it to my boss. Getting it from the university became my excuse. While I was in Tiranë, I went to see my friend who worked for Swissair at the Dajti Hotel. There I met a family friend who asked me what I was doing. I confided in him and I remember saying desperately, "It can't get any worse. I see no escape." He told me that there were some foreigners who were starting a project, the Small and Medium Enterprise Development Program (SME), and suggested that I go for an interview. I was reluctant, but he insisted. I went to the ministry of finance and was the twenty-fourth person to be interviewed for the job. In fact, they had already completed the interviewing process and had made their choice. However, I told them that I had never had an interview before and asked them if they would interview me anyway so that I could see what it was like. They agreed and when we were through, they asked me to wait outside in the corridor. When they came out of their office, they offered me a part-time job doing interpreting, with a promise that I would have a full-time position as soon as one was available. I refused because I didn't want to commute from Librazhd.

After that, I went back to Librazhd and there I met an Albanian man who wanted me to work for his company in Tiranë. I agreed as long as he would open his office where I told him to: next door to the SME program. That way I could do both jobs.

Leaving Home

I simply said to my father, "I'm leaving." Although my father refused to accept the fact that I was going to leave home and go to Tiranë to work because I had always been a well-behaved daughter, I told him that I was determined to go. He thought I was crazy and irresponsible and he was very angry with me. Although I had spent a great deal of time away from him, he still didn't like to lose control, even though I was 27 years of age at this time. I now understand that it was hard for my father because I was the first to leave home. My uncle also reacted negatively and put a great deal of pressure on him. It was the way they had all been brought up. As you know, it was very unusual for young Albanian girls to leave their parents' home unless they were getting married.

My mother, on the other hand, was very supportive and encouraged me. She told me to go and helped me to get in touch with cousins with whom I could stay. I actually ended up staying with my cousin's mother-in-law who was in her eighties. I did the shopping and carried water up to the apartment and she did the cooking. It worked out well, but she worried about me. We had no electricity and no water in the flat. Often we heard gunfire on the street. No one was on the street when I returned from work alone at 8:00 P.M., and I too was afraid because I could hear the guns then. It was times like these that I remembered the safety and quiet of Librazhd, but I remembered too that there was nothing there for me. The women just gossip about each other and I didn't want that.

Everything has worked out well and I have been successful in my work. After a short time as a part-time translator with the SME project, I became the assistant to the credit manager for procurement. My job was to work with Albanian clients to determine their needs and then find equipment that would meet those needs through an agency in England. This was an activity that had never before been practiced in Albania and so I had my first opportunity to travel outside of the country for a week of procurement training in England. This job and the travel experience opened a whole new world for me. I learned more about what I wanted to do in the future; it helped me to begin forming my goals. I also knew from this experience that I would have to learn more skills in order to be successful and to attain my new career objectives. For that reason, I was driven to apply for other positions that would expand my knowledge and give me an opportunity to further my career.

The Fast Track

My next job was as the personal assistant and interpreter to the team leader of the European Committee Phare Program agricultural project in the ministry of agriculture. There I worked long hours and performed a great variety of duties, including interpreting for high-level people and, later, managing the office. I left this job for twice the salary and half the work. Actually, I found that I was bored in my new position, but it gave me more skills, including working in a bank and doing public relations. Fortunately, I had an opportunity to leave after only six months, because I was accepted for a six-month training program designed to prepare the future leaders at the European Commission (EC) in Brussels.

The program in Brussels turned out to be another turning point in my career. The work I did in visual media and communications taught me much about the activities of the EC and I learned more new skills. I also had an opportunity to meet people who were supportive and encouraged me.

Just before I completed the training program, I learned that I was accepted to Surrey University in England for a master's program in tourism. I was lucky to have this opportunity to spend 15 months in England studying. However, when I came back to Albania I had nothing to do and found that my goals were unclear. By this time I had done many things and had many ideas, but not a great deal of focus. I started working on a freelance basis with an Austrian firm on a tourism project. Then I discovered the Albanian-American Enterprise Fund. I had an interview and was hired on the spot. I started working there on the January 15, 1996, and learned just two weeks later that I was accepted for a research fellowship in England. This time I asked to defer the fellowship for a year so that I could get the experience I felt I needed at the fund.

I am leaving at the end of this month to go to England on an internship program and am on the waiting list for an administrative position in the environmental and tourism division of the Council of Europe in Strasbourg. I think it would be quite a challenging and competitive environment to work with the Council of Europe. Truthfully, this intimidates me just a bit, but also makes me very excited. I think it would be good for my future.

I don't really know what my future will hold, but I know that I want a career and am not willing to sacrifice that career totally for a family. I want a husband and children, but later. Then I will be able to make some compromises.

For right now, I am happy with my life. I have bought a house in Tiranë and have moved my family to be with me. At first, I was thinking only of my sisters. I knew there was nothing for them in Librazhd and that they would have more opportunity here. Then I thought of my mother. I knew that her mind was never at rest. Plus, it was time for my parents to get something back; they have been giving and giving all their lives.

I have been successful in my work and have also become more tolerant. I understand now that when I was small my mother was hard on us because she wanted us to have the opportunities that she never had. She wanted the best for us. Now that we have grown up, she is softer.

The Source of Her Strength

It is my personality, my character, to be strong. I take after my mother in that respect. Nothing can scare me. I have done hard work all my life, so I am not afraid. I have always believed that I could be successful and I have never had anything to lose. I would describe myself as pushy and determined. Also, I have always had hope.

I was never given things and have always had to do things for myself. I had no one I could rely on except my father and I didn't want what he had to offer. Then, I couldn't risk relying on a husband. I am very independent.

For all that, I have been lucky, especially during the time I was abroad. For example, when I was in Brussels, I had an excellent landlord, Jorgen Henningsen, who gave me an apartment to live in. He has been very influential in my life as I found him and his circle of friends—all of different nationalities—to be very supportive of me. They trusted me and believed in me. They reassured me that I was as good as they were, even though I grew up in Albania and had not had the advantages—educational and others—that they had had. I found strength in their encouragement.

The Role of Faith

I grew up in an almost totally nonreligious family. My grandmother observed the Muslim tenets strictly and my mother used to, but learned not to. My father told her that we girls would pick it up if we want to. My mother still believes in God, but doesn't practice. I don't believe in God and the Muslim rituals don't attract me. I like the services in the Christian churches, but I am basically indifferent. I have read a great deal and am simply tolerant.

Liri and the Future

Although Liri has been identified, somewhat arbitrarily (based on her age) as part of the middle generation of Albanian women, she exemplifies the best of the new generation of women: those of any age who made the most of the new freedoms and opportunities in their country. For this reason, Liri is a transitional figure. She has clearly inherited many of the characteristics of the Albanian women interviewed in this book. She is hardworking, strong, and determined. However, she is one of the first women to focus her strength and intellect on achieving her goals in the new world that is Albania today: an Albania that is no longer isolated, that is taking its place in the modern world. For this reason, she is a trailblazer and an example for the next generation of women.

Part IV
CHAOS AND HOPE

Chapter 16

The Younger Generation of Women in Albania

The women who constitute the younger generation are those between the ages of 16 and 29. The oldest members of this generation, those born before 1978, might be thought of as a transition generation. They were born into the zenith of communist power and success in their country and yet lived most of their formative years in the period after the break with China when the downfall of the system was steep and rapidly accelerating. The youngest members of this generation were born into the declining years of the communist regime and the poverty that came with it. These youngest women are actually coming to maturity in the chaos of the establishment of democracy. All of the women of this generation faced the maturing experience of being eyewitnesses to a revolution in their country and adjusting their lives and actions to an entirely new set of rules and expectations.

In many ways the women of this generation are repeating the experiences of their grandmothers. They are coming to maturity at a time when the old order is passing and the new has yet to be clearly defined: at a tumultuous time in the history of the country when new ideas and ideals are being introduced. Maybe for this reason their outlooks and ambitions seem more like their grandmothers' than those of their mothers.

Three metaphorical earthquakes have rocked Albania in the short history of this generation, each having an impact on the lives of these women and subsequent events in the country. The first of these was the severing of relations with China in July 1978, when Albania began its isolated march toward self-sufficiency. The second was the death of Enver Hoxha in April 1985, which opened up the potential for a change in the government's isolationist policies as well as for social and economic reforms. The third was the cataclysm in 1990 and 1991 that preceded the coming of a democratic government in March 1992.

Isolation and Deprivation

In breaking relations with China, Enver Hoxha announced that Albania would from then on be self-sufficient. He exhorted his countrymen to make the necessary sacrifices and to expect to rely on no one but themselves to achieve their economic objectives. Sadly, his oft-repeated words, "The Albanian people would rather eat grass than give up their adherence to their Marxist-Leninist principles," came true quite literally for some people because of this radical and short-sighted policy.

After July 1978 Albania no longer had the grants and loans from external sources that the country had been relying on for so many years. The industrial projects that had been started with Chinese funding, technology, and technical assistance either stopped or progressed at a much slower pace than previously. Heroic efforts were demanded of the people by the government to meet the agricultural and industrial objectives.

It is testimony to the intelligence of the Albanian people and their hard work that many of the projects that were begun by the Chinese were, in fact, completed by their Albanian counterparts. The technical aspects were planned and carried out by homegrown technical experts and the labor was provided largely by "volunteers." In this manner the huge steel mill in Elbasan, the hydroelectric power plant at Fierzë, and the oil refinery at Ballsh were completed. In addition, the production of coal, chromium, and copper were increased. All of these efforts provided much-needed products for export and reinforced Hoxha's commitment to his isolationist economic program. These projects also gave Hoxha examples of accomplishments with which to exhort the people to greater production.

It should be noted, however, that during this time the needs of the Albanian people were not adequately met. Household appliances were scarce and rationed to the privileged few. In addition, although the quality of the products produced was reasonably good, the methods of production were inefficient. The goods produced often cost more than the price to purchase them outside of Albania. In addition, an environmental nightmare was created in the geographic vicinity of many of the factories, especially in Ballsh where the oil refinery was and in Laç where there was a large chemical fertilizer plant. Although agricultural production levels were reported to be sufficient to feed the people in 1976, they could not keep pace consistently and over the long term with the continued rapid growth of the population. All industrial and agricultural products that could be exported were, leaving the people increasingly exhausted, hungry, and poor.

As the quality of their lives spiraled down, their fear of reprisals for "crimes" against the state increased because in this period Hoxha's policies became more and more repressive as his own paranoia increased. Many people suffered from persecution at this time. Groups of "traitors" were "discovered" by Enver Hoxha in almost every field of endeavor. Some people were reportedly imprisoned as traitors for complaining that there were inadequate goods to purchase or that the quality of the bread was poor. The most shocking event, however, was Mehmet Shehu's death by "suicide" in December 1981.* Because Hoxha's hand was so evident in the death of this loyal and dedicated official, a majority of the Albanian people could see clearly the extent of Hoxha's sickness and the potential threat to all Albanians.

For all of these reasons, the final years of Hoxha's regime were characterized by increasingly persistent and strident propaganda that also became increasingly ineffective as people saw the growing disparity between what they were told and what they knew to be true in their own lives. The failures of the system became more obvious as the people perceived that their sacrifices were being made in vain.

The Death of Enver Hoxha

For all the growing disenchantment, the day that Enver Hoxha died in April 1985 was marked by tears. Since the population had grown so rapidly in the 40 years of his rule, most of the people—possibly as many as 80 percent—had known no other leader. The future was unknown and they felt a huge loss. Perhaps to reflect this public feeling of loss, or in an effort to simply reinforce the continuity of the past, the Central Committee of the PLA rushed to rename schools and other public institutions after their former leader and to erect statues of him in all of the primary cities.

As Hoxha's personally chosen successor, Ramiz Alia—the president of the country since 1982—took over as first secretary of the Central Committee of the PLA in a deceptively smooth transfer of power. Deceptively smooth because the divisions were already in place between the hardliners who sought to enforce the ideas, teachings, and policies of Enver Hoxha and the moderates who were open to or actively encouraged change. Hoxha's widow, Nexhmije—who served as the director of the Institute of Marxism-Leninism—led the hardliners, while some of the younger members of the Political Bureau were open to economic reforms. As a result, Alia found himself in a difficult position. How could he moderate between

*See footnote on page 192.

the two groups? What options did he have for meeting the increasingly critical problems of his country while remaining true to the ideals of his mentor and predecessor?

Due to these competing pressures and opinions, Alia's 6½ year rule from mid–1985 through the end of 1991 was characterized by growing conflict. While Alia's role is still a hotly debated one, the following elements of this period are clear:

1. Whatever Alia's personal goals or desires,* the desperate economic condition of the country and its people could not be ignored and, in time, the government had no choice but to turn to the outside world for assistance. This process, however, was at first extremely tentative and reluctant. The government was only prepared to open up and meet the demands of the potential benefactors, most of whom focused on remedying the country's human rights abuses, because the situation had become so desperate. Hunger was extreme and industrial production had all but collapsed from lack of spare parts and from worker vandalism and absenteeism. Further, many thousands of people had fled the country under extremely dangerous and difficult conditions.

2. Alia's pronouncements and policies were presented in "double talk" that made it unclear what the policies were. New ideas that would constitute a change from the policies of the past were clothed in the slogans and dogma of the Hoxha era. In addition, the Sigurimi continued to work actively to root out dissenters, and individuals were continually exhorted to report on their neighbors. As a result, it was a dangerous time. People didn't know what position they were supposed to support and couldn't trust anyone.

In the later years of Hoxha's rule and continuing into this period, the impact of foreign television and radio was enormous. Hoxha himself had believed that he could use the media for his own purposes while controlling what the people saw and heard. However, Albania's proximity to Yugoslavia, Italy, and Greece meant that the people—those brave enough to defy the government's laws against watching or listening to foreign transmissions— were increasingly aware of events and the life of the outside world. Therefore, many Albanians, especially those in the cities and those who were well educated, listened to the Voice of America and the BBC. They heard reports

---

*It has been suggested that Alia himself was in favor of economic reforms but his long-term collaboration and friendship with Nexhmije Hoxha led him to take only limited action. Others suggest that he himself was a hardliner and that he only introduced cosmetic reforms to appease the forces of change in the government and the country.

of current events that at that time included the fall of the Berlin Wall and the collapse of the other Eastern European communist governments. Many also saw Italian programs that showed them what life in Western Europe was like, directly contradicting the propaganda of the government. More poignantly, they saw the glitzy ads for consumer products and cat food at a time when many of their own people were literally starving. The impact of television and radio on the change in the Albanian people's attitudes and beliefs and on their revolt against communism cannot be underestimated.

Two Years of Hell

The average Albanian would probably say that the entire period leading up to the elections in March 1992 was hell, but the crisis was at its worst in 1990 and 1991. These two years were characterized by hunger, despair, and chaos. Agricultural production dropped to critical levels due to drought and inefficiency of production methods. Toward the end of this period, production fell even further, due to worker rebellion and absenteeism. Industrial production fell for similar reasons. The drought that reduced agricultural output also reduced the hydroelectric output, leading to an inadequate supply of electricity for industrial production. The government's tentative and limited relaxation of the restrictions on trade, communications, and other contacts with the outside world gave the people an immediate passion for change: a zeal to be part of the modern world. At the same time Alia's rhetoric, still based as it was on the propaganda slogans of the Hoxha era, made the people despair of seeing the changes they so urgently wanted. Even when reforms were announced, the people saw them as too little and too late. Many, especially the young people who represented the vast majority of the population, no longer had faith in their leaders or the tolerance or endurance to wait for changes.

Although there had been a few isolated demonstrations prior to 1990, a demonstration in December 1989 by the students at the University of Tiranë (then called the Enver Hoxha University) touched off a wave of protests that did not end for two years. Although the students' issues were mainly the lack of adequate heating and food, there were also those who were advocating democracy. Another significant early protest occurred in Shkodër in January 1990, where people demonstrating for religious freedom and protesting the lack of food tried to bring down the city's statue of Stalin. In both of these cases the government's reprisals against the protesters were severe and included long prison terms for some of the activists.

As 1990 progressed, there were rumors and reports of other antigovernment protests, including more student demonstrations, attacks on party offices, and worker strikes. These protests gained supporters and became more angry, widespread, and gradually became more focused on political reform. Perceived gains from these activities—including the government's initiation of a de–Stalinization program in December 1990—seemed inadequate to those who were dissatisfied with the system, and yet served to encourage them to push for further reforms. One of the most significant demonstrations was the anti–Hoxha demonstration in February 1991. One hundred thousand people, led by university students and professors, gathered in Skanderbeg Square in Tiranë and succeeded in toppling the huge statue of Enver Hoxha that had stood on a broad pedestal there.* Throughout 1991 and until the elections that brought the Democratic Party into power in March 1992, the student protesters were increasingly joined by the workers. Strikes were staged and almost all public property, including schools, hospitals, parks, and factories, was destroyed or vandalized. Some counterdemonstrations were launched and police reprisals against the protesters continued.

In addition to the demonstrations, there was a virtual flood of people leaving the country by whatever means they could find. For example, in July 1990 many thousands† sought political asylum in the embassies of the European nations. They braved police barricades and stormed the walls, preferring to risk their lives and camp on the grounds of the embassies in the hope of escaping, rather than remain any longer in their homeland. People became so desperate that in increasing numbers they also sought to cross the still heavily guarded borders to Yugoslavia and Greece, many of them losing their lives in the effort. The trickle of people who braved this route turned into a flood in January 1991, at which time the Greek government reported that almost 5,000 Albanians had successfully entered Greece in a two-week period. Then in March and August 1991 many thousands§ more swarmed onto cargo ships and other boats in the ports of Durrës and Vlorë and successfully crossed the Adriatic to Italy. The total number of persons who fled Albania during this two-year period is not fully documented. However, some estimates suggest that as many as 200,000

---

*In December 1994 a bumper car ride was set up on this spot and in December 1995 it was joined by another carnival ride.

†"Three thousand sought refuge in the German Embassy, another 3,000 in the embassies of Italy, France, Greece, Czechoslovakia, Poland, Hungary, and Turkey." Jacques, The Albanians, p. 657.

§Some of the larger boats were reported to have carried as many as 8,000 people each. As many as 20,000 people are reported to have arrived in Italy in a two-week period in March 1991, with thousands more arriving in Italy in August of the same year.

people, most of them young men, were successful in their attempts, although some were subsequently repatriated. Although the pressure to leave the country has continued and the total figure for émigrés, both legal and illegal, is now estimated to be as high as 500,000, these flights to freedom in 1991 were significant for being the largest and most desperate mass migrations of this period.

On the political front, the government's announced reforms were increasingly liberal and yet fell short of the expectations of the people. Finally, however, after pressure from protesters inside the country and from outside forces—including other countries, human rights organizations, and the United Nations—Alia's government agreed to multiparty elections at the end of March 1991. Although three new parties, in addition to the Communist Party, participated in the elections, the opposition parties were handicapped by the lack of access to media and the poor transportation and communications within the country. Therefore, the Communist Party won 68 percent of the seats in the Parliament, primarily based on support from the rural and remote areas where the majority of the people lived. However, the election was also characterized by police intimidation of the opposition and ballot-box stuffing.

Although the Communist Party drafted and presented a new and more liberal constitution in the first few days after the election, popular discontent remained strong. This resulted in the Democratic Party's withdrawal of its 75 delegates from the Parliament at its first meeting on April 15, 1991.

A general strike began on May 16, involving more than half of the workers in Albania. It lasted for more than two weeks and brought the economic crisis to a head. As a result, protesters successfully demanded the resignation of the prime minister, Fatos Nano. The government then entered a caretaker period in which half of the senior governmental positions were held by Communist Party members and the other half were held by members of the opposition parties. New elections were set for March 1992. During this time, the economy remained in crisis. Workers left the country or simply did not work, so factories and stores were closed and agricultural production and distribution ground to a halt. The people survived only with the help of food aid from the international community.

The democratic reform began in Albania with the parliamentary elections that were held in March 1992, when the Democratic Party took 66 percent of the vote by promising a clean break from communism. Dr. Sali Berisha, a cardiologist, became president and began an aggressive program of privatization and economic reform that were designed to lead Albania into cooperation with the Western countries and eventual membership in the European Union. Following this election, Albania was quieter politically, and aid and other economic improvements brought relief to the people.

The success of the new government's programs can be measured in the improvement in the overall standard of living of the people; the rapid privatization of property and the reform of land ownership laws; the increase in foreign trade and both financial and technical assistance; and the vitality of the retail trade. However, this new government combined a laissez-faire approach to the economy with the strict centralization of power that characterized the communist regime, leading to further despair and chaos that erupted in violence again in early 1997.*

The World Turned Upside Down

Remember we were only 12 and 13 years of age when these changes happened. Our whole world turned upside down. There were scandals and corruption. The old political leaders who were previously revered turned out to be scoundrels. We needed someone to take care of us, but had to look after ourselves. Our generation had to understand that all the things we were told before were outright lies. We had to find the strength to face this reality.

I remember that I was in front of my house in February 1991 with my neighbors and heard a group of people shouting "Enver Hitler!" I also saw Hoxha's monument, the one I had looked up at so many times, being dragged through the streets on the ground [Adia, age 18].

Although the entire period after the break with China with its ever-declining prosperity affected the younger generation, it was the two years from 1990 through early 1992 that had the most radical effect on these young women. This period was one of uncertainty and fear for all of the Albanian people as their desperation and their rage were acted out by so many and with such violence. Many people, especially the young—both university students and workers—took part in pulling down the statues and destroying all of the symbols of communist rule. Others, continuing to fear government reprisals or concerned for their own safety, watched and suffered from the results. For everyone the situation was extremely critical. Crimes of all types occurred in this chaotic and desperate time, as rape, theft, shooting, and destruction of property all became common.

For the young women, this was a particularly difficult time because they personally were at great risk. Frequently, they themselves witnessed the

*These recent events are detailed in the Epilogue; see page 289.

demonstrations, the destruction, and the crimes on the streets, and feared for their own safety. In addition, their parents, also fearing for the safety of their daughters, restricted them severely, refusing to allow some even to go to school. As a result, a large number of young women left school at this time and never returned.

Not only were the lives of these young women changed in this way, but their entire worldview was shaken. Everything they had been told before—many of them by their own parents, who were now supporting or actively engaged in the conflict—was being challenged. The world changed from a predictable place, however difficult or limited, to an uncertain and dangerous place. The shift shook their faith in their government, in the people around them, and, sometimes, even in their parents. There was literally nothing left: no food, no rules, no place to go. Many of them lost their brothers, fathers, uncles, and friends to emigration, leaving them to bear their fears alone and without the traditional protection that male relatives offered.

For all the improvements brought by the eventual establishment of a prodemocracy government—not the least of which was a certain amount of public order—the people have been living in the aftermath of the revolution, especially with the destruction. The younger women of this generation have had to go to schools with no windows and study in drafty, unheated classrooms. In addition, especially in the cities, many come from families where one or both parents are unemployed, or working at jobs for which they are vastly overqualified.

These young women live in an economic and emotional uncertainty that did not exist before. Neither they nor their parents understand well the rules of the new game: this world where education and jobs are not provided—but are competed for—where there is freedom—but no security—where the economic differences between the rich and the poor become greater each day. There is impatience to realize the benefits of democracy and a free-market economy,* but there is no guarantee that the future will bring all the things they want.

The unfortunate result of this is that many—perhaps even most—of the people of all ages still want to leave the country, and many have achieved

---

This impatience is reminiscent of that described by Edith Durham in her book, High Albania, in which she reports a conversation with a Mirditë clan chief just eight weeks after the establishment of the 1908 constitution. "Our lively guide explained to me, before an applauding audience, that, so far, 'Konstitutzioon' was a dead failure. 'It promised to give us roads, and railways, and schools, and to keep order and justice. We have had it two whole months, and it has done none of these things. We have given our besa till St. Dimitri, and if it has not done them by then—good-bye Konstitutzioon!'" Edith Durham, High Albania, London: Virago, 1985 (original publication date 1909), p. 327.

that goal, some at enormous personal cost.* Some young women are so desperate that they marry a foreign man, any foreign man, in order to get out; others accept offers of work that lead them to prostitution in other countries. Still others are sold by their parents and other relatives, often with the girls' acquiescence, to be prostitutes. Those young women who stay in Albania struggle to make the most of what they are offered: just as their mothers and grandmothers had done.

There are two distinctions that need to be made among the women of this generation. The first is based on age, distinguishing the women in their twenties from the teenagers. The women in their twenties almost belong to a separate transition generation. Most of them finished their education—whether through the eighth grade, high school, or college—prior to the coming of democracy. Some of them actually completed their courses of study, while others were taken out of school by their parents; still others longed to continue, but did not have the financial capability to do so. They were mostly raised as their mothers were raised, with limited expectations and an emphasis on compliance and dedication to the family. As a result, it is not surprising to find the majority of unmarried women living at home and a large number of the married women living with their husband's families, in accordance with the societal norms of the past. And yet, the world has changed dramatically and this has had a profound effect on these women's expectations and outlooks.

The second distinction that needs to be made is between the young women living in the cities and those living in the villages. Many of the young women in the cities, especially, have gained opportunities their mothers only dreamed of. The emigration of young men has left a void in the society and the young women are actively seeking to fill professional roles that the young men might otherwise have taken. In many of the villages, however, the young women have seen a return to the ways of the past, when the lives of the women were circumscribed by tradition and the strong role of the father in the family: when women were not educated beyond a certain very basic level, then were restricted to the home and land to work until a husband was found for them.

The societal changes have been dramatic and are most visible among the teenagers and younger children. For these young women, television and

---

*The cost can be measured in terms of both money and risk factors. A false Italian tourist visa (for three months) costs $1,500–2,000 on the black market and a false American immigration visa with the new "counterfeit-proof" hologram costs about $17,000. Boat operators do a thriving business taking people illegally to Italy across the Adriatic from the port city of Vlorë for $500–1,000, even though there are frequent reports of drownings and deaths by fire and other mishaps at sea.

the contrasts that they have seen there between their own lives and those of the people of Western Europe and the United States have had a profound effect. An increasing number of Albanian families have had the financial capability to buy televisions and have drawn inferences about the world, their peers, and the societal norms of more advanced countries from the foreign shows they have seen. These shows, along with greater personal freedom and the improving economic circumstances, have influenced many parents to become overindulgent of their children. As a result, many parents today, especially those in the cities, give their children previously unimagined freedoms and material goods. At the same time, many of the young women have concluded that full freedom from parental authority and full satisfaction of their material desires are their due. Many believe that the older generation is too steeped in the past to understand them as new Western women. At the same time, these young women do not know the past intimately—only the failures. They cannot know what their parents have experienced because they have seen only the changes brought about in the recent past. They are impatient with the old order and eager to experience the benefits of the new order. The seeds of conflict between the generations have been sown and have taken root.

Not only have images and expressions of Western culture bombarded the Albanian people but also new scientific and professional information, as well as new and old religious beliefs. It is a time of searching for personal and national identity, for understanding and knowledge, and for a path for the future. The young women are part of that search, and many of them are even leading it.

Chapter 17

The Lives of Young City Women

The Transition Generation

The stories and outlooks of some of the women of this group are virtually indistinguishable from those of the middle generation of Albanian women. For example, in Berat we met Alma, a 26-year-old mathematics teacher from a nominally Muslim family. Our impression was that not much had changed in her life in this transition period except that she was now released from the burden of the party's military training requirement.

Both of my parents loved education and allowed me to go on to study at the university. Although the party decided that I should study mathematics and I was not allowed to choose, I decided that it wasn't a bad idea.

The only difficulty I have ever had in my life is that I hated military training. It was especially difficult for us girls because we were not offered the proper conditions for personal hygiene.

I am optimistic by nature. I believe and I hope that my personal future and that of my generation will be better than that of my parents. I also believe that the future is not far away and that the signs of the brightness are already visible.

Like many in her mother's generation, Alma reported that faith had played no role in her life. She dismissed faith with the following words, "I believe that it is absurd to think that there is a God who puts everything in order."

By contrast, in Korçë we met three young women who exemplify well the changes and opportunities that have been presented to women in this transition period, and the stresses and changes that they have begun to create in the society.

Anxhela, a 29-year-old librarian, told us,

I was born in 1967 in Korçë. My parents are simple workers and I am the older of the two children. I finished secondary school here and attended university in

Tiranë. Although I graduated with a degree in mechanical engineering, this isn't what I wanted to study. At that time, however, there was no choice or competition.

I married just a month ago under an arrangement. We were introduced and saw each other for two or three months; then I gave my approval.

I work at the American Free Library here and I like it. It is easier and more interesting than the shift work I did at the local enterprise, even though I was the head of the shift. My goals for the future are to continue working here and to be able to do more sewing in my free time. One day I would also like to have children.

I think I am strong because I am so happy that democracy has come into power. It will be nice if it stays because I am given much freedom now. The change isn't complete in just five years, but it is significant for us. I argue with people of the older generation because they haven't changed. For example, when I got married the older people insisted that we give dowry gifts, but I refused.

Anxhela was wearing a cross and I asked if she did this because it is the fashion* or because it is an expression of her faith. She responded, "I wear a cross because I believe. I attend the Orthodox church and study the Bible with an American missionary."

We also met two sisters, Viola (25) and Shirli (21) in Korçë. They are the granddaughters of a well-known and respected physician and have had a privileged upbringing. Not the least of the advantages they have had is a spirited mother whose joy of living and optimism are evident to all who meet her. Viola and Shirli too have had experiences that would not have been possible under the communist regime and, at the same time, have felt the pressures that have come with the changes.

Viola, a doctor, told us,

I specialized in medicine at the university and have been fortunate to spend three months in England specializing in gynecology.

Although I have faced many challenges in preparing for my profession, the most difficult moment I have had in my life came when there were so many changes in Albania. Lots of people left, including some of my friends. I felt that I would end up being totally alone.

I have been fortunate in my life to have such wonderful parents. My mother is a joyful person all the time. If she is not in our house, it is quiet. If she is there, the life is there. She is like a child for us, someone to play with. My father is a doctor, as was my grandfather, and that inspired me to become a doctor. In our family, our father is the mind and our mother is the hand.

In the future, I am looking forward to practicing as a gynecologist. I will also have a family. No, I don't think that having a career and a family will be difficult. I believe that those women of my generation who want to succeed will be able to.

I draw my strength from doing my best and don't worry about what is under

---

It has been the fashion recently for rock stars seen on MTV and other Western television shows to wear crosses, and many of the young Albanians have started wearing crosses to imitate them.

the control of others. I have my dreams and determination. Failure doesn't matter to me because I learn a lot when I fail.

Shirli, who was named for the American actress Shirley Temple, told us,

I am now at the University of Tiranë studying classical music—voice—and am going into my fourth year. My goal is to have qualifications in classical music everywhere in the world. For that, I hope to go on for postgraduate studies in voice, and longer term I hope to have a great career in singing opera. Later, I will have a family, but my career comes first. When I do marry, I do not expect it to be an arranged marriage, but a marriage for love.

My strength comes from my passion for music and from my family—my parents and sister—who have always helped

Librarian Anxhela in Korçë.

me. My mother, especially, because she has been my mentor and cheerleader.

When asked about the role of faith in their lives, these two young women from a nominally Orthodox family showed clearly the changes that are occurring in Albania today. While Viola said that faith had played no role in her life, Shirli, who was wearing a cross said, "Five years ago someone was here from Italy and spoke to us about God and I believed."

Afroviti's Story

Delina Fico, director of the Women's Center in Tiranë, suggested that we interview Afroviti, the 29-year-old publisher of a city newspaper, both because of her personal accomplishments and because of her strong commitment to helping women. We met her in Pogradec in her newspaper office. Her story is one of hard work, change, and new possibilities.

In 1967 I was the second of three girls born to a simple family in Pogradec. My parents worked in agriculture. My father is the nephew of a well-known writer, Lasgush Pogradeci.*

I remember that as a child I always liked to read and was fortunate that I had the possibility to do so. I was good at both literature and math. Although I wrote from the time I was in secondary school, I picked up mathematics thinking that I would be more successful in obtaining approval to go to the university.† Anyway, although I continued to have the desire to write, I didn't want to be a teacher of literature.

I graduated from college with excellent grades and returned to teach in a village near Pogradec for one year. In 1991, however, I returned to the university for one year for a postgraduate degree in math. When I completed my studies, I was assigned to work in a remote village. I couldn't understand why they asked me to go so far even after my postgraduate degree.

In 1992 I married for love. I had met my husband in school in Tiranë, but he too was from Pogradec. Also in 1992, I published a book of poetry, *Wild Quietness*. I borrowed the money and paid all the expenses myself. There was a local literary newspaper in Korçë and I began to write for them. This was the beginning of my life as a journalist.

After our daughter was born, I went on writing, but was appointed to work in the Department of Education, qualifying teachers of math. It was hard work because I had to go from one village to another. I stayed in that job for just two years.

There are many things in my life that I would like to forget, including my troubles when I began writing. The newspapers in Korçë were political and I had no knowledge of the political aspects of things. Although I had participated in the demonstrations in 1991 with the other students and the teachers, I was very naive. For example, a few days ago I found a speech I had written, but never gave, in which I called upon the university to change its name from "Enver Hoxha" to something else. This speech now sounds very naive because things have changed so fast. We could never have imagined that things would change so quickly.

It was at this time that I started thinking about the fact that Pogradec did not have a local newspaper. There had been a successful Communist Party paper for a few years prior to 1990, but it was closed at that time because it no longer had the party's financial support. I wanted to start a nonpolitical newspaper, one not aligned with any party. I made my idea known and learned that time and again there had been an idea to do this, but there was no printing press in Pogradec: the closest one was in Korçë.

In 1994 I began the paper on my summer holiday. My husband was dead set against the idea. He thought I was crazy, especially considering the financial aspects. However, the owner of an offset printing press in Elbasan offered to help me and we began, publishing only when we had enough money to do so. It was very difficult at first and for a long while I had to do everything myself—gathering information, writing, and going to Elbasan. I don't know how I did all this, but

---

*Llazar Gusho. See chapter 11.
†At this time, the second or third child in a family was usually not given permission to go on to college if the first child had done so. However, math was not a popular subject and offered a path for some second-borns.

my husband helped me a lot. Later he gave up his work as an economist to help me and we found many kind supporters.

In the fall of 1994, we went to Tiranë to seek support for the paper and met with the head of the association for independent (nonpolitical) newspapers, and he in turn led us to the Soros Foundation. They offered to help us to get laser printers and we were able to have part of the printing process done in Tiranë, with the remainder still being done in Elbasan. It was also a great help that we met journalists in Tiranë, but there was a period of time that still terrifies me to remember. We had to stay in the capital city for three days, covering all of our own expenses. Sometimes we stayed awake for 48 hours at a stretch. We weren't making any money and people thought we were crazy and asked us why we were going on with this project. Maybe it was just my passion, I don't know.

Ever since the beginning of the newspaper, we have also come under serious pressure to align with one of the two major parties. At the time we began the local government in Pogradec was dominated by the Socialist Party, while the national government was ruled by the Democratic Party. These two parties offered us financial assistance and other support if we would align with them. Despite the pressure—which occasionally took the form of threats—we maintained our independence tenaciously. As a consequence, our newspaper has continued to be critical and independent.

Also, in 1994 the Women's Center had a round-table conference entitled "Women and the Media." I was invited to attend and this was the first time that I started working with women. There, I met professional journalists and learned of their experiences, which were very different from mine. They had received specialized training, while I had learned only from experience; and they only wrote, they didn't also manage a newspaper. At a break I met Carlo Bolini, the editor of a Tiranë paper. As soon as the next session started, he spoke to the group and pointed out that there was a woman editor-in-chief in the group (the only woman editor-in-chief in Albania, as it turned out), and I was asked to speak to them. After that I had ongoing contact with Delina Fico, the head of the Women's Center, and later had an opportunity to work with Reflexions.* I had the idea from these experiences that I could form such a women's group in Pogradec and since then have done so.

With all of the challenges this young woman has had to face in achieving her goals, from where has she drawn her strength? She answered this way,

The newspaper has been an adventure and, luckily enough for me, it has ended well. I am afraid I am an egotist or maybe I am just a strong-willed person. I always had to work hard as a student and what has come after has been easier.

Also, it is a period now in our history when you meet quite a number of people who call themselves rich. Some have made their money through the restoration of their property and some have made their money illegally or by theft. At 29 years of age, I have experienced all sorts of things: periods of poverty and other economically better periods. I have never thought of being rich, but I expected that when I graduated from college I would live better than others because my husband

A nationwide women's group focusing on education and training.

and I would be living on two salaries. However, with all the changes we were really living in poverty.

I have also been lucky that my mother has helped me quite a lot in raising my daughter and am very fortunate that my husband has supported me, despite the fact that he was against the project from the beginning. It is actually he who has encouraged me to go ahead.

What role has faith played in my life? That is a more difficult question. I come from an Orthodox family, but I have not had a spiritual link with God. My father was religious and gave me icons to kiss. We have always had celebrations, and I remember the time we had to keep them secret. Whenever I was in difficulty I always called for God's help, but I have only gone to church at Christmas and Easter. I love the candles and the atmosphere when I go. My husband is a Muslim, however, and I am very tolerant about religion.

Recently, I have suffered spiritually as a result of several deaths, and I find myself wondering about death and trying to understand it from a religious point of view. First, my father-in-law was killed in an accident, then the police chief, a well-loved man in Pogradec, was shot and killed, and then another violent killing took place here. I have been wondering how it is that very good people have died. I have also started kissing the cross that I brought back from a recent trip to Italy.

The Teenagers

In our traveling and interviewing, Ksanthi and I found the teenagers in the cities to be particularly articulate and mature. They have an optimistic outlook and a keen desire to succeed. In Tiranë, we interviewed a group of teenage girls from the foreign language high school.* These girls are primarily from prominent and intellectual families. In responding to questions about their lives, they spoke of the two years preceding the democratic reform and what these events meant to them.

Eges, 18, told us,

Our parents fought for changes, but we were trembling. We were afraid for our mothers and fathers because we heard rifle shots in the street while we were at home alone.

Another problem was that of refugees. The parents in my neighborhood were in the streets calling after the young men and women who were fleeing the country, trying to keep them from going. They feared what might happen to their children.

Margarita, a 17-year-old from Kavajë, added, "During the first demonstration in Kavajë, I remember people going along the road—only boys. My mother said 'don't go out' and 'don't do this,' but it was a new experience.

They were all seniors in the English program so the interview was conducted in English.

I was curious so I looked out and saw people throwing stones and crying 'Enver Hitler.' I didn't know why this was happening."

These teenagers also explained what these events meant to them and how they changed and shaped their lives and their ideas.

Ejona, 18, explained, "We had been taught to love and admire our country, but became confused. There were so many things destroyed that we found little left to admire. Lots of girls were raped during this time. We had to stay in the house or be accompanied by our parents whenever we went out."

Adia, 18, continued, "We didn't understand why people were leaving. We had been taught differently. We couldn't understand. We learned from them that our country was 'bad.' What our people lack now is nationalism. Our generation is disappointed and we are still living with this disappointment.

"The world changed and we were changed. The first thing that changed was our uniforms. We no longer had them. Then our classes all changed. We used to have 'Politics' class, but we all just said what our parents told us. After the change, every class was a politics class and we put our souls into it. The classrooms were colder than ever because the windows in the classrooms had been broken. There was no water or electricity and we were afraid in the streets. We were terrified and confused."

When asked how they saw themselves and their futures as a result of these changes, Fjorela, 17, pointed out, "In the past we had not a prayer of knowing ourselves. Now we are free to express our attitudes and feelings. We are free to know ourselves better."

Sabina, 18, added, "We now have to find something true within ourselves to find ground to rely on. We have to start thinking our own clear thoughts. Before we were never aware of where we were going or what we were thinking."

Edita, 17, continued, "This experience, especially seeing the people fleeing the country, made us decide to make something different of our lives. These people were escaping from a reality they couldn't accept. It made us stronger to cope with reality. We are being brought up in a better way. We don't want to leave the country. We want to make it better. Another problem is that even though we have our dreams—our plans to become a famous doctor or whatever—there is often no light when you need to study. You can only think how good it would be to get out of the dark. Your dreams go off in pieces."

Ejona also noted that "The ability to choose is what we have gained. But now that it is possible to achieve our educational and professional goals, there is much competition and corruption. You try everything, but

The teenagers in Tiranë with Ksanthi.

you can still fail because of corruption.* We all want to get a good education: a good preparation for life and for what we are going to be. One other problem is that the schools and universities here are not so challenging."

Here there was a general discussion of how discouraging it is to work hard and get good grades and then have to compete with others whose parents pay the teachers and college officials to let their children into the university.

Characteristically of this generation, more of them report finding strength in themselves. As Adia explained, "I find strength as a survivor. That fact gives me self-confidence." However, family continues to figure strongly as a source of strength, as Sabina explained: "My father gives me inspiration. He is fond of work and his career. Career comes first, even though he loves his family. My father specialized abroad and has always made a way in his career. A career is best for me because it is the future. I must always get ahead. My personal dream is for a career in international relations or psychology: dealing with one person's world or the whole world."

For Matilda, age 17, her strength comes from her mother. "My mother has been a good example. She has strength I've never seen in another woman. In the way she educated me with stories and legends, in everything she does and says, she is strong. She has been a good example for me."

Ejona added another person who had made an impression on her. "My family—parents, grandparents, aunts, and uncles—all affected me. We are close and do many things for each other. But the greatest source of inspiration I have received has been from an American, a Peace Corps volunteer who taught us English last year. He really affected my life—my thoughts and my way of living."

When asked what role faith has played in their lives, there were those who spoke of their religion.

Eges, who is Orthodox, told us, "I believe in God and find strength in Him. If something goes badly for me, I explain it as follows: 'I try hard to succeed, but if not, it was written in this way.' In other words, I will face the disappointment as the will of God and learn from it. When things go well for me, I thank God because I feel that gratitude."

Edita, who is Muslim, said, "My faith in God makes me more self-confident. My faith in God gives me faith in myself."

Margarita added, "My family is Christian (Orthodox) and I believe in God. I believe and hope—I just feel it. My mother dyed red eggs and maintained the faith. I like to go to church and pray there. I like it that someone is taking care of me."

Alba, who is 18 and from the city of Vlorë, also said, "I trust God. I don't trust so much in my own abilities. God is the only way of help. He is my friend and He never lets me down."

Others spoke in more generally spiritual terms. For example, Adia said, "I am not a good believer. I believe on some occasions. However, I find a friend inside myself. I believe in that friend, my God inside of me. I also have faith in my mother. She is the perfect mother and career person."

Matilda added, "I believe in God, but I am not a churchgoer. I don't pray every day, but when I do prayers just come out of my spirit. I say 'thank you, God' when I succeed."

Only one member of the group said simply, "I am an atheist."

Outside of Tiranë, the teenage girls put less emphasis on political events in their lives and greater emphasis on changes in their families and their own lives and futures. Majlinda, 18, was typical of teenage girls we met in Korçë. She told us,

> My mother is an engineer and teaches mechanical engineering. My father is a technologist and received specialized training in China, but he is not working in his field now. He is selling furniture. My parents married for love and have had a happy marriage. My uncle is a well-known singer. In fact, I come from a family of singers. My father sings all the time as do his friends.* The song is beautiful in my family.
>
> My mother has made many sacrifices to help us enjoy life. We used to live in the house next door to this one, but since my father comes from a very large family with eight children, our family of four had only one room, so we all had to work, study, and live in the same area. My mother went on studying by correspondence while she was raising us.
>
> I would like to be like both of my parents. My family speaks of a difficult life. Even when my father was unemployed, he tried his best to make life good for us. When my father was unemployed, we all tried to make up for my father being out of work so we made vodka at home. I have always helped. It is the example of my family. All that I have done so far makes me think that I can do much more in the future. This will give me strength. Also, I would like to become someone and have something of my own. At first I thought I would study management, but a cousin persuaded me to study marketing. After graduation, I plan to start an employment agency with my friend. I want to do something good.

When asked about the role of faith in her life, Majlinda, whose family is Orthodox, replied, "My friends and I are frequent churchgoers. I believe in God and pray when I have problems."

Alma and Anxhela

In Shkodër we met two teenage girls from Catholic families, Alma and Anxhela. Although she comes from a divorced family, Alma—who is studying mathematics at the university in Shkodër—described herself as a typical 19-year-old girl from a Catholic family.

*Majlinda's family gave us a sample of their singing that evening. Her father and another uncle sang typical Korçë serenade music as well as partisan songs, some of which were written by Dhora Leka, whom they admire greatly.

I am the child of a divorced family. My parents had married for love. It was unusual at that time for people to do so and my mother's family disapproved strongly, but my parents married anyway. They divorced when I was three years old and I have felt this terribly. My mother's father was greatly shocked by the divorce and died soon after. There were many rumors and much gossip about my parents, and this started quarrels between them. This led to their divorce.

By law I had to live with my mother and had to go and meet my father from time to time. It was always difficult to leave the parent I was with because I was afraid that I would never see that one again. I noticed my friends having two parents and I felt the loss of the other parent. The worst consequence, however, fell on my mother. She was a worker and she had lived a hard life. She came from a poor peasant family. My grandmother had given birth to 11 children, 8 of whom had died due to poverty and lack of medical attention. I admire my mother because she never sunk into despair. She is a very strong woman. Everything I have in me I get from my mother and I dedicate myself to her.

My father continued to live in the village after the divorce, although my mother and I moved back to Shkodër. I remember that when he brought me back to Shkodër after a visit, my parents never met. There was always a distance that I had to walk by myself between them.

I am engaged myself now to a man I love. His family is more emancipated than most and the divorce of my parents has not affected my engagement. We were engaged when I was 17.

I am enthusiastic and optimistic about my future. I always dreamed of going ahead with my studies. My dream was to study in Italy or America, because I wanted a diploma that would be valued everywhere. When I got engaged, however, I gave up the dream of studying overseas. Even though it means that I will be educated here in Albania, I want to be someone in life. I am happy with the man I am engaged to. Since the man is good, I don't think I will repeat my mother's history.

Where have I found strength? I have always believed in God and am a regular churchgoer. Whenever I have a problem and want it resolved, I go to church and pray to God that I will be successful. My maternal grandmother played a major role in this respect. She always told me stories of Jesus, and the miracles of the Zoja.* I was little, but I believed. My prayers have been answered and God has created favorable circumstances for my desires to be fulfilled.

Anxhela, who is 17 and speaks good English, told us,

I haven't suffered so many bitter experiences as my mother. My life could never be compared to hers. However, one thing is that I would have liked the communist regime not to have ever existed. When I was a child, we were like parrots. We had to do what we were told. On celebration days we had to go out and applaud the leader and do what the others did because it was an order.

A decisive moment in my life came four years ago when I was finishing school and wanted to go on to the foreign language school. Only the children of Communist Party members were allowed to go there. I knew I couldn't be favored, and

*She refers to the mysterious healing powers attributed to an icon of the Virgin Mary, the Lady of Shkodër (Zoja e Shkodres).

Alma in Shkodër.

yet I desired it so badly that I often wondered how I could do it. That was the year the regime broke and the Democratic Party won. For the first time in my life, I was free to choose. A competition for the school was held. Because I had good grades and worked hard for the competition, I won first place. I had told myself that everything depended on me; that if I were skilled enough I would succeed. I finished high school with top marks and am now taking my exams. I achieved what I wanted: to study English and other foreign languages (Italian, Spanish, German, and a little Turkish).

I dream now of attending a good university, abroad, if possible. I think I would get a better education outside the country because the conditions are so bad here. I want to study English and psychology, either or both of these. I want to use my education to become a worthy person for my society, for my parents, and for myself. I would also like to have a family, but it is early to think about that now.

[When asked from where she has drawn her strength, Anxhela answered,] First from God. He has always enlightened my way and He has given me such good parents and family to count on. Second from my parents: their comfort, protection, and encouragement. Without these I wouldn't even be half of what I am. I like all the characteristics my mother possesses, but more than anything else I admire her strength. She has always been close to me. Whenever I have followed my mother's advice, I have been successful. Without her I wouldn't be where I am. I dedicate my life to my mother.

Chapter 18

The Lives of Young Village Women

The distinction between the transition generation and the teenagers is not as great in the villages, especially the most remote villages, as it is in the cities. However, there is still a great difference between their expectations and dreams and the role of faith in their lives. While the expectations of the village women of the transition generation have been raised a great deal, those of the teenagers have been raised even more. At the same time, the circumstances of their lives have not improved significantly. In fact, for some their lives are more circumscribed now than at any time since the period prior to the War of Liberation. The biggest difference is between the lives of the village teenagers who are no longer in school and the ones who are still in school. Those girls who are still in school continue to have hope and determination.

Luz i Vogel

ON THE ROAD TO LUZ

Since most of the interviews we had done to date had been with women in the older and middle generations, Ksanthi and I went out in search of young women. We were also interested in finding a village with some distinctive characteristics that was also relatively close to Tiranë. Kozeta Mamaqi asked to accompany us to do some interviewing for a radio program and so the three of us set out together. Our original destination was the village of Shen Gjergj in the district of Tiranë, but we changed our minds when we realized just how difficult it is to get there. We chose Luz i Vogel instead, because it had special meaning to Kozeta and tied in with her story, and also because it was accessible.

We went by car on a Tuesday morning in early October, just after the opening of the school year. It was a lovely sunny and breezy day, warm and picture-perfect Albanian weather, when the sky is so wide and blue that you feel as if you might fall into it. We took the Kavajë Road out of Tiranë and wound around to Durrës, talking all the way. Next we went along the coast, then turned inland. The road in Kavajë has deteriorated to being almost impassable and we bumped and thumped our way to the other side of town. From there we headed south for several miles to the turnoff to Luz. Fortunately, Kozeta remembered the turn and we were able to find our way easily.

Luz is a small village located on a flat plain in the central coastal area of Albania. It is exposed on all sides and there is no contour to the land. There are a few low-rise apartment buildings, some other low buildings—including the elementary and high schools and a few grim shops—and some scattered houses. From the center of the village there was no green visible: no fields, no trees, nothing. The most striking feature of the village was its dirtiness: there was dust and dirt everywhere, and the only color came from the trash strewn in all directions.

Since we arrived unannounced, we went directly to the school to see if we could find someone to help us. There we met some of the teachers and had an opportunity to learn about the village from them. We then put together a group of teenagers from among the students. Finally, we met with some of the older members of the younger generation in a home.

A memorable moment came in the middle of the day when we were ready for our picnic lunch. We found a sheltered spot with some rocks near the school. We sat there among the discarded soda and beer cans, the candy and potato chip wrappers, and the dust as we shared our cheese and bread and fruit with each other.

The elementary school is a one-story, whitewashed building with broken glass, dirt, and ducks in the yard outside. The noise coming from the building was deafening. However, there we had an opportunity to meet Mihane, one of the teachers, and to talk with her in a quiet place. She and her husband are both from Luz and are both teachers. Mihane told us that the village has a population of 5,000, but that almost all of the boys 17 to 25 years of age have emigrated, most of them illegally, to Italy, some to Greece. She continued,

As grim as the village may look now, it was worse before the liberation. The situation changed a bit during the years after the liberation. Although much was spoken during the years of "Monism" (communism) about how little difference there was between the living conditions and circumstances in villages and towns, in fact the gap was large. I remember that the situation was such that we could not buy food. We were given very little rations. Thanks to democracy everything is totally changed. The standard of living is much higher. Almost all of the families have furniture and televisions now. The economy of the village is mostly agriculture and diary products, but the emigrants have contributed greatly to improve the standard of living.

There are 600 children in the elementary school, all of whom are from Luz. In fact, there are so many children that we run the school on two shifts. The high school is for the entire area and has only 160 students. There are so few students in the high school because during the transition period, the situation was very confusing. People were afraid to let their children come one and sometimes one and a half hours on foot to the school. At that time, the enrollment fell to just 17 students. It is back up now, but it is mostly girls as the boys have emigrated. They leave the country very young. It is the girls who go on to high school and some even go on to university in Tiranë.

Mihane also told us that the village is almost 100 percent Muslim, although a few Orthodox have married into the village.

THE SCHOOLGIRLS

We interviewed eight 17-year-olds in a classroom in the high school, standing or sitting on desks for want of chairs. The walls and the stone floor of the room were dirty, there was a stylized picture of happy farm workers on the wall, and there was an old wood stove in one corner. The girls were dressed in slacks or blue jeans and spoke openly and easily.* The energy level was high and the time flew.

Ornela, an outspoken and direct young woman, told us of her difficult life and the challenges she faces,

If I speak sincerely, my life has been full of difficulties. My parents divorced when I was very young and I have lived with my grandparents. They have taken care of me since I was born and are my real parents. I stayed with my grandparents because my father was almost always drunk. At one time I was ashamed to see my parents because people here talk much and gossip. It isn't the fault of the people, it is the fault of the regime that allowed this behavior to continue. But, for example, they speak badly of a girl whose parents were divorced. It mostly doesn't bother me because there is a saying in Albanian that I like: "From a bush a rose comes out and from a rose a bush."

In my opinion there is a difference between town girls and village girls. Many village girls understand life well and want to do what they like, but they can't do what they want because of social opinion. What I mean is that I am a girl of 17 with lots of dreams and wishes, but I can't put them into reality. I can dance and sing, but if I do these things, I will be the subject of gossip. I want to love, but I can't because it will be commented upon. Here the girls live for others and not for themselves. However, a girl in town lives a different life.

*Many of the names of the participants in this group, and the names of family members, have been changed because their comments were so honest and direct that I fear repercussions for them, at home or in the village, if their comments are attributed.

The major problem here is stress between generations. There are parents who understand, but even when they share our opinions they too are afraid of social opinion.

Olta interjected, "I will make it concrete. Many girls, for example, would love to continue in school, but can't because their parents think that school is a place for love stories. There are many killed dreams among young girls in our village."

Mirsa agreed,

My family is emancipated and my parents understand me, but they put the breaks on my dreams because of the mentality of the people here. It will take a while for this mentality to change.

What are my dreams? To dress beautifully and as I like, to love freely, to travel outside of Albania and see what Western Europe is like. I would also like to go to college because I am a good student, even considering the poor conditions we have here. [Ornela interjected, "God is great and will help you realize this."] I am not unusual in this desire to learn, but the teachers are not very demanding and we expect that they will close this school because the number of students has declined so far. Many are interested in school, but are much occupied with the cows and sheep.

Ina also spoke of the destructive power of public opinion:

I have led a quiet life. I have wonderful parents who are warm and full of love. However, when I was young, I competed for ballet. I didn't win and that was a shock, but what came after was the real shock. I wanted to go on dancing, but couldn't. Why? Because all the village gossiped about me. They called me a "bad" girl. Even the children in school brought this opinion of me from home. When I was only 12 I received a letter accusing me of being a prostitute. I wanted to make up for this opinion so for three years I stayed closed up and away from others. Thanks to my good parents I overcame this difficult situation. They understood and helped me to be myself. I also thank my friends here who understood me.

What about my future? Dancing and ballet were my dream, but that dream is over. Because I am ambitious by nature, I think now that I might go on to be a clothes designer. I also paint beautifully. People like my paintings, but behind my back they say, "A girl going on in this will never have a family or a decent life." I also love to write. I have already written a novel.

How has this social environment and the difficulties it has created affected these young women?

Daniela responded, "I have followed attentively what has been said and I agree, but what hasn't been said is that there is still optimism among us. We are not dead people."

Mirsa added, "We want to do away with all pessimism that sometimes comes up among us. We are the generation that will go forward and put an end to this kind of mentality."

When asked how they envisioned their future, many of them responded poetically and with passion, as Mirsa did: "I see a clean, clear sky. A dove flying freely in a clear blue sky over a deep blue sea. I am the dove and my only dream is to fly freely and not have my dreams cut, to have no one hinder my flight. I would love to be famous. I believe strongly in God to help me realize my goals."

Ina stated more simply, "I would love to feel complete freedom. I am free now, but I want to be freer. I want to be famous, not only in Albania, but outside. I am determined."

With reference to marriage, they all desired to marry for love, many drawing upon their parents' experiences as Olta did: "My parents were married under an arrangement, but my mother's father was a communist and my father's father was an anticommunist. After four years of marriage, my mother's father asked her to divorce her husband, but she refused. You see, she had given birth to two children and she did not accept the demand to leave her husband. She was one of eight children and never went to see her parents again or took part in family wedding ceremonies. As for me, I wish that no one would interfere in my future life and family."

Mirsa added, "My parents were married under an arrangement and saw each other first on the day of the marriage. My father says that he married a beautiful girl and now he has five beautiful girls and one boy. Although they have been happy, I will choose when I marry."

Where have these young women found strength to meet the challenges of their lives?

Ina told us, "The primary source of my strength has been my family. I mean by that my parents. My parents are the main driving force for me to go on. I also have great confidence in myself. I think that a woman should appreciate herself. If she doesn't she will never expect to be successful."

Teuta's response was characteristic of this generation: "If I have a strong desire and a big passion, I can realize it. If there is no passion and no talent, you don't expect to realize your dream."

Mirsa's viewpoint was different: "For me, God is on the first plane. God is the greatest source of strength and I rely on him. Family and economic conditions and a strong belief in myself are also key."

Olta added, "We find strength in ourselves, in our hearts, in our families, and above all in God because God thinks of all people. I don't believe in hoxhas or priests, but I believe in God and I pray to him. God understands me better than anyone. He is my hope."

Ornela concluded this discussion with her thoughts: "It depends on a person's economic and spiritual situation. Courage gives one optimism and hope, and hope will be the last thing to die for me. God created us and my hopes depend on what God has thought of me, because after you have something bad comes something good."

When asked what role faith played in their lives, Daniela answered, "For me God occupies an important part in my life. I hope that God will help me much because I believe and pray to him. I have read the Bible and am impressed by the words of Jesus Christ, who says 'Blessed be he who believes in me.' My family is Bektashi and our faith includes belief in Jesus Christ."

Mirsa said, "I have read the Koran. I believe very much in my faith. I believe in God and respect religion. Reading the Koran is part of one's culture and it helps me to respect other religions."

Meli spoke with tears in her eyes, "For me God is in the first plan and stands above all else. My father respects all of the religious feasts and is very strict about religious rituals."

Teuta also expressed her faith: "When I go to bed I pray to God for everything, for my wrongs of the day, for things that trouble me, and for my family. I have much faith in God."

Rudina also said, "I don't believe in hoxhas or priests, but I do believe in God and that he will help me. I pray only for his help."

THE TRANSITION GENERATION IN LUZ

After this meeting in the school, and after our picnic in the trash, Mirsa set up a group of older members of this generation at her home in a severely dilapidated apartment building with a poorly equipped interior. It was a poor home and spoke of a poor quality of life in the village, but the spirit of the group—which included Ina's sister, Erjona, and Mirsa's sisters, Griselda and Elsa—was surprisingly optimistic.

Erjona, 21, told us,

I am one of three girls in my family. I graduated from high school and have stayed at home for the past four years. I would like to go on to university, but cannot because of economic and other problems in my family. For example, my older sister went on to study for economics, but she didn't finish. She quit to get married to someone she loved. My parents have a fear that the same will happen with me and that is not acceptable to them.

Because we come from a formerly persecuted family, I hope to be given the right to study to become a teacher, but by correspondence . My grandfather was a member of the Balli Kombëtar and spent five years in prison.

Right now, all day, every day, my life is monotonous. I do housework and work in the garden and in the field, in our family's plot. I do most of the field work because my older sister is married and my younger sister is still in school.

I am also now thinking of my family, but in the future, I expect to have an arranged marriage, not because that is what I want. However, a matchmaker will propose someone. I would like the chance to agree, but I do not expect to have that opportunity. I would love to marry for love, but there is no opportunity for me to meet someone.

I find strength in my hope for the future. My optimism helps me ignore the monotony in my life. I simply hope for a better future.

Griselda, Mirsa and Ana's 25-year-old sister, told us,

I have finished my studies at the agricultural school (vocational high school) and am now at home. I am not engaged or married. There are now six adults living in our household (a two-bedroom apartment with a living room) so I do housework because I have no profession or education of any value. After I finish the housework, I listen to music or read the newspaper or poetry. I would like to be a hairdresser and to have a salon like my friend, Aida, but I can't afford to do that.

Considering the living conditions and the environment, by which I mean the social opinion, I don't think life is beautiful here, but I hope that the future will be better. I would like to marry for love, but let it be what it may. I have been offered a young man, but I haven't decided. At least, I hope I will have the decision.

My primary source of strength is my family, especially my mother and sisters. We communicate well. We pour out our hearts to each other and help one another. We are also a religious family. We all hope that God will help us realize our dreams.

Mirsa and Griselda's sister Ana, 18, then spoke:

I finished high school and am now at home. I don't work in the field, but only in the house. I do the housekeeping, cooking, and cleaning. When I am done, I listen to music and dance. I have no opportunity to go to college because of my family's economic situation. I too would like to become a hairdresser. In fact, it is a great desire I have. I don't think of marriage or engagement yet because I am too young.

The greatest difficulty I have faced in my life is when I left school. I had such nice friendships. I enjoyed being with my classmates and we all loved being with each other. [She cries.] Life at home is monotonous and boring. Only my faith in God—this has given me strength.

Aida, 25, is an energetic and determined young woman and one of the fortunate ones in Luz. We first met Aida in her beauty salon earlier in the day. It was a bare concrete structure with one broken chair and a mirror. A young woman sat on the chair with a dirty towel around her shoulders as Aida cut her hair. The only other evidence that this was a hairdresser's establishment was an old electric curler set made of rusting metal.

I am one of seven children, five girls and two boys. I am single, but engaged to a man I love. How did I meet him? One day he stopped me on the road in his car and asked me who I was and who my family was. Luckily enough, a cousin of his gave him more information about me and my family. My family accepted him and we will be married this next summer. My fiancé is by origin from a village near Berat and now works in Italy. I was engaged once before two years ago for love, but we had to break the engagement through no fault of either one of us. People spoke badly of us.

I have been working in my own beauty shop now for two years. My sister attended a hairdressing course in Durrës for nine months and she taught me what she learned there. I make 6,000 new lekë [about $60] per month. My dreams are beautiful and I hope that they will be realized. I especially dream to have a house of my own.

The people who love me give me strength: my family and the people around me. Also, we say that God holds us in his hand, and that God throws us down with one hand and lifts us up with the other. I am thankful to God that he gave me a boy—my future husband.

Valshaj

On the way back from Luz i Vogel, as we were driving along the Durrës Road toward Tiranë, we saw some young girls working in the fields and stopped to interview them. They told a similar story to that told by the transition generation in Luz. Aida, Irena, and Bedrana were sisters. Aida, 20, told us,

I am the oldest girl in my family. I finished high school and am now working in the house. I spend my spare time reading romances and novels and watching television. When I have time, I work in the garden. Our father used to work in the mine, but now he does all that comes along. For example, he is currently working for an Italian firm that makes visors. My mother looks after the cow and we girls look after the house and help with the cooking. For fun we sometimes walk in the boulevard of Maminas [a slightly larger village close by]. Most of the village girls here spend their time in the village and at home embroidering.

We have all had a difficult life and thank God that democracy came and gave us a better life. Also, thanks to my father's hard work, we have had a good house for 20 years.

In the future, I hope for a better life. There is something characteristic about the village: most of my friends were engaged and married from the age of 16. I am lonely sometimes because my friends aren't here or are leading very different lives. I am the only 20-year-old girl in the village not married, but 2 weeks ago I was engaged to a boy from Tiranë. A friend of our family arranged the marriage. I was happy that it was in my hands to say yes or no.

From where have I drawn strength in my life? I think that all of us find strength in work and in God.

[Bedrana, 18, went on,] I finished high school last year and now I work in the house. Occasionally, I have a good time with my friends. Many of my friends are now married, but there are some other single girls like me who are my friends.

The sisters and their friends: Bedrana, Ornela, Dorina, Irena and Aida.

I look forward to a good future and to having good friendships. I would like to be a hairdresser. I was studying in Maminas, but now I will go to Tiranë to study.

I have gained my strength from my mother's great love. She gives much love and warmth to me. She is not an obstacle for any of us to do what we want.

[Irena, 16, added,] I finished eighth grade and didn't continue because it was a difficult period. My parents were afraid of girls being raped and injured so they wouldn't let me go to school. I am now at home and responsible for the garden while my sisters work more in the house.

In the future I would like to be a singer and a dancer. I also love poetry and would like to write.

I think that just the difficult life in the village has taught us a lot about being strong.

As we were talking, some other young girls came and joined us sitting in the field. Ornela, 17, told us,

I am engaged and will be married next week. I am marrying a man from another village whom I love. Even if my parents had not agreed, they would have had no way to say no because I had made up my mind and I had given my promise. My fiancé is nine years older and is a businessman doing importing of goods to Albania from Turkey.

There are six children in my family and my parents work in agriculture. I only attended school through the eighth grade. It is fanaticism that doesn't allow girls to finish school.

In the future I dream of going abroad. Of course I will go to Turkey as my husband works there. I will have a child and meet all my child's needs. I don't really think much about the future; marriage is first.

When asked about the source of her strength, Ornela shrugged and then when asked about the role of faith in her life, she replied simply, "I am Muslim and I believe strongly in God."

Aida interjected here, "Don't you know that God gives you strength?" and Ornela responded, "That doesn't mean that I can rest and let God do it all for me. I have to work hard, too."

Dorina, 15, turned out to be Irena's best friend and the only one of this group of young women in Valshaj who was still in school. She told us,

I am in the second year of high school and I don't care that people say that the only reason girls go to school is to meet a boy. It doesn't bother me; it's just gossip and my parents and I know what my behavior is like. It's just like the villagers to gossip, especially the old women who say things about everyone's appearance. Enver left them to their fanaticism. I keep going to school to get more knowledge. In the future, I would like to go on to university, but I don't know if my family can afford it.

I find strength in my love of life. It gives me the strength to face life successfully. Also, I believe in God. God gives me strength and courage. People can live if they have the courage to face life.

In the South

The young village women in the southern part of Albania appeared to be more focused on emigration, primarily to Greece, than any other women of any age whom we interviewed. This may be for any one of a number of reasons. The first is simple geography. Greece shares the southern border of Albania. The second is that there is a legitimate Greek minority living in southern Albania by sheer circumstance and because of where the borders of the modern countries of Greece and Albania are drawn.* Finally, there are traditionally close commercial and trading ties between southern Albania (especially along the coast) and Greece, which date back centuries.

*Although the border is not officially in dispute at this time, there are Greeks who view southern Albania as northern Greece, part of the province of Epirus, as well as Albanians who view what is now northern Greece as part of the original Illyrian kingdom and therefore part of southern Albania.

HIMARË

I stopped in Himarë as I was passing through on a pleasure trip along the Ionian coast to the southern city of Sarandë. The trip along the coast from Llogarë, high up in a mountain pass, down to the coastal village of Dhermi and then on to Himarë is stunningly beautiful as the narrow and twisting road leads through olive groves and provides sweeping views of the shoreline and clear blue water. This area is not developed because it was considered to be of military importance in the communist regime. Therefore, it is probably the most unspoiled coastline in Europe. The old village of Himarë sits atop a hill overlooking the sea, but the modern village sits directly on the water.

Ksanthi referred me to the English teacher at the high school in Himarë as someone who might be able to help me find women to interview and to translate for me, Bukurie. All I knew was her first name. I went first to the school, which sits on a bluff overlooking the village and the sea on what is clearly one of the potentially most valuable pieces of property in the village. The school itself, though of relatively recent construction, is a shambles, with no windows and a dusty, dirty lot around it. Since it was early on a Saturday afternoon, school had just finished and there were no teachers or students to be found there.

As I was walking back to my car, a woman who was working in her garden called out and asked if she could help me. I explained what I was doing and whom I was looking for and she sent me to the center of town to a café, owned apparently by a relative of Bukurie's. When I got there, I found the café closed so I tried asking in another. A man there directed me across the street, where I met someone who told me that Bukurie's apartment was in a building just behind the waterfront. When I found her and explained my purpose, she kindly set out with me to assist.

As we walked, Bukurie explained,

Himarë was a cooperative before the democratic reform. The women here received very low wages and found it hard to make a living. So, the minute democracy came, the people left. Most of them went to Greece or the United States, where they had relatives. Many people here pretend to be Greek in order to get Greek visas, and most of the people who go to Greece from Himarë go with legitimate visas.

[She explained what she meant by "pretend to be Greek."] Most of the people in Himarë speak Greek, although they are predominantly ethnic Albanians. The Greek language came here many years ago through trade with nearby Greek islands and was taught in the schools here, which were run by what was at that time the Greek Orthodox Church [before the establishment of the independent Albanian church in 1908].

The people go to Greece and work for wages that are lower than the wages earned by the Greeks, but they are happy because they are employed and earn more than they could make here. Most of them go to Greece to make money, but return to Albania because it is their home. This emigration has had a devastating effect on the schools in Himarë because many of the people who have left are the teachers. Therefore, the remaining teachers are instructing in fields in which they themselves have inadequate training. The students are not being well prepared and are bored, so many of them are trying to leave as well to get an education in Greece. The class sizes have fallen and the school is in danger of closing.

Through Bukurie I had the good fortune to meet two girls who exemplified this trend. Viki (18) and Dorime (16) are sisters, the second youngest and the youngest of a family of six girls.

Dorime explained her family's circumstances,

My father, who is 64, was a bus ticket clerk, but he is now out of work and my mother, who is 52, works in a bakery. My parents were married under an arrangement and it has been very hard for our mother. I admire her because she is strong in decision making and very calm. She has worked hard and has done what she had to do to support her family. My father hasn't been helpful to her so she has had to survive. She is still an optimistic person, despite all her troubles. Our father was nice to us, but hard on our sisters. He was frequently depressed and that made him demand more from them. Our second sister worked as a dressmaker and that helped our family financially when we were young.

When asked what she had learned from her mother, Viki explained more about their family,

What lessons have I learned from my mother? I would have to say that the lesson I have learned is that every problem in my life I want to be able to solve calmly, as she does. In Himarë there is a characteristic of the women that they do the hardest work and have the full burden of the family. Here in our family the division of the jobs has not been correct. Father worked, but he used all the money for himself: he drank it. Therefore, my mother had to work extra hard. Our grandmother raised us when our mother was at work. Also, when our father was drunk, he hit my mother and sisters. We felt sorry about this and sometimes we were frightened, but for us it was a way of life.

Dorime added, "Things have changed now. He is older and doesn't drink anymore because he has a health problem."

When asked about how they saw their futures, Dorime responded first, "I would like to be a lawyer, but you have to study hard and that's difficult for me. I have an aunt and cousin in America and would like to go there to study."

Viki stated her goals in this way, "I left school at 17 years of age because I want to go to Greece. I didn't find school interesting here. Maybe in Greece I will find a course in computers that will help me get ahead in life.

Sisters Dorime and Viki.

I already have three sisters in Greece. At some point I hope to get married, but for love, and have children."

Where have they drawn strength from to face the family and economic difficulties in their lives? Dorime responded, "From ourselves. I can deal with things and just know that I will survive. I am just that way—strong." Viki agreed and added, "I don't expect others to help me. Who else better than me. I will find force within myself."

When asked what role faith had played in their lives, Viki responded for both, "We both believe very much. Faith in God is related to faith or belief in oneself. We will always go forward in hope that God will help us."

BELLOVODË

Near Vithkuq in the Korçë region the daughters of Viktori told us about their hopes and dreams, as well as about the importance that working in Greece has for their family. Florenca, 20, the middle daughter began,

We have lived neither a good nor a bad life. My father has worked in the mines and my mother has worked on the cooperative and been a housewife.

I have finished two classes of secondary school. I have especially good memories of the time when I was in school. None of the girls in the village has completed secondary school because there is no school here and the families are afraid to send their daughters to another village. Besides, there used to be a bus to take us to school, but the bus doesn't come any more.

After I stopped going to school, I went to Greece to work, to care for two children. [Her grandmother who was sitting with us interjected here, "All the young people want to leave the village."]

I am engaged to a man from another village whom I met in Greece. It is technically an arranged marriage, but I chose him. We will be married next week and have our honeymoon at the beach. So, for the immediate future I am looking forward to my wedding and then returning to Greece to work for some time. My husband's family is there, but when the conditions are better in Albania we will return. I also want a family and a better house in my country.

The most challenging time in my life was when I first went to Greece and I didn't know the language. It was good that I was with my father. Now I can speak Greek well and I get on well with my work as a baby-sitter. It took a lot of strength, but I had a desire to know what life was like in Greece and I wanted a better life than I have had here. That gave me strength.

What role has faith played in my life? I believe strongly. Whenever I have found myself in difficult times I have prayed for help. It is inside me.

Margarita, 23, the oldest of the daughters, told a similar story,

I finished middle school: it was another time and democracy had not yet come. I am now married, partly by arrangement and partly for love. We have been married for three years and have two children. My husband and I live in Athens where he works in a department store and I have been a housewife.

My immediate goal for the future is to start working. I would like to get the best job that I can. I would also like to attend a course for some sort of skills— sewing or something.

I find strength in myself. I am courageous.

Brunilda, 17, said,

I still live at home and have not yet been to Greece to work because I am too young. I spend my time watching television, embroidering, and helping my mother look after the children. My oldest sister leaves her youngest child with us when she goes to Greece.

I expect that in the future I will go to Greece and see what the world is like outside. I would like to marry a man who is more beautiful and richer than I am, but who is good like me.

In the North

HOMESH

As the remotest village we visited, Homesh typified the changes that are throwing the lives of the young women back to those of an earlier century.

There are higher hopes and optimism based on what they wish for, but for many the direction of their daily lives is backward rather than forward.

For those in the transition generation, there has been a change for the better as evidenced in both Nasije and Fiqirete's words. Nasije, 28, the oldest member of this generation whom we interviewed in Homesh, told us of her childhood and her dreams,

I was the eldest of eight children. Like many children, at that time, we dreamed to lead a life where we had enough to eat. We knew that others led a better life and our plan was to work hard to bring about a change in our own lives.

I was married at the age of 23—one half for love and one half arranged. I liked my husband. He had been married before, but his first wife died, and he had two daughters from that marriage. We now have two daughters of our own. Although my life is better now because we have everything we need, I have other challenges, including raising the children from his first marriage. It's okay, however, because I love my husband and have good relations with his children.

I find force in my outlook for a better future. To have a boy: that is the specific aspect of my dream. Also, I dream to have the girls' dreams realized. I want them to receive an education and live a better life. I'd like my two daughters to be like their two half sisters: well educated and polite.

Fiqirete is 24 and the wife of the singing tractor-driver, Besniku, who is also Hatixhe's son.* Fiqirete told us of the difficulties she faced in the past and the great changes that have occurred for her. In listening to her, we sensed healing and resolution of old wounds.

I didn't attend school beyond the eighth grade because I was the sixth child out of nine and had to work in the cooperative. Most of the work I did was hard: opening new land on top of the mountain.

I have been married now for three years and have one son. Although I was married under an arrangement, I had a year-long engagement and it has worked out well. I never thought of marrying in any other way than by arrangement. After all, where would I have met a man to fall in love with? I worked all the time.

I don't work now because I married into one of the wealthiest families in the area, the Dema family. They owned much of the land in Homesh and much of that has been restored to them. Therefore, I have had a vast improvement in my life since I got married. In the future I hope that we will be even better off economically and that we will stay here in the village.

What role has faith played in my life? I have always believed. I always fasted during Bajram, even though in former times people came to us to give us biscuits as a test.

BRIGHT SMILES AND TEARS

We interviewed a number of young girls in Homesh, including Suela, 16, the stepdaughter of Nasije, and the granddaughter of Hide. This beautiful and

*See page 61 above.

articulate young girl with long brown hair told us of her life and dreams with clarity, fierceness, and passion.

My father is an electrical mechanic and my mother was a cooperative worker who died 6 years ago in childbirth at the age of 29. She had been married for 11 years, under an arrangement, of course. I really admired her because she was courageous. She wanted us to look good and dress well and she worked hard to make a better life for us. Mother didn't live long enough to find a moment of happiness for herself. She sacrificed to the maximum for us and she was extremely careful and caring. My mother prepared me to be a good woman. She said time and again, "When you learn how to do these things, I won't be around." Did she understand that she would not live long? I don't know, but I do know that my mother and father had problems and their relations were not good. They didn't understand each other well. They were so young. I think that men don't always understand women. My mother, for example, wanted to change things for the better in the family. She liked to buy new and beautiful things for the house, but my father was against her. That was one cause for trouble in the family. However, I never thought that my good mother would die so young.

For the future, I want to go to school to learn English and Italian and to attend the fine arts school to become an actress. I would like to become someone and do something that would satisfy me and others. I think of marriage, but not now. There are people who think it is their duty just to marry off their daughters. This would ruin my dreams!! Society hurries to get daughters married now because they need to work the land. [Her friend, Anita, commented here, "fanaticism has come back with the return of the land."] Education has a great impact on the character of the people; otherwise they fall victim to their parents and the society.

What I find in me will make me successful, I think. I will find strength in myself.

In response to the question regarding what role faith has played in her life, she replied simply, "I believe in God, but I don't pray."

Suela did not see herself as typical of the young women in Homesh, and our interviews with the other young women there bore out this opinion. We met one evening with a group of 9 young women ranging from 15 to 22 years of age. They were all friends from a certain part of the village. These attractive and sweet young girls cried and smiled, but were almost unable to talk due to the emotion they felt.

Bukuroshja, whose name means "beautiful young girl," is well named. She is 18 years old and is one of the fortunate ones who was allowed to finish high school. She told us about her family and her future. "I am from a family of five children, two boys and three girls. I am close to my mother and admire her because she is hardworking and has done her best to raise good children.

"What is my outlook for the future? I have many desires and dreams. I would like to create a family and lead a much more beautiful life."

Suela in Homesh.

Edlira, another beautiful girl of 18 who also finished high school, told us, "There are so many ways in which I would like to be like my mother, but mostly I would like to be a good dressmaker. My dream for the future is to become a good dressmaker."

Teuta, another 18-year-old, the third of 5 children, added this about her life, "I finished school only through the eighth grade because my father wouldn't let me finish high school, even though I wanted to. I admire my mother because she has worked hard to raise me. I have inherited everything good from my mother.

"My outlook for the future? I think I will probably be married by arrangement, but I would like to know him first before marriage. I don't know if I will. My dream? I don't know. Life in a village is not bad, but I think it is better in a city."

Majlinda is 17 years of age and the only one of these girls still in school. She is in her third year of high school. She told us only the most basic things about her family and stated simply that her outlook was "to lead a better life."

Mirela, 22 years of age, said, "I was fortunate to have finished high school. While I was there, I ran track and played basketball and other sports. I enjoyed these activities a great deal and miss them. Although I am not working now, I did work briefly as an elementary school teacher.

"I cannot foresee my future. Marriage, of course, but considering the hard life in the village, I can't see staying here and getting married here, even though the village is beautiful. It is difficult to find the right man because we are so closed here. If the opportunity were given to me to fall in love with someone, my family wouldn't object. I don't believe that I will be forced into an arranged marriage.

"What impresses me about my mother is the way she has tried to raise all of us. I admire that she is a good housewife, despite all of the other work. She is very gifted and talented at embroidery and needlework. I would not like to lead the life my mother led economically, but I would like to have the relationship my parents had as an example."

Ylvija, 21 years old and fifth of a family of 6, cried and smiled throughout the interview, explaining, "I am sensitive by nature." The extent of her dream is "to become a professional worker at making mattresses."

Adelina is 18 years old and the eldest of 5 children. She finished high school, but now works at home. She told us, "I have been engaged under an arrangement for nine months and I like my fiancé, even though I didn't know him before. He is from another village in the region."

When we asked Adelina about her dreams, she simply shrugged and tears formed in her eyes.

Three of the girls in Homesh: Ylvija, Edlira, and Mirela.

Selvija, 15, didn't speak for herself as she was too overcome with emotion. Her friends explained that she was sad because she had wanted to go on with her studies, but her father wouldn't let her. She now works in the field and in the home, waiting for her father to arrange a marriage for her.

What was the emotion that overwhelmed these young girls as we spoke? We discussed our impressions with our 17-year-old hostess, Anita, after the interview. She explained that their sadness had to do with the restrictions placed on their lives and the contrast they felt between their lives and those of girls in the outside world. Although they spoke with optimism of leading better lives, they also spoke with enormous sadness that their schooldays, filled with learning and fun, were over and that they really had very little to look forward to: work in the fields and around the house, arranged marriages, and a circumscribed life.

A particularly poignant moment came when I asked the girls if they had any questions to ask me. They were shy at first, but finally managed to ask me where teenage girls in the United States meet young men. As I thought about the answer, it was my turn to cry because I had never thought much before about the social freedoms that American girls have and didn't want to throw the contrasts in the face of these young girls.

As we rose to leave, they began treating us like talismen. They wanted to be as close to us as they could. They wanted their photos taken with us;

they carried our purses, books, and bags in solemn and, for some, barefoot procession through the fields when we left; and touched our arms and hands when we were walking, to guide us and steady us in the muddy and uneven terrain, even though we showed no signs of needing this assistance. Every time I turned to one of them, she smiled and frequently a tear rolled down her cheek simultaneously.

When I told the girls in Tiranë about this interview, they did not believe me. How could such a life for young women like them still exist in their country? Clearly, the future is mixed for the women of this generation and much needs to be done to improve the circumstances of the young women in the villages, especially in the areas of family economics and social conventions.

The stories that follow illustrate some of the dramatic changes that have occurred for some of the young women in Albania and suggest a bright future for many others.

Chapter 19

Valbona Selimllari:
Instant Stardom

As the first "Miss Albania," Valbona is both well-known and much loved. However, I decided to interview her with some trepidation, fearing that she might not in fact be representative of her generation or that she might be arrogant and unpleasant in accordance with my stereotype of beauty queens.

We went to pick her up at her parents' home on the boulevard in Tiranë. Although Ksanthi and I had received directions from her, it turned out that the young man who was our driver, Sokol, knew where she lived because he had lived next door as a child, and remembered Valbona as one of neighborhood children with whom he had played. When we arrived we only had to wait a short while for Valbona to come down to the car, and when she arrived she greeted Sokol casually and asked about his family. My concerns were dispelled immediately in the warmth of Valbona's personality and smile.

Valbona was born on May 23, 1972, and grew up in a simple family of people from Përmet. She is one of 4 children: 3 girls and a boy. She describes her brother, who at 13 is the youngest of the children, as "the lion of the house." Although her father studied engineering, he did not graduate from school. He was an excellent mechanic, however, and found work as a mechanic and later as a driver at the Kinostudio (the Film Studio). Her mother graduated from high school and was an upholsterer.

Valbona is good-hearted, and her story is one of luck and success.

The Beginning

I had a good childhood. I lived in a good neighborhood where I had many friends and a good area in which to play. Also, I grew up in a happy family.

Although my father cried when I was born because he had wanted a son, as time went by we became closer and closer. In fact, we have always been much closer than my mother and I have been. Some of the qualities that I really admire in my father are that he is nice, quiet, straightforward, and direct. He also has a good sense of humor.

I think that my mother is like most Albanian women. They are strong and so is my mother. She has a good personality and is also powerful. Since my father was gone a great deal of the time, she has had all the problems of housework and the upbringing of us children. I think that is why sometimes she has been hard on us.

Very often I am asked who I am like and I respond that I have inherited something in my character from both parents. I have, for example, inherited some of my mother's strength and therefore have been able to cope well with the hard work I have been asked to do. I am also just like my father in some ways. For example, he only gets really furious when someone does him an injustice, and I am the same way.

In addition, my grandfather had a great influence on my life. He was always very confident about everything that had to do with me. I was not a beautiful child. In fact, when I was born I had a small head and a big nose. I was better looking by the time I was three, but I was still not good-looking, even when I grew older. Maybe it was the way I did my hair or the way I dressed, but my sisters were always more beautiful than I was. It was my grandfather who had confidence in me and encouraged me. He always said to my parents, "Don't think of it! She will be the most beautiful." My parents were also upset about my grades in high school and my father used to say that I would be fit only to clean pigsties if I didn't study more. However, when my grandfather heard all this he said, "Say what you like, but God will send her everything." I thought these were the words of a saint and I looked up to him. In fact, my grandfather's confidence in me was justified, and I was so sorry that he died at the age of 94 before I became Miss Albania.

When I was young I was a gymnast and I loved this activity. I started when I was eight years of age and competed on a team called Dinamo, which placed first for three years in succession. However, I gave it up in my second year of high school because the team was disbanded. Even though I loved gymnastics, I never dreamed of being a sports girl. Since I was a child, my dream has always been to do something to give people pleasure. For example, when I saw something on television that was pleasing, I wanted to be a television personality and be able to give viewers that sort of entertainment.

The Opportunity

When the first Miss Albania pageant was organized in Albania in 1991, I was a quiet girl. I didn't walk in the boulevard like the other young people. I thought it was just a show and a waste of time. I didn't find pleasure in being with these groups of people. I just went to my aunt's house or visited in my friends' homes. However, in my family, I was always the one who had the most freedom because I am an independent spirit like my mother. From time to time my mother would tell me not to do things, but I didn't like to obey. During this time I was at an age when

Valbona Selimllari.

I knew what I had to do and was not likely to be led astray. Therefore, I didn't worry my parents. As a person, I value independence and freedom highly. I don't want anyone to interfere, even my mother.

Anyway, I did nothing to enter the competition to become Miss Albania. It so happened that a sister of a friend of mine insisted that I take part in the competition. She was much older than I and, though I gave no answer to her, she enrolled me without my knowledge or that of my parents. When I found my name on the list, I told my mother. It was the first time that I did not tell my father something first. I wasn't afraid of my father's opinion, but I decided that I would go forward, no matter what he or my mother said. I had decided that I would find a way to make them agree. In any event, my mother was not enthusiastic and my father did not know until four days before the performance.

At the beginning of the process, I found it difficult. I was sometimes overcome by emotion and at other times the organizers said that I was stiff—that I was wooden like the trunk of a tree. Despite this, something inside of me told me that I could succeed, so when the actual performance came, I was quite myself—another Valbona. I presented myself well and won. It was a wonderful experience. Although I have heard of the jealousies among the contestants in American competitions, there were no jealousies here. I got along well with the other girls because they liked me and I shared everything I had with them. I also helped them with their makeup because that was something I was good at. We had all borrowed our clothes from family members and had a great time together. We didn't really care who won.

The night before the big day, I had a beautiful dream. I rarely remember dreams, but this one is like a film and I remember every bit of it. I dreamed of being a superhero. While flying I caught hold of two girls. I didn't want to drop them for fear of hurting them, so I put them down gently and flew away again myself. The next morning my little brother gave me a necklace that he had found in the street. It had a pendant of Saint Mary and Jesus on it. I wore it in the performance and I won. I'm so sorry that I have since lost it. It wasn't valuable, but it was meaningful. I took both of these to be omens of success.

As a result of being Miss Albania, I have had many opportunities. I study acting at the art school now. I am asked to act in advertisements as well as in roles in the theater. Many people love me and have helped me.

The Future

I am in a bit of a dilemma now over my future. First I thought I might work in television. I adore Vera Grabocka* and would like to be just like her. However, during these years at the art school my interest in television has been shaken in favor of the stage. I would also love to be in films, but I haven't yet tried. I have learned that often it is not enough to want to do something. Other things have to happen as well.

I have faced some difficulties in my life and in my current circumstances. There are many talented people and a great deal of competition. If these artists don't have the moral support of others, they sometimes fail. I feel that I am surrounded by people who love me and are willing and eager to help me. They must see something good in me. I must also work and I find that I work as much for others as I do for myself. If I am unsuccessful, I will be the reason. If I don't work, I won't succeed.

Also in the future, I wish to get married and have children—two or maybe three. I don't want to have an only child because I loved so much having sisters and a brother. We always had each other as friends. I am not engaged now. I had a boyfriend before but it didn't go well. I know that my personal life will affect my career, but I couldn't sacrifice my life in this manner. I would have had to have sacrificed too much for this relationship. When I do find the right person, I will

*Vera Grabocka is a television announcer working for the Albanian television company. It was she who took the initiative to organize the first Miss Albania competition, and she has been successful in organizing all of the subsequent competitions.

marry for love, not under an arrangement. I can't do things I don't feel. I don't like things "as if." I know that it's my profession to act, but in my life? No, I won't do it. I know that I will have to be strong to be a good family woman and a good artist. I would like to be successful in both parts of my life. I will also try to find a man in my life who will love me in the way I deserve and who will support me in my career: someone who is a friend.

The Source of Her Strength

I have this characteristic in my personality to meet the difficulties I will face in the future. I know that I am strong enough to meet the challenges of a family because I have cared for my sister and my brother as well as for my nephew. I know I can cope with family life. I also know that my parents and my husband will help me as well. In return, I will try not to cause my husband problems that are a consequence of my profession. The young man I loved before was an educated person and an artist in spirit, but he felt bad when I had to play a role. He found it so difficult. I want someone who will understand me. I am confident that I will succeed in finding a way to help my future husband understand or I will take roles that will not challenge my relationship. I am fanatical about this.

Also, it is important that I respect myself. I haven't changed inside since I became Miss Albania. I am the same Valbona. I believe that my parents are proud of me and my accomplishments and I owe them a great deal. They have been and always will be my greatest source of strength.

The Role of Faith

Faith in our family has never played a role. We have never gone to the mosque or observed religious practices. Sometimes I believe and sometimes I don't. I remember listening carefully to and enjoying my grandmother's stories about fairies. They made me superstitious, but that is all.

Summary

Valbona is a totally modern young woman with independent thoughts and ideas. In contrast to the women of the older generation, she has an opportunity to express and act on those ideas: to craft her life as she wishes. Even so, she puts traditional relationships first: her relationship with her parents and siblings and the relationship she expects to have with her future husband. At 24 years of age, she is poised to make great contributions to her country and to exemplify the best in her generation of women.

Chapter 20

Magnola Liço: The Transformation of a Life

Magnola is a highly motivated, poised, and attractive 19-year-old who spoke to us with confidence and enthusiasm.* She is currently a first-year student in the informatics (computer sciences) department at Tiranë University and is studying finance and economics through a correspondence course.

Her story is special because she was born in exile—in a remote village—and yet with the coming of democracy she now has the opportunity to study in a field of her choice and to travel. Recent history has changed her life and she was prepared by the encouragement and optimism of her parents to take full advantage of the opportunities presented.

The Family

My family had a bad biography. My father's father, Muhamer Liço, was from Korçë. He had studied to become an attorney in the United States and learned many democratic ideas. When he returned to Albania, my grandfather began publishing a newspaper that spoke about democratic life in America. When the communist regime began the special trials of intellectuals in the early postwar period, my grandfather was tried. In 1945 he was shot for his ideas. His brother, who is my great-uncle, Eduard Liço, stayed in the United States and was a founder of VATRA† and wrote articles against the regime.

My mother's father, Artif Golje, was from Dibër. He served as a major in Zog's army and studied at the military academy in Italy for 15 years. In 1945, when my mother was just two years old, my grandfather was imprisoned in Burrel prison and died while being tortured for his anticommunist beliefs. My grandmother was

This interview was conducted in English.

†In 1912 VATRA, the Pan-Albanian Federation, was founded in the United States by Fan Noli and Faik Bej Koniza, among others. This organization consolidated all of the Albanian nationalist associations.

Magnola Liço

told to divorce my grandfather, but she refused. Later, when my mother was a child and she mentioned her father's name, the secretary of the Youth Organization told her to deny that he was her father. She did not accept this.

A Village Life and Future

As a result of their bad biographies, my father was limited in the amount of education he could receive and both of my parents were given jobs in villages outside of Tiranë. My mother taught school in a village and my father worked as an economist, also in a small village outside of Tiranë. However, in 1967 when the class struggle intensified, my parents were sent away from Tiranë to the village of Ndernenas, about one and a half hours from the city of Fier, with my brother who was only three years old at the time. It was a type of exile in that they were made to work in the fields rather than in their professions and to live in housing constructed for people such as themselves. This housing was segregated from the village and a Sigurimi family lived at the head of the street to keep watch on them.

They were not, however, required to check in with the police on a regular basis and still had the right to travel to Tiranë when they wished.

I was born in 1977, ten years later. When I was very young both of my parents worked from 6:00 A.M. to 6:00 or 7:00 P.M. I either went to the nursery or stayed at home alone while they worked. However, when I was nine or ten, my father began working nights looking after the cows and so he was at home with me during the day.

I started school in the village when I was six and went to that school through the seventh class. Although I was a good student, I was not given good grades because the teachers were not likely to give children of families in our political group high marks.

There were 3 or 4 children in our class from these families in the village. We knew we were different, in part because we had no other family members in the village. There were even villagers who called us "enemies," but on the whole the villagers were kind. I had friends among all the people in the village and since we had the right to travel to Tiranë we didn't feel totally isolated. In addition, since my brother began working in the fields when he was 16, we didn't feel so much suffering because we had 3 people in the family working.

Once I remember, when I was seven or eight years old—I had just started school—my mother spoke to me [about why we lived here]. She said, "I am telling you the story of why we are here in this village because I think you should know. I also know that you can keep secrets and I trust you." She then told me the story of how they were told to leave Tiranë and move to Ndernenas; how they had come there with my brother when he was small; and of the changes in their lives that this had brought about. She told me of our status, with an explanation that was not intended to nourish hatred or thoughts of revenge in me. I didn't learn the whole story until much later when I was older and I was never taught to hate: to be angry and hurt, but not to hate.

Afterward in 1985, when I was eight years old, I remember one day when I was in school and we were told that Enver Hoxha had died. All the other children started to cry, but I found that no tears came to my eyes. I remember my mother taking sick leave from work because she knew that she too could not pretend to be sad over his death. However, on the day of Hoxha's funeral, as I was a child, I was affected by events and began to cry. My brother shouted at me to stop crying saying, "It's a happy day!" All the families like mine were happy, but we didn't dare tell each other because there were spies among us as well—people who were corrupted.

My brother, for example, was asked to work for the Sigurimi. It was not so easy to escape the pressure he had from these people, but my father was very quick to give him a good suggestion. He told him, "Say to these people, 'I have a bad habit. Everything I hear during the day, I say at night in my sleep. I can't help it.'" They stopped bothering him immediately after he told them this.

There were not many opportunities for me to continue my studies in the village. The village school only went up through the eighth grade. If I was to go on studying (if I had permission), my only option was the agricultural school that was an hour and a half away from our village on foot. I might have gone to Tiranë and lived with my uncle there, but it is uncertain whether that would have been allowed. However, my mother is a strong and optimistic person. She accepted the lot that fell upon her and she never complained to us of her troubles. At the same time, she encouraged me to think of a better future. She always kept telling me, "Your destiny is not here in the village. I can't imagine you to be here for long. You must always study hard and appreciate the opportunity to learn." She wanted me to go on with my studies because my brother had to go to work in the fields at such an early age and never had the opportunity to study. My mother did not want for me also to start working in the fields, marry a village boy, and remain in the village.

The Transformation

After 1985, as I was growing up, the class struggle became less severe so we were able to breathe a bit more freely. Then a miracle came. In 1990 my family was able to move back to Tiranë. Although I had been to that city before, passing holidays and summer vacations there, it was a great release that we were able to move there, away from the village. We were allowed to move in accordance with a new law that permitted families that had housing available to them in Tiranë to move back. It was difficult at first because we lived in a single room in my uncle's apartment and my parents had no work. However, my uncle in the United States, who had heard how much we had suffered, helped us and then my father found work as an economist in an institute and my brother got a job working as a mechanic.

I was 14 years old at this time and thrilled to have an opportunity to start learning English. Also, I heard my parents talking about the recent events in Romania and Bulgaria: the coming of democracy. My family and I hoped that a change would come soon to Albania. When the embassies were opened, my uncle suggested that we all try to leave. We were afraid, however. We had only been in Tiranë for three months at the time and didn't know what would become of these people. We remembered also our cousins and friends who were still in exile and worried about what consequences they would suffer, even if we were successful.

When the demonstrations began, my family, friends, and neighbors took part in them. It made me feel happy and very lucky because it meant the end of the regime. I saw the doors begin to open for me, for my generation, and for my class of people. We would be allowed to study and to get good jobs.

My life has changed so much since that time. I have had the opportunity to study and am getting the top grades in my class (now that the teachers no longer have to keep my grades low because of my political status). I am studying informatics and finance at the same time to improve my employment options in the future. In addition, I have learned to speak English. As a result, my uncle, who is now working in the Albanian embassy in Pakistan, asked me to translate for some businessmen who were here in 1994 and they invited me to visit Pakistan later that year. Therefore, I have had an opportunity to travel outside of my country, a dream I never entertained before.

I am optimistic for the future because I see an opportunity for all of my generation to work in their chosen professions and everything being for the better. The main thing is that there will be no more class struggle, which will be good for everyone.

The Source of Her Strength

My parents have been my primary source of strength. They have always kept me believing that the future would be open to me. They trusted me and encouraged me. Every good I have had came from them.

Faith has also had a great role in my life. My parents are Muslims, but I have changed and become Orthodox. I have read a lot of books with religious themes, I have attended church, I listen to religious programs, and I have read portions of the Bible in English and Albanian. I think everyone needs something to believe in. We need to believe in God. It is important in good and bad moments. I pray especially when I am in difficulty.

My parents are not upset that I have converted, although they ask me from time to time why I wear a cross. They want to know if it is because crosses are fashionable or because I believe. I always answer, "Because I believe."

Summary

Magnola's story is both unusual and typical. Her life circumstances and the radical change in her future that democracy brought make her unusual. However, the zeal for knowledge and her faith in God, herself, and in the future make her typical of urban girls in her generation. Magnola's determination and thirst for knowledge will benefit her and make her a force in the shaping of her country's future.

Chapter 21

Juliana Kurti:
Poetic Promise

Ksanthi and I met Juliana on our first trip outside of Tiranë in the group in Berat. At that time, she was an attractive 17-year-old high school senior, who had already won awards in English and successfully completed an Albanian translation of one of Ernest Hemingway's books the year before.*

At that first meeting we were enthralled as this young woman spoke of her life, her hopes, and her dreams. Her observations were keen and her expression of them poetic. When she began, she spoke first of her perception of the ideal of an Albanian woman, using her aunt and her mother as examples;

Historically, the Albanian woman stands above all other human creatures. She has had to suffer spiritually and materially, even in love. The family has been a pillar with the woman supporting the family and vice versa....
The Albanian woman has been a big harbor where all find shelter....
She represents a big sculpture and life has engraved on her the important moments in her family's life. She has always dreamed of something in life and that has kept her going....
My Aunt Vigerje's life work is to give comfort even to a piece of stone....
It is a characteristic of Albanian women to sacrifice for their children. My mother says she has forgotten the sacrifices and problems because her children are so good. Most Albanian mothers are like this. Sacrifice is the best understood word in their language.

When we heard Juliana speak, we knew that we wanted to hear more and arranged to talk with her further. Hers is the story of a modest but talented and determined woman of astounding sensitivity and perception.

This interview was conducted entirely in English.

265

The Challenges of a Young Life

My father was originally from Vlorë, but after he completed his university studies he was sent to work as an agricultural economist in Skrapar. Skrapar was a new town to which so many intellectuals were sent by the party that it became an intellectual center. There he married my mother who was working as an economist in the technology bureau. They lived there for ten years, but in 1988 my father asked to be moved from Skrapar because it was far from our family and all of our friends had already moved. He also wanted a better life for my brother and me. I was ten years old at the time and I found the move very difficult because I was young and fragile.

I come from a quiet family and have had a very normal life. I am a good student and have many friends. The everyday challenges of my life have included facing people who want to provoke me or tease me. In Albania many of the teenagers want to put into difficult situations those who pursue their studies and succeed. They tempt them to give up their ambitions and to join in the fun of unimportant things. You can get tricked or deceived very easily. You may have a specific aim in mind to become a doctor or an economist, but your peers work on you to give up these goals. Is it jealousy? I don't know, but there is a great deal of peer pressure to have fun: go to the discos and participate in other frivolous activities that take you away from your studies.

The Time of Political Change

This was especially true during the period of change that took place in 1991 and 1992. This was a time when everything was in chaos. The teenagers, many of them, believed that school wouldn't be so important after the change. I am happy that my parents encouraged me by telling me that school would always be important.

During this period, I saw children in the gymnasium going on strike. I didn't know the reason why they were breaking the rules. They talked roughly and didn't obey the teachers. There were so many options to going to school—leaving the country, going to work—that many of the teenagers decided to leave school. What could I have done at 14 years of age with no education and no profession?

Also, during this time it was dangerous on the streets. Everyone was afraid to go out, even strong men. There were so many instances of rape and theft. People just couldn't go outside. I was afraid, but I felt safe because my family took good care of me.

The events of this time changed forever my view of the world. It paralyzed my attitude in a certain way. It broke something inside of me. The world was not as nice and beautiful as I had thought. It had violence and things I never expected to touch me and my life. They frightened me. Something was crippled inside me. I can't explain because it was very deep, but I lost my faith in people. That matured me. It made me see things more deeply and from another point of view. After that, I had to study people carefully before making a connection with them.

Juliana Kurti.

This period of time shocked me, really shocked me. I believed and hoped that other days would come when I wouldn't have this feeling.

A Death

However, 15 months ago a friend of mine died in a car accident with her mother. It changed more things inside me. Life is not as long as we think it is. I understood, for example, how much I had loved that friend and how much I love all of my friends. I hadn't thought I loved my friends so much, but now I understand that the absence of even one of them is important. After a while, I had to push the bad part away and I began to see the beautiful things again. I began to appreciate the little things—to love life more.

At first, however, I saw the black side of things. I thought I would always be in shock, but I took my courage in both hands and thought that I must exploit every second of my life. It's unforgivable not to. You have to suck the essence of life, that sweet syrup, every moment.

As we get older, we realize that we make connections with people in the same way as the basic elements in chemistry. The love for life makes you take care of things that you never cared about before, to pay close attention to coincidences and friends and even to unimportant things. It makes you more sensitive to the world around you. It was this experience that made me more open to everything and especially to other people. I am more expressive now. I believe that you have to do things at the proper time because life is so short. If you don't say the word now, you might never get to.

The Future

My first aim is to study to be a doctor. I will achieve this goal because it is very important to me. I also want to be a well-formed person. I have to strengthen my qualities as a human being to make connections with people, even in my job. Having a good family is also important to me when I get married later. I want to make my parents proud of me. I'd also like to be patient and reasonable like my mother and to find in my marriage the compatibility that my parents have in their marriage. There are no hidden things in our family. We are open and everyone talks about the problems.

I know that it is difficult to balance a family and a career. I won't say that I won't experience difficulty, but they are both important to me. Maybe a family is more important. I try not to delude myself, but I am optimistic. I try not to discourage myself with difficult things. I just do what I have to do right now. I try to take life as it comes today and accomplish today's obligations.

One way or another I believe that with my capabilities, desires, goals, and even my illusions I will be able to make a difference. There is even a small part of me that would like to be a politician. In that role I would bring the real intellectuals and most respected and loved people into leading positions. I would encourage cooperation between the people and the leaders and would work to open up new opportunities for women.

The future for the women of my generation is mixed. For the intellectual women, they can study and, even with the hardships, they have the potential to succeed. For the nonintellectual girls, it's difficult to say. They will get married. Maybe they will have a simple job, but they will be primarily focused on their families. However, I am optimistic about my generation. Everything has changed. The intellectual interests of women are greater now and there are more opportunities to fulfill their desires: education abroad, jobs, and fun. There is liberty of choice.

The Source of Her Strength

Since I was 14, in that period when I saw that life had so many negative things, I wondered where I would find the strength to survive. At first I thought it might be faith in God.* It was temporary: it didn't last. Later I realized that it is a thing that is born inside of you. It is a love for life. It is only in strong people, almost a physical part of them.

My mother helped me. She told me, "Life is all a competition. Your whole life will be that way so you don't have to worry about the little losses." Even when I lament now she says, "It will always be that way, but I know that you have the mental and physical strength to get through this. You should say to yourself, 'I will do this.'" I have internalized the confidence my parents have in me.

My father has also told me stories of Albanian women who were as strong as men. These historical women came from the region that my father was from. I can't remember the actual stories at the moment, but I do remember that the women were strong and energetic like me. My father has always told me, "You are my sword and will break the world into tiny pieces. You will achieve your goals in life."

My family is a typical Albanian family and most of my friends have found the same things in their families as I find in mine. The particularly strong relationship I have with my parents is not typical, but the values, love, good upbringing, and good education are the same. Their families have tried to create a good future for them.

My friends have helped me too. For example, a close friend of mine saw me in a moment of desperation on a rainy and cloudy day and said to me, "It is you who has gathered the clouds. Think of blue skies and happier times." Two hours later the sky was blue.

I will find the strength to succeed because I would not like to be saying when I am 40 years old, "Half of my life is gone and I have not fulfilled the dreams of my youth to build some towers of song on a lofty parapet."

Summary

Juliana's quiet force and determination combined with her sensitivity to people and situations are exceptional, yet in some ways typical of the young women from intellectual or privileged Albanian families. Also, like many members of her generation, she is strong and independent, confident in herself and her ability to succeed. She credits her family, her heritage, and herself for that strength.

*Both of her parents are Muslims.

Part V

SOME CONCLUSIONS

"When a man walks, the leaves of the tree tremble.
When a woman walks, the roots of the tree shake."
"*Kur ecen buri, gjethet e pemes dridhen.
Kur ecen guaja, rrenjet e pemes tunden.*"

—Albanian Proverb

The stories presented in this book speak for themselves, but the main objective of this book is to answer the underlying questions that had formed in my mind regarding the Albanian women's response to their difficult lives: What has given the Albanian women the strength, the force, not only to survive, but also to live meaningful and fulfilled lives with good-heartedness and optimism? Is it possible that faith has survived? Is there another explanation of where this strength has come from? Tradition and the role of women in the family and in society? The will to survive? A replacement of religious or spiritual faith with faith in the dictator or communism?

Part V summarizes my observations regarding the Albanian women's sources of strength.

Chapter 22

The Role of Faith in Albania

It is not a reasonable conclusion that religious faith is a significant source of strength for the majority of the Albanian women whom we interviewed. Specific religions were rarely mentioned as a primary source of strength. Religion in Albania has historically been secondary to nationality and ethnicity in the Albanians' self-definition. Some even say that the religion of the Albanians is determined more by "the sword," or political expediency, than by actual faith. For example, historians have called Albania at the time of Skanderbeg "the last bulwark of Christianity in the Balkans." However, the argument goes, Skanderbeg's personal renunciation of Islam when he returned from Turkey to defend his country was as much political as it was a return to the faith of his forebears. Following this line of reasoning, many people argue that the conversion of the Albanians to Islam under the Turks was also a simple economic and political expedient rather than a conversion of belief. This theory also explains why the Albanians, in general, were so accepting of the policy of atheism under communism. Finally, it is argued that so many young people are now drawn to Christianity, especially the evangelical message of the American and Western European protestant missionaries, because they wish to be allied, or associated, with the politics and attitudes of the Western world, or because they hope to gain economically from their friendships with Westerners.

Diana Çuli expressed this theory most clearly:

The Albanians are not religious in general. They have changed religions every 100 years to survive under various occupiers. The renaissance writers said "the religion of Albania is Albania." Now, people change their religions to get jobs in Greece and Italy. The young girls wear crosses because it is fashionable. They want to be like the Americans and Europeans. There is no strong faith in Albania: it is pure pragmatism.

My opinion is that faith in God is not a true source of strength for the women of Albania. Impotence turns people to God, but here it is more a sense of fatalism, a belief in fate or destiny: "Ah, this is my lot."

Having spent time with women all over the country, I disagree with this theory in its essence. It is true that religion was rarely raised as a primary source of strength by the women we interviewed. However, it is astounding how frequently women stated in their interviews—especially when they were asked directly about the role of faith in their lives—that faith had played a major role in their lives, giving them strength beyond that which they gained from other sources. This is especially significant after so many years of religious persecution and official atheism. Although the nominal religions of Albania—which were identified in the early part of this century as Muslim (70 percent), Orthodox (20 percent), and Catholic (10 percent)—have fared badly in the past 50 years, they have shown remarkable tenaciousness. In addition, from the interviews presented here, it appears that the faith of the people—that is faith as belief in God—seems to have less to do with the tenets of religion than with a profound spiritual sense.

Traditional Religions

CATHOLICISM

Based on the responses we received in Shkodër in the Catholic community where women of all ages identified their faith in God as their primary source of strength, it is clear that the Catholic faith, at least in some areas, has survived well throughout an extended period of persecution. This is true, even though Catholicism has the smallest proportion of adherents of the three primary faiths in Albania. Therefore, in Shkodër, I interviewed our hosts Marie and Pjerin Sheldia about how the Catholic faith has been maintained there. Pjerin began,

In my opinion, there are two reasons that faith has been preserved in Albania, despite everything. First, belief in God has been strong although the people have been ignorant. Sometimes the less education they had, the stronger they believed. It was an unshakable belief. For example, I remember an old woman who had two sons who attended the Franciscan school. One was given the opportunity to teach there. You cannot imagine how poor this family was: no fire to keep warm, no light to read by. The boys went out and studied under a street light. However, in the time of Enver Hoxha, just after the Liberation, both boys were arrested. People asked their mother how she felt and she responded, "God knows best. Let him decide. May God's will be done." Later, one son died in prison and the other died shortly after his release from prison. The old woman was left with no children and no grandchildren. When people asked her about this she replied, "It is the will of God." This woman exemplifies the simple, unshakable faith of this community. In former times faith was not discussed; now people ask questions. They want to know why and what material benefit there is for them in believing. Only those people who have faith as a family tradition just believe.

Secondly, the women have kept the faith alive. They are strong and the bravery of the Albanian women is such that they were able to cope with all difficulties just like men.*

The Catholic faith has been kept alive in this community because it has been a tradition in most Catholic families to memorize the prayers of the rosary. They were said by all the members of the family every night, and the family would never go to sleep without saying them. They also said a shorter prayer before dinner. We have nourished our children secretly with love and respect for God and told them that they were not to mention such things in school.

Marie, a teacher, gave us an example of this, "There was one time when I was responsible for teaching my son's class. Afterward, my son questioned me about the things I had said. I replied, 'Remember, what you hear in class is a lie. What you hear at home is the real thing.'"

Pjerin continued,

Remember too that even in former times—that is precommunist times—we had no missals or Bibles. There are some prayer books that were translated into Albanian prior to the Liberation. (Pjerin showed us one that had both the Latin and the Albanian translated by a Jesuit priest, Padre Mark Arapi, in 1941 or 1942.) It was dangerous to have these, but some families did. There were also books published earlier about the lives of the saints and the history of the church. During communism, taking the sacrament of communion was rare. One might go secretly to the priest's house and take it on a special occasion, such as a marriage, but the Sigurimi were always watching and even the neighbors were paid to watch the priests' houses. If caught, the priest would be publicly denounced.

Can you imagine that the priests of this country who had studied in a total of 24 universities abroad, mostly in Italy and Austria, were sentenced to a total of 800 years in prison? Even so, the priests were very brave. They said, "We don't impose anything on anyone, but will continue to serve people who wish it. If you want me to deny my faith, I won't." This was a common reply of the priests.

I remember one particular occasion. There was a meeting that we were required to attend where a report was given naming a particular priest. We knew that he would be arrested. He was well-educated and had such a brave attitude at that meeting as to make all the others admire him, even though they didn't provide a word of support for him.

Others have suggested that the Albanian women of all faiths represent the most religious segment of the society. This observation has been variously interpreted as a function of their relatively low level of education and culture compared to men or that this is due to the economic dependence of the women, which leads them to a certain fatalism. However, since it is frequently the women in other cultures as well who are identified as the most religious segment, this may also be that as women marry and raise children they turn to their faiths, to God, in the miracle of childbirth and nurturing of their children. They are thankful for the birth and health of their children and yet are aware of their own limitations in raising them in safety. Women tend to believe that the future and destiny of their children are in God's hands.

The persecution of the Catholic faith in Albania seems to have made Catholicism stronger. It appears that the example of the priests—their conduct under torture and those who died still professing their faith (as Drita Kosturi and others related)—provided a profound inspiration for their congregations. The commitment of the families to their faith and the instruction of children in the tenets, rites, and liturgy of the Catholic church also clearly formed the basis for the continuation of the faith. The young girls are now exploring for themselves what faith means and are drawn to the church as a symbol of freedom and hope in the future.

ORTHODOX

In the interviews with Orthodox women in all parts of the country—faith was rarely raised as a primary source of strength, and many women, especially those of the middle generation, reported that faith had played no role in their lives. Some of the common responses regarding the role of faith in their lives frequently showed ambivalence: a desire to believe or a feeling that they should believe.

"I liked to believe. I went to church with my mother-in-law, but I didn't continue after the churches were closed. I go again now when it is possible. I want to learn."

"While religion was outlawed, nothing was spoken of religion in our house. We were taught to be atheists, but now I see that my father was a religious man. Now I believe, but I don't have a fanatical belief."

"I know very little of religion. I try to make myself believe, but I do everything with a critical eye. I do believe in something."

"I like to believe because it gives me pleasure to observe the religious holidays."

"I don't believe in God. I only believe for my daughter's sake. If there really were a God, he would have to think of all the suffering of the Albanian people."

There were, however, people who were committed to perpetuating the Orthodox faith. In August 1996—at the recommendation of Father Luke Veronis, an American Orthodox priest supporting the Albanian Orthodox church and training new Albanian priests—we interviewed two sisters who are reputed to have been almost singlehandedly responsible for the continuation of the Orthodox faith in the predominantly Orthodox city of Korçë. We actually met with Dhimitra aged 85* and Marika aged 90, their

---

*Dhimitra's health was very poor and she was bedridden so we conducted our interview at her bedside. We learned later that she died in September 1996, about five weeks after this interview.

sister-in-law Frangji, and their friend Berta and asked them to tell us how the Orthodox faith had been maintained in Korçë. Despite their ages, they appeared to be prepared to talk all night. They explained that they always have energy and enthusiasm when they are talking about their faith. I have merged all of their comments into a single presentation because all four women spoke from the same experience and faith.

Although we had not much formal education, our mother nourished in us a love of reading. She always said, "Read other books, but don't forget the Bible." So she also nourished in us a love of religion. We later formed a group of 40 women called the Sisters of Christ and worked with these women to teach them the word of God and how to maintain their faith.

When the communist period came and the churches were all closed down, we were desperate and felt a sharp pain in our spirits. We organized the women to pray continuously for 40 days and nights without rest. We kept on praying to God with each person taking a 2-hour period. All day and all night God had to listen to our prayers. Of course, we did this secretly, most of us in our houses.

All the religious people who wanted to continue the religious rituals gathered at our house, usually after dark, leaving one by one in the early hours of the morning. They did not call our house the Cicos' house, the name of our family, they called it Stephen's Place for the martyr. We sisters used to cover the windows with blankets because we didn't want the people to see in or hear us praying. We were the hidden apostles.

There was not a single Orthodox house in Korçë without an icon and a candle to light on special occasions. When the communists told them that they had to give them up, they did not give them all up. That became evident after the fall of communism because every household had some. Where had they been all this time? In the bottoms of vegetable barrels? In walls and ceilings? Who knows. One Orthodox woman in Shkodër refused to give any of her icons to the Sigurimi, so one day they came to take them. She calmly allowed them to take them and then on the way to the door she said, "Oh, I have a very large cross and you have forgotten to take it." When they turned around and demanded to see the cross so that they could take it also, she crossed herself then put her legs together and stretched out her arms in the form of a cross. "Here it is. You can't take this!"

Most of the Orthodox families also had the Bible and the liturgy in Albanian or Greek in their homes. However, they had to celebrate and pray on their own. We have celebrated all the fasts, even though we had no priests to lead us. There was one priest from Vlorë who came to us. We had known him before and he continued to serve as a priest secretly. We had to send word to him using a password to get him to come for communion services. Since we supported ourselves as dressmakers and he worked with sheep and other animals, we frequently wrote to him, "My sister needs wool for her work. Please come and bring her some." He came as an ordinary man, a common villager, to our house as a family guest.

We had three children in the house at that time and we were afraid when the priest came that the children would report it. So we waited for the children to go to sleep before beginning our worship. Frequently the priest would then say the liturgy until 3:00 A.M., and after 6:00 A.M. other women came, one by one, to receive communion.

There were priests in Korçë, but they no longer practiced as priests. There were only two practicing priests in all of Albania. The fact that persecution of Orthodox priests was not massive is that they surrendered, they gave in to the demands that they not pursue their priestly activities. Those who refused to obey these demands were sent to prison or killed.

It was just like war—there was so much suffering. Whenever someone knocked at our door, we feared arrest. Also, our brother was sent to exile for five years because he said something that was construed to be pro-Greek: just for a casual comment at a wedding ceremony. We were always followed by the Sigurimi. Once Dhimitra was told that someone on the Party Committee wanted to ask her questions. As she was waiting to be called, she went on with her prayers. Someone came and said, "Why are you here?" When she said "I don't know," they told her she could go home. She responded, "My prayers have been answered." Another time a Sigurimi asked, "We hear that you continue to preach and worship. Is that true?" Dhimitra answered, "We don't need to because the families know when the feasts are and worship on their own."

When the churches were closed, we never stopped worshipping or baptizing, and marrying people, but, of course, these were all done at night with someone on guard at the gate. We baptized 40 children during this time here in this house or in the houses of others. Secretly we did this. We knew how much we risked, but God was with us. We did it all with His help.

When we first arrived for the interview Dhimitra said to me, "God loves Albania very much." At the end of the interview I asked her why she believed this when everything they had told us of persecution and danger pointed to the opposite, and when many Albanians who have lived most of their lives in poverty and desperation feel that God has abandoned them. She responded, "We thank God that he has made us suffer because these sufferings made us feel much closer to God." Marika added, "God made many miracles during this time. Also, these sufferings brought us closer together. It made us much more patient and able to put up with all our sufferings. God has not forgotten us because it has made the young people more religious now. Before there were very few young people who went to church and now there are many." Frangji noted, "When you are happy and live in happiness you do not call on God. When you suffer, you turn to Him."

Although there are clearly many Orthodox people and families in Albania who fervently maintained their faith throughout the period of communism, the Orthodox faith, in general, appears to have fared less well than Catholicism. Based on what the Orthodox sisters said and my own observations about the Orthodox community—particularly as we found it in Korçë—it appears that the fervency of the faith and its role in the lives of the women was not strong. This may be due in part to the Orthodox community's generally strong adherence to the ideals of communism and the benefit they derived from their political orientation, coupled with the fear of the possible consequences of observing their faith. However, there is also evidence, particularly in what the Orthodox sisters told us, that the Orthodox priests may not have set as inspiring an example as did the Catholic priests in Shkodër.

ISLAM

External evidences of the Muslim faith are prevalent in Albania in the number of mosques and the regular calls to prayer, but Islam in its most fundamental forms is absent. For example, there is no veiling and there are only rare examples of Muslim attire. Within the families, however, the feasts and many rituals are observed. For example, the blood of a goat is spread on the threshold of a new home to purify it, a goat or lamb is killed for the feast of Bajram, and fasting from dawn to dusk is observed during the month-long festival of Ramazan. However, a deeper understanding of the religion appears absent.

This is particularly understandable in light of the types of Islam that were established in Albania and their fate in the past 50 years. The Sunni-Anafit form of Islam, which was the dominant Muslim faith prior to Albanian independence, was based on a juridical and bureaucratic system that was virtually eradicated simply because the system was not allowed to operate under communism. The hoxhas were persecuted and the system did not stand. In addition, religious instruction and catechism were minimal among the people, so that there was no firm basis for understanding or preserving the Sunni religious traditions.

While the Sunni sect has been poorly maintained, the mystical order of Bektashi has had a profound affect on all Muslims and seems to be the dominant force among that community today.* Since the Bektashi faith relies upon the mystical connection of the individual with God rather than on the intercession of priests or hoxhas, the maintenance of faith is primarily an individual matter. The people are left to believe as they wish, to find their own spiritual connection. In addition, since the Bektashi faith recognizes the teachings of Christ, it suits the religious tolerance of Albania. Finally, the mysticism of this sect ties in well with the nature of Albanians and with the informal beliefs of many.

These elements are especially evident in the profound statements of two young Muslim women from the central Albanian village of Perondi. Marinella, 18, told us that her primary source of strength was "faith in

---

*Albania has been the world center of the Bektashi faith since the Turks disbanded the predominantly Bektashi janissaries in 1826 and many of them returned to Albania, which had been their native country.

Two women climb the mountain overlooking the city of Krujë to worship at a Muslim holy shrine located at the top.

God." She continued, "I have tried to learn more about Islam, but have found only information about Christianity. Although I am a Muslim, I have the spirit of Jesus Christ. I have always believed in God and have never lost faith or hope. It is not success that has made me optimistic. I try to put into practice what I have read about Jesus Christ. I don't know how it came or how it happened, but I have such a strong belief. My optimism comes from God and I try to transmit it to other people."

Aliona, 20, said,

> Thinking of the lives lived by my parents and grandparents, I am thrilled and my flesh crinkles at the stories of their sacrifice. My mother and grandmother have been my base. However, my love of life and of my parents as well as what I have read in the Bible regarding respect and love for others is my source of strength. I don't care for any specific religion, but I believe in God. God belongs to all of us. We are creatures of God. I can't explain it, but in democracy my generation has found such strength in God. I am optimistic. I think we'll have a brighter and better future, but this depends on us, the youth. This transition period doesn't make you feel confident, however. I pray to God: "Let all the world lead a good life, but let Him think especially of my country." Although I am grateful to the people who have helped us during this period, I say let us sacrifice as our parents did. There is an Albanian saying "We can't keep the house with borrowing flour."

What Exists Now

Unfortunately, an analysis of the specific aspects of the Albanian women's faith is not within the scope of this book, but certain observations are possible, based on our conversations. Whatever specific religion the people have practiced or identified with, there are several aspects of faith that are consistent among the women we interviewed.

1. The women interviewed showed a high degree of tolerance for those of other faiths. Countless times we were told that Muslim and Christian neighbors celebrated with each other on feast days, as Marie did in Shkodër. "When I finished university, I worked in a school with Muslims and Catholics. We were united, we were friends. We talked about our faiths, but only in private. We went to the Muslims' houses at Ramadan and they came to our houses at Easter."

    As evidence of this religious tolerance today, the government of Albania recognizes two national holidays for each religion: Orthodox Easter and Christmas, Catholic Easter and Christmas, and Big and Little Bajram. Rarely in the interviews or in my daily life in

Albania did I hear or see religious prejudices or intolerance, and frequently I witnessed lifelong and intimate friendships and good marriages between Christians and Muslims.

2. The Albanian women's concepts of God are remarkably similar. Specifically, it appears that, regardless of their religion, the women seem be in relationship with a God that is both immanent in everything, and also an entity that is outside of everything: its creator, a force that can intervene in the lives of the people and come to their aid in time of trouble. This seems to represent a melding of the traditional Bektashi and Christian concepts of God. The Bektashi faith has traditionally been seen as a pantheistic faith: one in which "the belief in God and the universe are ultimately identical."* This contrasts with the dominant Christian tradition that Marcus Borg refers to as "supernatural theism," meaning "a supernatural being 'out there,' separate from the world, who created the world a long time ago and who may from time to time intervene within it."† The result is an inclusive concept of God called panentheism: "a way of thinking about God that affirms both the transcendence of God and the immanence of God,"§ thereby allowing God to be in everything and yet separate.

3. In this concept of God among Albanian women, a common aspect seems to be that God is unpredictable in dealing with people and their lives. It is the role of the believer to accept the resulting changes in their personal fates as Job did, with continuing faith, prayer, and understanding.

As these commonalities suggest, the statistics above showing the religions of Albania by percentage of the population is more reflective of the history of the people than it is of their actual faith. This is especially true as time goes on and new forms of the traditional religions and totally new religions are introduced into the country. Missionaries representing the fundamentalist Islamic sects, the charismatic and fundamentalist Christian denominations, and the Baha'i faith, as well as those supporting the reestablishment and strengthening of the indigenous churches, are finding a thirst for spiritual guidance and are having a profound impact on the religious mosaic of the country. While the people themselves fear divisiveness based on religion, such as is evident in the countries that composed

---

*Wordsworth Dictionary of Beliefs and Religions, *London: Wordsworth Editions, 1995,* p. 390.
†*Marcus Borg,* The God We Never Knew: Beyond Dogmatic Religion to a More Authentic Contemporary Faith, *San Francisco: HarperCollins, 1997, p. 11.*
§*Ibid., p. 32.*

the former Yugoslavia, they also seek a deeper meaning in life and a spiritual connection. Many of them retain their cultural or family religious ties even while espousing the faith of a new religion. They see no conflict in being both Muslim and Christian, or Orthodox and Baha'i.

Some people, both expatriates and Albanians, have explained this by discounting the faith of the Albanian people as basic superstitiousness: a desire to cover all bases. However, it can also be attributed to a pervasive and profound sense of personal connection with an all-embracing God who is not bound by the tenets of any one church or religion. So many times women like Maqi, who is Orthodox, and Lume, who is Muslim, told us, "We, Muslims and Christians, all of us, are worshipping the same God." Similarly, a Muslim woman in Perondi said, "I don't care for priests or hoxhas, or churches or mosques, I have always knelt down where I was and worshipped my God."

In all three of the primary faiths—Catholic, Orthodox, and Muslim—there is a clear pattern of belief by generation. Although many women gave up their religion—or at least the practice of it, the women of the older generation have, for the most part, clung to the beliefs of their forbears and maintained them for themselves. On the other hand, the women of all faiths in the middle generation whom we interviewed were much more likely to report that faith had played no role in their lives. Interestingly, some of the most profound statements of faith, such as those above, came from the youngest generation of women. Still, for the majority of those interviewed, faith or religion was not their primary source of strength. From what source, then, does their strength come?

Chapter 23

The Spirit of the Albanian Women

A number of responses that were given, when taken together, provide the key to understanding this unusual force that the Albanian women have: the force that enables them to triumph over the adversities of their lives. While there is a common expression of fatalism in the addition of the words "Ish Alla" (If Allah wills) or "me kismet" (with luck) at the end of statements of plans or hopes, the women have not, for the most part, given fatalistic responses when asked to identify their source of strength. Also, their lives are too vital to be a reflection of pure fatalism.

All of the primary responses fall into areas of connectedness: family, hospitality, tradition, and faith. Albanians are open and connected people and they derive this attribute from their history and culture. Diana Çuli explained, "The Mediterraneans are social and open people, but also the psychology of war was a fact of life in the Balkans. This made the population linked with each other and made the traditions strong and created the national identity. Poverty and survival made people stronger."

Their Success at Survival

As Diana's statement suggests, their very survival through the adversities in their lives has given the Albanian women confidence and force beyond measure. Suffering and surviving have been regarded through generations as values, and the very fact of surviving brings strength and hope.* The strength gained by the women in overcoming difficulties is admired

---

*When I think of this phenomenon, I am reminded of the words of the Apostle Paul in his letter to the Romans (5: 3, 4), "And not only that, but we also boast in our sufferings, knowing that suffering produces endurance, and endurance produces character, and character produces hope."

and displayed in stories and everyday speech. However, the women generally seem to regard this strength not as an individual attribute but as something drawn from the family and the community. For example, Dhora Leka's mother said to her, "If you don't suffer, you don't know what suffering means and you don't remember the needs of others."

Their Interconnectedness

The pure fact of surviving and drawing strength from success, however, still does not fully explain the force and optimism we found among the Albania women. Clearly, a strong factor in shaping the character of the women is their interconnectedness: the family ties, the traditions of the country, and the community of women. The following are two most commonly identified areas of interconnection.

Family. The women's parents have given them the strength to overcome their difficulties and optimism for the future. The love the women have received from their own parents, their parents' sacrifices and dreams for them, the mutual assistance, and respect of an extended family structure: these form the basis for strength. The reciprocal love between parent and child, the simple pleasure of seeing a child play and grow, and the universal desire on the part of the parent to see the child live a better life: these are the stuff of dreams and also the building blocks of hope for the Albanian women.

Culture and Traditions. The traditions and stories that glorify the sacrifices and courage of early generations of women give today's women a sense of identity by providing a cornerstone or frame of reference. The examples of these women, whether national heroines or their own grandmothers, set the standard or expectations for the current generation of women's response to life.

Of all the traditions of the country, the most significant is that of hospitality. It is through acts of hospitality that the Albanian women express their deepest desires for connection with others, including strangers, and shape the community in which they live. Marjorie Thompson defines the essence of hospitality as follows: "Hospitality means receiving the other, from the heart, into [one's] own dwelling place."* That "dwelling place," she explains, can be either a physical place, such as a home, or an emotional space that we invite others to enter. "Hospitality is essentially an expression

*Marjorie J. Thompson, Soul Feast: An Invitation to the Christian Spiritual Life, Louisville, Ky.: Westminster John Knox, 1995, p. 122.

of love.... It is the act of sharing who we are as well as what we have."*
Thompson goes on to say that hospitality is not only giving, but also
receiving: a mutual sharing. This spirit of sharing and giving is ever present in the community of Albanian women and gives them strength to
overcome adversities. It is manifested in the neighbors and friends who visit
in times of joy and times of need, supporting others in their community
and giving them courage and hope for the future. They sit with the griev-
ing and listen to their pain, and they celebrate with the joyful and share
in their joy. Understandably, then the women, who were cut off from this
community and sharing, suffered greatly as they faced death and other
tragedies alone.

In conclusion, I have found that the Albanian women are women of
spirit who demonstrate a powerful form of spirituality. The spirit of each
of the women is composed of both her very essence and her bond to that
which is outside: whether it be the family, the community, or God. The
spirituality these women demonstrate is in their longing and active search
for this bond or connection between their essence and the forces outside
them. As the women draw from these outside forces and internalize them,
they derive a powerful strength to meet the challenges of their lives: a
strength that gives them optimism and hope. Then they willingly share
this spirit with others: family members, friends, and even strangers.

*Ibid.

Epilogue

On March 13, 1997, my family and I were ripped from Albania, from our friends and neighbors there. It would have been wrenching to leave under any circumstances, but to leave under a forced evacuation with gunfire all around us was extraordinarily painful.

It all seemed to happen so fast and yet—in retrospect and with the benefit of reading the free press outside of Albania—we soon realized that these events had clearly been coming for some time. The Democratic Party headed by President Sali Berisha won a landslide victory in the aftermath of the fall of communism, with promises of personal and economic freedom and an aggressive push to join the countries of Europe, ultimately as a member of the European Union. After the elections the government met with extraordinary success in bringing in much-needed foreign assistance to meet the housing, infrastructure, agricultural, transportation, educational, and economic and financial needs of the country. The international aid community and the Western nations provided assistance enthusiastically, both because of the strategic position of Albania in the Balkans and because the country had nowhere to go but up. Therefore, they reasoned, there were not old, industrial or economic structures to tear down or restructure. Albania was virtually a blank slate, so many of the problems of the more developed Eastern European countries could be avoided. Optimism was high in the early years of the Berisha government, and progress was made through a combination of the extreme laissez-faire approach of the government in some areas and the influx of funds from foreign aid organizations. What the international aid community did not factor in sufficiently was the deep-rooted nature of the old political structure.

"The Albanian people are good people, but they are unlucky in their government," said one of our neighbors shortly before we left. In fact, this became evident in late 1994, when the old political patterns began to be repeated. In the fall of that year there was a referendum on a new constitution. This constitution would have provided for a strong president and a relatively weak Parliament and prime minister. In promoting the constitution—

which had been drafted almost exclusively by the members of Parliament from the Democratic Party—President Berisha took a strong line with the people, saying that a vote for the constitution was a vote for democracy and a vote against it was a vote for communism. He also made the vote personal by saying that a vote for the constitution was, in effect, a vote of confidence in him. When the constitution was defeated, the face and tone of the government changed dramatically. One of the two deputy prime ministers, Mr. Kopliku, was removed and the majority (8 out of 11) of the cabinet ministers were replaced. Many of these ministers had been from Korçë and were replaced with people from the northern part of Albania, because these ministers from the south were not considered to be sufficiently dedicated to Berisha and his ideas. These events represented the clear turning point toward what became an increasingly autocratic regime, having its roots in the political history of the country.

Progress was made in the period following, but, as I have explained earlier from a more naive perspective, there were many frustrations on the part of those providing assistance. Political divisions were deep. We heard an increasing number of stories about Albanians who had lost their jobs or were denied contracts with the government because of their affiliation with a party other than the Democratic Party or because of their prior positions within the communist government. Programs that called for cooperation among government officials, governing bodies, or even individuals, were unsuccessful in part because of the depth of the animosities, old and new.

Because there was so much chaos, with poor and erratic governmental management, oversight, and lawmaking, much of the appearance of progress came from illegal activity. For example, the housing that was so desperately needed was provided, not by the government or by a free market in which communities were planned and construction undertaken in an orderly fashion, but by people taking or buying land from the state or private owners and constructing on the land without permission. Vast amounts of agricultural land have been lost to this unplanned and disorganized growth, and the acreage of the cities has mushroomed. In Tiranë, for example, new, unplanned construction represented 50 percent of the physical area of the city by the end of 1996.

The prosperity of the families and their ability to buy consumer goods and costly imported fruits and vegetables came largely from overseas remittances from husbands and sons who had emigrated, legally or illegally, to Italy, Greece, and other countries. These monies were also invested in the proliferating pyramid schemes for which the people were promised enormous returns. As a result, funds did not go into building the country's industrial and agricultural base. Many people, used to being given everything under the communist system, simply lived off the income from their "investments," choosing not even to search for work. Easy money also came from drugs—growing, exporting, and selling marijuana—and from other smuggling operations such as oil to Montenegro during the embargo and illegal émigrés to Italy. In addition, the Italian, Turkish, and particularly the Bulgarian mafias jumped into the chaos to take advantage of the situation.

In fact, lawlessness of one form or another—from seeking bribes for college admission, the administering of medical services, to evading customs duties on imported goods—was much more the norm than the exception. Routine transactions frequently required payments up front, and obtaining a scarce commodity—such as a telephone—often required large payments in the thousands of dollars to technicians and office personnel. In their ignorance of free markets and capitalism, many Albanians defined this lawlessness as free enterprise, and it flourished in the absence of an effective government that included all parties and had the support of a broad base of the population.

The beginning of the end came in the spring of 1996 when the parliamentary elections took place. The Democratic Party would, most likely, have won a majority of the seats in the Parliament, but the president needed to have 75 percent of the seats in order to assure his reelection for another five-year term in the spring of 1997. Therefore, the Democratic Party used every means to win the election. Friends, American and Albanian, who served as polling monitors and election officials reported seeing people beaten and intimidated, the ballot boxes stuffed, and enough other irregularities to nullify the validity of the vote. While dirty tricks were apparently played by all or most of the parties, it is estimated that the Democratic Party's activities swung the vote by 25 percent or more. The postelection report of the official observers was negative, and a number of countries called for Albania to repeat the elections. President Berisha's response was to accuse the commission's decision of being the work of European socialists and others working against democracy in Albania.

It was during this same period leading up to and following the election that the first wave of violence began in Albania. In March 1996 the newest VEFA* supermarket in Tiranë was bombed, killing several employees and some pedestrians on the street. Most people thought that the event was related to the organization rumored to have ties with the Italian mafia and

---

*VEFA is the oldest and largest of the pyramid schemes. Styling itself as an investment company, it has purchased assets and established businesses in all regions of the country. The name of the company is everywhere, on products from flour to beer, on conventional billboards, and, ironically, on an electronic billboard on top of the Palace of Culture in Tiranë's main square.

to be running illegal as well as legal operations. However, President Berisha proclaimed it the work of communist terrorists seeking to destabilize the government. Later that year the home of a judge on the top floor of a Tiranë apartment building was bombed in the night, injuring his young daughter. The bombing was thought to be the work of gang members who were protesting the judge's decision against one of their members.

The growth of pyramid schemes reached a frenzy in mid- to late 1996, with people selling their homes, land, and livestock to cash in on the promised profits. At the same time the link between the funds and the government became stronger and clearer. In the preelection campaign there were billboards with a photo of the Democratic Party candidate for Parliament from the district on the righthand side and the words "Sponsored by" and a list of two or three pyramid schemes on the lefthand side. Later it surfaced that some of the people who ran the pyramid schemes were related to or good friends of senior Democratic Party officials, including the president himself. In October, when investments in the schemes began to reach a fevered pitch, the International Monetary Fund appealed directly to the Albanian people to consider the risk they were taking putting their money into these funds. This appeal was followed immediately by a statement from a senior government official that the funds were good for Albania and that the Albanians could get rich by investing in them. These assurances by government officials in turn led to an even greater influx of funds in the last three months of the year. Even as late as December 1996 President Berisha himself made statements supporting the activities of the funds, which further encouraged the Albanian people to invest their money. Whom were the Albanians going to believe? The foreigners who were only in Albania temporarily and had potentially no personal interest in them, or their elected leaders who presumably had their best interests at heart? In a country where television and radio are still controlled by the state (the Democratic Party in this case) and rumors continue to be the most prevalent form of news—despite an impressive number of independent newspapers with relatively high journalistic standards—the rumors flourished and the creators of the pyramid schemes, their supporters, and some members of the government used the gossip to their own advantage.

As 1996 unfolded, therefore, we witnessed one tragedy after another. We heard the bomb blasts from our home and passed the wreckage every day. We watched our friends and neighbors invest their money in the pyramid schemes, despite our warnings. We shared the international aid community's concern over the course of the elections. We also saw a sharp decrease in the enthusiasm and optimism among both the international community and the Albanians. There seemed to be a giving up of hope as it became harder and harder to do business in an honest and productive manner. We also saw more and more people seeking to leave the country. Our next-door neighbor bought illegal documents to go to Italy with her son and daughter, to be with her husband who had already gone illegally. Frequently, women would come to my door or stop me in the street to ask for my help to get a visa to go to the United States. Neighbors would ask for help filling out an application for a visa or the lottery.

In retrospect, all of these signs indicated a looming crisis, although at the time we were relatively oblivious to their meaning as our own lives were challenging and full. However, when we returned from our Christmas vacation in the United States in mid–January 1997, the tenor of the country had already begun to change. A startling statement about this period was made by our housekeeper, Dije, who attended my birthday party on January 30. She remarked that while the Albanians talked of nothing but the pyramid schemes and their concern over possibly losing their money, the expatriates talked about a street dog that one of them had rescued. The pyramid schemes had suddenly started to collapse and there were the first demonstrations in the streets of Tiranë. It looked at first as if the government would take reasonable steps to alleviate the problem by freezing the assets of the various companies held in the state banks and distributing them to the depositors in some rational manner. However, when the large Vlorë-based Gjallica Company declared itself insolvent, a spark was ignited that started a fire, one that almost totally engulfed the country. Vlorë has been a center of much illegal activity, and lawlessness has been a way of life for some there. Many people turned to violence. What started as a protest over the collapse of the investment funds turned political as the people accused the government of allowing these companies to operate and indeed benefiting from them. Both accusations had a certain amount of at least circumstantial validity. Moreover, rumors—such as the one that government-armed vehicles had come to Gjallica's offices the day before the insolvency and had taken all of the funds away to be given to senior government officials—fueled the rage in Vlorë.

During the months of January and February we felt somewhat schizophrenic watching the news. If we watched the Albanian news channel, we saw calm protests and a few angry words. However, if we watched EuroNews, CNN, or the Italian news, we saw armed protests and violence. It seemed that the foreign press was indeed looking for violence to report, as the government accused, because Tiranë remained very calm. Also, although Albanians in other cities—including many of our friends and neighbors—were distraught about losing their savings, it appeared that the worst of the violence would be limited to Vlorë. However, as the situation became more political in that city and as the government began using the secret police to employ ever stronger and more violent means to suppress opposition leaders and journalists (especially Albanian journalists), the situation erupted.

The political aspect was further highlighted by a student hunger strike that began in Vlorë in which one of the key demands was the resignation of President Berisha. It reminded people of the success of the student hunger strikes that occurred in 1990 and helped bring an end to the Communist Party rule of Albania. The hunger strike spread to other cities after forceful means were used by the government to end the one in Vlorë.

The violence was brought to our doorstep as the husband of one of the women who had helped me with the book was beaten, the journalist father of our son's schoolfriend was beaten, and a good friend's family was smeared in an official Democratic Party newspaper, resulting in threatening phone calls presumably from the secret police. My Albanian friends warned me to speak in code on the telephone because all of the phones were tapped. I had direct evidence of this several times when I was trying to tell someone in the United States or Italy what was happening in Albania. If I was truthful or negative, I was cut off and could not call the person back. We began to understand the price that the Albanians were paying for the calm in Tiranë and for the illusion of democracy.

It was not until the March 1, however, that the situation began to deteriorate rapidly. Although my husband's contract was due to end on March 15, we had planned to stay at least until the end of May so that I could finish writing this book and he could work on a short-term consulting job. March 1, a Saturday, was a beautiful sunny and warm spring day. There was a protest scheduled for Tiranë, but I decided to go ahead with plans to take the children to a social gathering of families with preschool-aged children and toddlers. The children played outdoors in the sun while the mothers talked about the next school year and the school options in Tiranë. It was a very positive group that was mostly focused on a long-term future in Albania. The next day the protesters in Vlorë threatened that if the president went through with his parliamentary reelection for five more years they would bring their protest to Tiranë. That evening the government declared martial law and a curfew. They also cut off the broadcasts of the BBC and Voice of America, accusing the foreign press of inflaming the situation.

During the night we heard the first gunfire in the center of Tiranë. The nearby offices of the independent newspaper *Koha Jonë* were fired upon and burned, reportedly by Berisha's secret police. The next day the Parliament voted for Berisha's reelection and he was sworn in for another five-year term. This move, taken against the advice of the Western nations, further enraged the protesters in Vlorë and other cities and the move toward Tiranë began. The first few days were deceptively quiet. However, because Berisha continued to blame the opposition and "red terrorists" for the violence and for exploiting the economic situation, the nights were full of dread as the secret police attacked and silenced suspected opposition leaders.

For our family, events began to happen quickly. On Wednesday of that week we were encouraged, informally, to begin packing to leave with all our household goods. We met with the moving company the next day. On the following Monday the movers told us that they would arrive the next day to begin packing. They arrived early on Tuesday morning and packed all day. That evening we took the children to our favorite restaurant for dinner, and as we turned into our alley at 7:15 P.M. we heard gunfire. It continued all night as protesters looted an army ammunition dump and people chanted in the streets. At 2:00 A.M. I turned to my husband and said, "We're too late. We aren't going to get out in time." The next day was tense but quiet as we continued packing. Then at about 5:00 P.M. the gunfire started again and went all night and into the next day without stopping.

What a beautiful day that Thursday was, warm and sunny. Our garden looked as it always did—like a peaceful haven—but outside the walls there was the constant sound of gunfire. The movers were coming to take our things away by truck, and my husband had gone to pick up our airplane tickets to leave that afternoon. At 9:00 A.M. a friend called to tell us that the airport had been closed because they couldn't secure the aircraft against attacks. Later my husband called and said that the port was also closed. The movers told us that it was not safe to move our goods because they would likely be stolen from the truck. An Albanian man we knew came to the door to warn of violence in the city and then explained that his clothes were dusty because he had just participated in the looting of the bread factory. He asked if he could help us and we declined.

I continued to say my good-byes to the neighbors, taking them small gifts, food left over in our pantry, and toys for their children. We hugged and cried; no, we clung to each other and said prayers for each other's safety. Many of these women had inspired me in the writing of this book, some I had interviewed, but all had been a part of my daily life and that of my family. We had celebrated Easter, Christmas, and Bajram with them, we had attended each other's children's birthday parties, and we had shared our everyday problems and concerns, talking in the street while the children played.

Afterward, with some missionary friends of ours and Ksanthi, Dije, and her daughter, Ada, we sat in our living room with nine suitcases, one cat,* carry-on luggage, and our house packed up around us, listening to the gunfire and exchanging concerns and thoughts. It seemed so incredible, even impossible, that this was all happening. Then a call came from the American embassy to stand by, with no explanation as to what that meant. Only that they were trying to arrange something.

At about 3:00 P.M. the call came to my husband to take the children and me with one small bag each to the American embassy housing compound; that we would be evacuated from there. I first said that I would not go without my husband, but then, under pressure from the people around me, I agreed. I made an effort to reorganize my bags to ensure that I would have some clothing essentials with me. (Later, I realized that I had been unsuccessful as I came out with a great deal of underwear and pajamas for my daughter and no extra shirts for my son or husband.)

The next few minutes are branded into my memory as we said good-bye to our friends, held on to and cried with Dije, Ada, and our neighbor, Maqi, and left the house. Our driver, Sokol, drove as my husband and I tried to carry on a normal conversation about what he would do next. As we drove through the streets with crowds of people milling around, we had no idea where the gunfire was coming from or if we might be driving into it.

Saying good-bye to my husband was the single most difficult thing I have ever had to do. He was told to leave immediately and we parted in the courtyard in front of the house where we were assigned to wait. After that it was tense and confusing, but we were fortunate to be with friends who had children that our children knew. There were 51 women with children. We were informed that we would be taken out by helicopter, but not when or to where. Finally, after dark, the helicopters came and we had to walk down the rough terrain of an exposed hillside with our children and bags. In the dark with the noise of the guns, the tracer bullets flying into the air, and some return fire from the U.S. Marines who had arrived in the helicopters, along with the noise of the helicopters themselves, it was the stuff of nightmares. As we started down the hillside, my daughter started to shake. Then as we crouched down over our luggage waiting our turn to board the helicopter, she turned to me with a trembling voice and said, "Can we go home now, Mommy?"

When our turn came, we stumbled down the hillside and tried to

*We were prepared to take our cat, Phineas, on the commercial airline with us, but were forced to leave him in the ensuing evacuation. Thanks to Deedee Blane, the AID representative in Albania, he was returned to us in good health in early April.

jump a muddy ditch at the bottom, during which I lost my left shoe. I was almost literally thrown into the helicopter with the two children so that I could not go back in search of it. We took off almost before we sat down. When I looked around, I saw that there were gunners on each side of the helicopter. We watched as the "fireworks" faded and were able to see the coast as we flew offshore, feeling both relief and incredible apprehension for loved ones left behind.

We had not flown very long when we touched down, so we presumed that we had not gone to Italy, but to our surprise we found ourselves on the deck of the USS *Nashville*. We were even more surprised when we were told that we would be spending the night on board the ship. At this point, the evacuation began to take on the element of an adventure for the children, and they enjoyed learning about the ship and playing with their friends. They even slept for a while in their berths that night. Although I had thought that nothing could keep me awake since I had not slept for nights, I found that the sights and sounds, especially the faces of those we loved as we said good-bye, were constantly before me and sleep could not come.

We stayed in the Adriatic Sea all night waiting for the USS *Nassau* to catch up with us. There was a possibility that our ship would have to invade the port at Durrës to evacuate a number of Americans and other expatriates who were trapped there. We later learned that the people waiting in Durrës had spent a harrowing night caught between gunfire and being trampled by Albanians trying to get onto any sailing craft they could. They were finally evacuated by an Italian vessel in the early hours of the morning.

At midday we were helicoptered to Brindisi, Italy, and from there had an eight-hour bus ride to Rome, where we were booked into the Sheraton Roma hotel. In Brindisi I learned that my husband had probably made it out in the Friday morning evacuation before they had to call off the effort because of gunfire directed at the helicopters, but I only knew for sure when he arrived in our hotel room at 4:00 A.M. Saturday.

We stayed in Rome, in a daze, until Monday, when we were finally able to get a flight across the Atlantic. As we headed westward toward safety and comfort, I was overwhelmed with feelings of gratitude for our lives, mingled with grief for Albania and its people. We had all thought that the time of biographies, secret police, and random violence had passed. I thought of all of the women we interviewed and the sadness they must feel at the betrayal they had experienced. I thought also of their strength and their optimism and wondered how they felt and whether or not they were safe. I thought with dread of what might have happened to people like

Afroviti, Diana Çuli, and Klara. I remembered the dreams of the young girls in Luz i Vogel and the sadness of the beautiful young girls of Homesh. The words that kept springing into my mind from my heart were, "I'm going the WRONG way!"

As I sit safely in the Adirondack Mountains of New York State finishing this book, I pray in gratitude and concern for the Albanian women, known and unknown, for the future of Albania, and for the opportunity to return to help bring peace and progress there.

Index

Abnori, Pjeter 115
Albanian Renaissance 51, 103, 273
Alexander the Great 48
Alia, Ramiz 209–211, 213

Baha'i faith 103, 104, 143, 282, 283
Bala, Foto 168
Balli Kombëtar 122, 123–124, 136, 139,
    149, 238
Balluku, Beqir 187
Bardhyllus, King 48
Bektashi 49, 64, 149, 156, 238, 279–281,
    282
Bellovodë 160, 162
Berat ix, 1, 57, 93, 142, 219, 240, 265
Berisha, Sali 97, 113, 213, 289, 290, 291,
    292, 293, 294
Biographi: A Traveler's Tale 17, 33, 67, 85,
    130, 133, 138, 140, 145, 161, 166, 167,
    187, 192, 193, 259, 260, 297
Bulgaria 50, 51, 262, 291
Burrel ix, 59, 115, 189, 259

Çajupi 6, 13, 174
Catholicism 48, 49, 75–79, 80, 117, 125,
    136–140, 169, 228–231, 274–276, 278,
    281, 283
Central Albania 73–74, 80–85, 140–144,
    156–160, 224–228, 233–242
China see People's Republic of China
Christianity 48, 49, 204, 227, 273, 281,
    282, 283; see also Orthodox Christian-
    ity; Protestant Christianity
Ciano, Count Galeazzo 52
class struggle 33, 103, 128, 129, 146, 166,
    169, 188, 190, 191, 260, 262
Code of Lekë Dukagjiini see Kanun
communism 7, 10, 11, 19, 22, 23, 32, 33,
    34, 35, 38, 39, 47, 52, 55, 58, 64, 67,
    68, 69, 75, 76, 77, 78, 79, 81, 86, 93,
    101, 103, 104, 108, 109, 110, 111, 112, 115,

129, 132, 133, 134, 140, 144, 145, 146,
    147, 148, 149, 154, 159, 166, 168, 170,
    179, 181, 185, 207, 211, 213, 214, 220,
    229, 234, 237, 243, 259, 273, 275, 277,
    278, 289, 290, 291, 292, 295; see also
    Communist Party
Communist Part 10, 11, 67, 78, 81, 87, 90,
    92, 94, 101, 108, 110, 122–124, 129, 133,
    143, 147, 162, 186, 188, 189, 192, 200,
    209, 213, 219, 222, 229, 266, 294; see
    also Communism
Congress of Berlin 50, 51
Congress of Lezhë 48
Congress of Lushnjë 52
Congress of Vlorë 52
Convention of Boston 51
Corfu 27
Çuli, Diana 1, 179–184, 273, 285, 298

Dado, Floresha 173–178
Dado, Peçi 174–175
declassed people (Kulaks) 63, 64, 85, 146
democracy 19, 39, 84, 87, 97, 103, 108,
    117, 121, 129, 140, 149, 150, 155, 159, 160,
    165, 179, 192, 207, 213, 215, 216, 220,
    234, 240, 246, 259, 262, 263, 281, 290,
    291, 294
Democratic Party 11, 140, 212, 213, 223,
    230, 289, 290, 292, 294
Dervishi, Ibrahim 110
Dhërmi ix, 243
Doda, Pal 113
Dumoulin, Jack 110, 111
Durham, Edith 55, 215
Durrës ix, 18, 22, 137, 170, 173, 186, 187,
    188, 190, 191, 192, 212, 234, 240, 297

Elbasan ix, 27, 222, 223
execution 76, 77, 93, 114, 123, 140,
    168–169, 170, 259, 278; see also persecu-
    tion

exile 3, 11, 33, 67, 75, 87, 92, 93, 109, 129, 146, 169, 170, 190, 192, 193, 194, 259, 260, 262, 278; *see also* persecution

faith 7, 10, 34, 64, 65, 66, 68, 69, 71, 72, 73, 74, 75, 76, 78, 79, 80, 81, 85, 86, 96, 103, 115, 116, 117, 127, 131, 132, 139, 141, 143, 149, 151, 155, 160, 161, 162, 167, 169, 178, 183, 194, 195, 203, 220, 221, 224, 227–228, 229, 231, 233, 237–238, 239, 240, 241, 245, 246, 247, 248, 257, 263, 269, 271, 273–283, 285, 287; *see also* religion
Fier ix, 74, 93, 117, 137, 260
Frasheri brothers (Naim, Midhat) 51, 109, 122, 147

Germany 52, 69, 70, 71, 87, 90, 92, 110, 123, 124
Gjergji, Andromaqi 1, 81–82
Gjirokastër ix, 92, 93, 110, 144, 168, 186, 187
Grabocka, Vera 256
Great Britain 123–124
Greece 27, 41, 42, 43, 48, 68, 69, 108, 122, 144, 150, 151, 169, 210, 212, 234, 242–246, 273, 278, 290
Gusho, Llazar *see* Pogradeci, Lasgush

Himarë ix, 1, 72–73, 180, 243–245
Homesh ix, 1, 30, 59–68, 134, 135, 151–153, 154–156, 158, 165–166, 246–252
Hoxha, Enver 32, 33, 34, 41, 52, 59, 65, 67, 68, 70, 84, 87, 92, 94, 95, 103, 108, 109, 121, 123, 124, 126, 127, 128, 129, 130, 131, 137, 139, 144, 147, 154, 155, 156, 159, 168–169, 177, 181, 185, 187, 188, 189, 192, 193, 207–211, 212, 214, 222, 225, 242, 261, 274
Hoxha, Nexhmije (Xhuglini) 77, 109, 209, 210

Illyria 47, 48, 53, 57, 108
imprisonment 3, 22, 38, 59, 67, 70, 77, 84, 87, 93, 110, 111, 112, 113, 114, 117, 123, 165, 166, 168–169, 170, 187, 190, 193, 238, 259, 274, 275, 278
internment *see* exile
Islam 10, 34, 48, 49, 51, 55, 64, 73, 80, 85, 103, 135, 141, 149, 150, 151, 156, 159, 160, 169, 178, 194, 203, 219, 224, 227, 235, 242, 247, 263, 269, 273, 274, 279–281, 282, 283
isolationism 103, 127, 128, 207–209

Italy 5, 16, 51, 52, 55, 60, 67, 79, 90, 109, 110, 116, 122, 123, 124, 136, 140, 192, 194, 210, 211, 212, 215, 221, 224, 229, 234, 240, 259, 273, 275, 290, 291, 293, 294, 297

Jakova, Tuk 94
Janissaries 49

Kadare, Ismail 129, 179
Kanun 32, 53–55
Kastrioti, Gjergj *see* Skanderbeg
Kastrioti, Mamica (Topia) 57
Kavajë ix, 192, 224, 234
Kiçi, Rrok 75
Klos ix, 59, 92
Kokolare, Musine 115
Konispol ix
Koniza, Faik Bej 51, 259
Kopaçi, Liri 197–204
Korçë ix, 1, 21, 27, 68, 79–80, 81, 89, 90, 100, 114, 122, 144–151, 167–169, 170, 219–221, 222, 228, 259, 276–279, 290
Kosturi, Drita 3, 107–118, 124, 276
Krujë ix, 280
Kuçovë ix, 73, 156, 159
Kukës ix, 186
Kulaks *see* declassed people

Laç v, ix
League of Prizren 50
Leka, Dhora 69, 87–97, 124, 228, 286
Leskovik ix
Lezhë ix, 48, 108, 175, 190
liberation *see* War of Liberation
Librazhd ix, 197, 198, 199, 200, 201, 202, 203
Llogarë 27, 243
Lloshnjë i, x, 99, 100, 101, 137
Luz i Vogel 192, 233–240

Macedonia 27
Mamaqi, Dashnor 186–187, 189, 193
Mamaqi, Kozeta 94, 185–195, 233
Maminas ix, 240–241
Marxism-Leninism 32, 34, 123, 129, 181, 208, 209
Montenegro 56, 75
Mussolini, Benito 52, 109, 123

Nano, Fatos 213
Nase, Nesti 168
National Congress at Vlorë *see* Congress of Vlorë
National Front *see* Balli Kombëtar

National Liberation Movement 123–124; *see also* Communist Party
Noli, The Rev. Fan 51, 52, 108, 117, 259
Northern Albania 6, 53, 59–68, 75–79, 134–140, 151–156, 165–166, 228–231, 246–252, 290

Orthodox Christianity 19, 49, 51, 68, 69, 73, 85, 96, 103, 141, 143, 149, 150, 151, 158, 160, 162, 169, 178, 220, 221, 224, 227, 228, 235, 243, 263, 274, 276–279, 281, 283
Ottoman Empire 6, 48, 49, 50, 51, 53, 55, 108, 121, 124

Pan-Albanian Federation *see* VATRA
Party of Labor of Albania *see* Communist Party
Pasha, Preng 116
People's Republic of China 23, 34, 93, 126, 129, 168, 181, 207, 208, 214, 228
Përmet ix, 185, 186, 253
Perondi ix, 1, 73–74, 156–160, 279, 283
persecution 7, 10, 11, 12, 20, 33, 35, 47, 49, 77, 82, 86, 107, 110–114, 123, 133, 145, 148, 165–172, 192, 209, 238, 259, 274, 276, 278
Peshkopi ix, 1, 59, 65, 134–136, 137, 153, 165
Peshkopjë ix, 4, 59, 64
Philip II of Macedonia 48
Pipa, Myzafer 111, 112, 113
Pogradec ix, 27, 143, 145, 170, 221–224
Pogradeci, Lasgush 172, 222
Polenë 79, 89, 149, 150, 151
Postribe Revolt 77, 111
Prela, Kol 114, 118
Prizren 50
Protestant Christianity 178, 273
Protocol of London 50
Pukë ix, 76, 167

Qemali, Ismail 52
Qirjazi sisters (Parashqevi and Sevasti) 148

religion 34, 127, 131, 132, 133, 149, 150, 151, 161, 188, 194, 224, 227, 238, 239, 263, 271, 273–283; *see also* faith
Roman Catholic *see* Catholicism
Romania 79, 100, 146, 147, 148, 161, 262
Rosafa 56–57, 75
Russia 23, 34, 50, 129, 146; *see also* Soviet Union
Russo-Turkish War 50

Sadedin, Frida 115, 116
Sarandë ix, 243
Serbia 55, 61
Shehu, Mehmet 192, 209
Shijak ix, 12, 192, 194
Shkodër ix, 1, 48, 50, 56, 75–79, 81, 102, 108, 109, 110, 111, 112, 115, 116, 122, 136–140, 149, 166–167, 211, 228–231, 274, 277, 281
Shupenzë ix, 59, 64, 65, 155
Sigurimi 11, 12, 33, 115, 129, 166, 170, 187, 190, 210, 260, 261, 275, 277, 278
Skanderbeg 48, 50, 55
Socialist Party 223
Southern Albania 68–74, 79–80, 92, 144–151, 160–162, 170–172, 173, 185, 219–224, 242–246
Soviet Union 23, 33, 34, 126, 168, 181, 188; *see also* Russia
Stafa, Qemal 108, 109, 110, 175
Stalin, Josef 32, 33, 34, 92, 146, 211, 212
Stillu, Pandi 100
Sunni-Anafit sect 49, 279

Tepelenë ix, 189
Teuta 57
Tiranë ix, 1, 4, 6, 8, 9, 15, 17, 18, 21, 22, 24, 27, 29, 39, 40, 59, 64, 67, 75, 80–85, 87, 90, 93, 94, 100, 101, 104, 115, 117, 127, 129, 137, 140–141, 146, 153, 168, 169, 170, 173, 182, 186, 188, 189, 190, 193, 199, 200, 201, 203, 211, 220, 221, 222, 223, 224–228, 233, 240, 241, 252, 253, 259, 260, 261, 262, 265, 291, 293, 294, 295
Tiranë Party Conference (1956) 92
Treaty of San Stefano 50
Turkey 48, 50, 55, 125, 128, 134, 212, 241–242, 273, 291; *see also* Ottoman Empire
Turkish rule *see* Ottoman Empire

United States 6, 30, 51, 55, 68, 70, 75, 84, 101, 114, 122, 139, 140, 144, 168, 169, 177, 180, 183, 216, 229, 243, 244, 251, 256, 257, 262, 293, 294, 297

Valshaj 240–242
VATRA 51, 259
Vithkuq ix, 18, 68–71, 160–162
Vlorë ix, 27, 92, 110, 115, 143, 174, 190, 212, 216, 227, 266, 277, 293, 294, 295
voluntary action 35, 65, 125, 126, 129, 132, 181, 208

War of Liberation 3, 32, 47, 52, 58, 64, 69, 76, 77, 87, 90, 94, 107, 108, 110, 114, 122, 123, 124, 145, 149, 159, 168, 186, 192, 193, 233, 234, 274, 275
World War II *see* War of Liberation

Xhepa, Margarita 99–106

Young Turks 51, 116
Yugoslavia 61, 62, 122, 123, 124, 156, 129, 146, 147, 159, 165, 186, 210, 212, 283

Zog I *see* Zogu, Ahmed Bej
Zogu, Ahmed Bej 52, 55, 66, 67, 73, 80, 89, 90, 108, 122, 148, 170, 186, 259